Ethical English

ALSO AVAILABLE FROM BLOOMSBURY

Ethical English

Teaching and learning in English as spiritual, moral and religious education

MARK A. PIKE

Bloomsbury Academic
An imprint of Bloomsbury Publishing Plc

B L O O M S B U R Y
LONDON • NEW DELHI • NEW YORK • SYDNEY

Bloomsbury Academic
An imprint of Bloomsbury Publishing Plc

50 Bedford Square	1385 Broadway
London	New York
WC1B 3DP	NY 10018
UK	USA

www.bloomsbury.com

BLOOMSBURY and the Diana logo are trademarks of Bloomsbury Publishing Plc

First published 2015

British Library Cataloguing-in-Publication Data
A catalogue record for this book is available from the British Library.

ISBN: HB: 978-1-4725-7683-5
PB: 978-1-4725-7682-8
ePDF: 978-1-4725-7684-2
ePub: 978-1-4725-7685-9

Library of Congress Cataloging-in-Publication Data
A catalog record for this book is available from the Library of Congress.

Typeset by Newgen Knowledge Works (P) Ltd., Chennai, India
Printed and bound in Great Britain

For Ruth Pike 1931–2012
who taught me to read

For Luke, Lydia and Jeremy,
whose reading continues to inspire

Contents

Foreword by
David Stevens, UK

Mark Pike has written here an important book, and one that should critically inform the continuing debate concerning what the subject English is all about. The emphasis on spiritual, moral and religious education within and beyond the subject offers all those interested in English pedagogy a stimulating and imaginatively communicated counterbalance to the current obsession with narrow target-driven teaching and learning policed by punitive, deterministic modes of assessment. At the same time, Dr Pike acknowledges these harsh realities of contemporary secondary school life in England and Wales (and by implication well beyond), demonstrating in diverse ways how it is possible still to teach in creative, liberating ways, and stay true to humane pedagogical principles and practices.

There is emphasis on philosophical underpinning, as befits the nature of the whole enterprise, but also an insistence that good practice, critically reflected upon, is central to what English teaching and learning is all about. Teachers of English and teacher educators, along with many others in different contexts concerned with the ways native language education may be going, will find Dr Pike's book immensely helpful, I think, in providing fertile ground for debate based on such a powerful textual reminder about the very basis of education itself.

I am vividly reminded of the words of Thomas Traherne, the seventeenth-century English poet and prose writer, who evocatively described both the opportunities and limitations of his own highly privileged Oxford education. In one of the autobiographical sections of his seminal work *The Centuries* Traherne discusses these contradictions; having initially paid tribute to the breadth of learning possible at this august university,

> Nevertheless some things were defective too. There was never a tutor that did professly teach Felicity, though that be the mistress of all other sciences. Nor did any of us study those things but as aliena, which we ought to have studied as our enjoyments. We studied to inform our knowledge but knew not for what end we so studied. And for lack of aiming at a certain end we erred in the manner. (Traherne, 1960, p. 37)

Dr Pike has in this book demonstrated that we need not err in manner or in proposed end, as long as we follow his lead in keeping the debate open and couched in appropriately imaginative terms.

David Stevens PhD
Durham University School of Education
Traherne, T. (1960), *Centuries*, London: Continuum.

Foreword by Thomas Lickona, USA

In the 2014 issue of the *Journal of Character Education*, Karen Bohlin, who heads an award-winning US school for girls, argues that what young people need most is the 'schooling of desire'. Good character must be made attractive and compelling to young persons. How can we help them come to believe that virtues – excellences of mind and moral character – are the path to a flourishing life? In *Ethical English*, Mark Pike makes it clear that in order to do that, schooling must nurture the human spirit. It must touch our souls.

In recent decades, the 'standards' movement in education – especially when narrowly focused on the skills needed for economic success – has militated against the nourishing of the human spirit. Fortunately, the increasingly global character education movement offers a bigger vision. It includes preparation not only for earning a living but also for living a life. Educating for character, as Mark Pike explains in this book, seeks to develop the whole person in two ways: (1) through the human relationships of the classroom and school that teach us, experientially, why and how to respect and love each other; and (2) through the academic curriculum when it inspires us to strive for excellence and to think about what it means to live life well or poorly. Although all areas of the curriculum can contribute to students' character development, *Ethical English* argues persuasively that English is the subject, par excellence, where young people are enabled to *reflect on their own character* – their virtues and vices, beliefs and values – as they encounter and respond to the characters in great literature, biographies and films.

Great stories, as Dr Pike reminds us, transcend time. As one of many examples, he cites Hogarth's 1732 series of paintings, *The Harlot's Progress*. Moll is a country girl who comes to London, is met by a well-known procuress, becomes a fashionable courtesan and then, falling on hard times, a street prostitute who is eventually imprisoned. She later has a son, but at age 23 dies an agonizing death from the venereal diseases that have ravaged her body. Dr Pike reminds us that Moll's situation is being enacted even now in the human trafficking that scandalously thrives in modern societies. In a world that is also flooded with pornography, it is all the more important, he points out, for young people to understand the reality of life for those working in the sex industry. Hogarth's moving series illustrates how stories have an important role to play in striving for social justice.

Ethical English also shows English teachers how their work is relevant to fields outside English, such as politics and citizenship education. Ethical English should bring a sense of personal freedom – to interpret the world in a different way from another person and to express that in speaking and writing. For this reason, *Ethical English* can be a powerful antidote to intellectual conformity and political correctness. *Ethical English* places a premium on allowing young people to come to their own informed decisions on a range of political and social issues.

Finally, it is English where students are most likely to grapple with life's largest questions: What is the meaning of life? What is the purpose of my life? What leads to authentic happiness? It is no accident that when people are asked to cite a teacher they felt especially close to, a teacher who particularly influenced their development as a person, they often name an English teacher.

In this interdisciplinary, horizon-expanding book, Mark Pike shows us how to sustain and broaden the English teacher's distinctive influence – and in the process, help young people make a good life for themselves and a better world for us all. School reform in general and character education in particular will find this an important work.

Thomas Lickona PhD
State University of New York at Cortland

Acknowledgements

Many colleagues and students as well as friends and family members have encouraged me with this book project. Frances Arnold, my editor at Bloomsbury, trusted me to deliver the manuscript on time and was brave enough to believe in a big picture book such as this in increasingly utilitarian times. Professor Thomas Lickona of the State University of New York, USA, was unstinting in his enthusiasm for a book that seeks to make a contribution to both English and character education. His expert advice on the manuscript and timely provision of articles and chapters offered moral direction as well as intellectual stimulation. Dr Philip Barnes, currently Reader at King's College, University of London, UK, gave his usual invaluable and enthusiastic support, scholarly perspectives on religion and made a copy of his book *Education, Religion and Diversity* (2014) available ahead of publication. Professor Paul Black at King's College, University of London, UK, helped me to see that AfL could respect the dignity of the child (after a talk I gave at King's in which I was sceptical of AfL). Jane l'Anson (Advanced Skills Teacher) showed me what this looked like in practice. Dr Michael Wilson, my immensely erudite colleague in the School of Education, University of Leeds, UK, provided meticulous critique especially with regard to ethics in education. Professor Mark Halstead very generously read the manuscript and advised on numerous points. Professor Roy Clouser answered my questions about 'divinity' beliefs more promptly than I expected. Professor Michael Reiss of the Institute of Education, University of London, UK, confirmed my suspicions about behaviourism and free will. There are too many names to mention in the very rich scholarly community concerned with moral and character education that inspired me to apply these perspectives to English. Colleagues on the board of the *Journal of Moral Education* and at the Jubilee Centre for Character and Values at Birmingham University, UK, and especially Professor James Arthur, have helped me think about moral and character education. My old friend Colin Lanfear provided scholarly dialogue, invaluable contacts and brought his skills to bear upon bibliographic searches while recovering from a knee operation. My first head of department, Halima Alam, modelled ethical English teaching when I was a newly qualified teacher. I am especially grateful to the hundreds of teachers and children that I have had the pleasure to teach (and learn from) over the last twenty-five years. Working with them in classrooms has helped to keep philosophical perspectives grounded in reality. In particular Helen Powell, Emily Hall and Ceri Restrick (classes of 2012 and 2013) gave their permission to refer to their experiences of learning to teach. I have benefitted immensely from my association with school leaders such as Ian Brew, David Page, Chris Drew, Jon Winch and Julie McGonigle who have shown me the importance of character in teaching, learning and leading. My parents, Ruth and Norm Pike, showed me the importance of faith and action. Closer to home, my children Luke, Lydia and Jeremy Pike helped me see things from the learner's point of view every day and ensured that such things as football matches, cross country tournaments, swimming pools, parties, movies, Monopoly, bedtime stories (with Jem) and fun featured during an intensive writing period while still teaching undergraduates and postgraduates. Lydia showed a range of virtues underpinning good character and helped me to edit the manuscript. Most of all, my love and gratitude go to my wife, Babs, who has encouraged me to write over the last 15 years. Without her expert critical analysis, detailed reading and efficient editorial skills I would not have fulfilled my ethical obligation to deliver the manuscript to London on time. Her love covers a multitude of my failings and helps me see the good way (Jer. 6.16).

Introduction: Why 'Ethical' English?

We have ethical coffee, so why not ethical English? We buy ethical coffee because we know we should treat the people who produce it decently. This is a social justice issue; we should not produce excellent coffee by exploiting people. We might even argue that coffee cannot be judged 'excellent' simply by tasting the end product. Ethical coffee is not produced for the maximum profit; it helps to support communities and enables people to live well. Equally, we need to look at the *purposes* not just *effects* of teaching and learning in English. Ethical English concerns how we value students, what we believe about them and how we treat them. It is about being humane and addresses what it is to thrive in life.

To suggest that English was central to educational success might be regarded as an example of great British understatement. According to Her Majesty's Chief Inspector, Sir Michael Wilshaw, 'There can be no more important subject than English in the school curriculum. English is a pre-eminent world language, it is at the heart of our culture and it is the language medium in which most of our pupils think and communicate. Literacy skills are also crucial to pupils' learning in other subjects across the curriculum' (Wilshaw, 2012). Over 75 per cent of the world's television is in English, 80 per cent of the written information on the Internet is in English and 95 per cent of the meetings at the United Nations are in English (Wang, 2006). English is not only the official language of 45 nations but it is the official second language in nations such as India where more people speak English fluently than in England. It is also the unofficial second language in China, where over 5 million students, who are non-English majors, are currently studying English in a thousand universities (Peng, 2011).

To benefit from what is on offer in school and society, 'English' is the passport; it liberates one to travel both intellectually and geographically 'without let or hindrance' (as the preamble to my British passport says). Communication and reasoning in and through English is central to learning in the twenty-first century. When a German pilot on a descent into Shanghai Pudong airport discusses the approach with the Chinese air traffic controller, they converse in English. When the Indian scientist or engineer meets Russian colleagues in Amsterdam their discussion is in English. Questions and answers, explanations and discussions, in mathematics and science, history and geography, occur through the medium of English all over the world. 'English' is more than one subject on the school curriculum; it is important to all of us.

Ethical English concerns us all because it is about who we are, where we have come from and where we are going. Teaching and learning English concerns values as well as literature and language. It may help us to empathize and to treat others not just with fairness but also with compassion and generosity. It is through English that students learn to 'read' people and situations not just written texts. Through English we learn about the world as well as words. Worldview formation does not occur only *after* we have learned to read and write, speak and listen in English; it occurs *while* we are learning to do so. Learning English does not just concern how to identify the right genre in which to write, the most appropriate register or tone in which to speak or the ability to 'crack the code' of grapheme–phoneme correspondence, of letters to sounds. It concerns how we can 'crack' life and how we 'sound' during it.

To get our tone and register right we need to become increasingly sophisticated 'readers' in plural, multicultural, cosmopolitan cultures. Yet teaching English also entails learning something of the history of the character of England, its values and beliefs, as its literature and language developed. How lives have been lived on one part of one small island, lying off mainland Europe in the North Atlantic, usually comes into it. The *Magna Carta* in England established the principle that its people should be free from arbitrary arrest and that the law should not defer to power or wealth. We speak of England as a 'free country' because of its ethos of personal freedom and liberty. According to King Alfred in the *Cura Pastoralis* all the sons of freemen (*freora manna*) should be *taught to read* and the Latin word *liber* which means 'free' also means 'book' (Lewis, 1960). One cannot be free to appreciate English (or England) without attending to some of its greatest literary works, many of which are informed by a Christian worldview.

England (not Westminster) was described in 1865, by the politician, John Bright, as the 'mother of all parliaments' (Jones, 2009, p. 1) and the English word 'parliament' is related to 'parley' in colloquial English, which is 'to talk, negotiate or discuss'. Discussion is always underpinned by values, which have been defined as 'enduring beliefs about what is worthwhile, ideals for which people strive and broad standards by which particular practices are judged to be good, right, desirable or worthy of respect' (Halstead and Pike, 2006, p. 24). Teaching and learning English concerns beliefs, values and identity as well as morality and character. Consequently, this book seeks to provide the 'big picture' and to address some of the 'big questions' about teaching and learning in English: What is English? What is the purpose of teaching English? What are the results of teaching English? Our answers to such questions, whether implicit or explicit, impact what is learned in English classrooms. They inform practical questions such as: What should be taught and learned in English? How should English be taught? How do different learners learn best in English?

Ethical English offers universities and school-based providers of teacher education a resource to enable new entrants to the profession, as well as experienced teachers of English, to evaluate their practice and develop as ethical professionals at Masters level and beyond. The final chapters in each part of this book are explicitly devoted to the professional learning of teachers of English but every chapter concludes with study questions designed to enable teachers to reflect and evidence their professional learning in relation to the *Teachers Standards* (2012) for England and Wales. While *Ethical English* draws most of its examples from the current professional context of English teaching in England, it is likely to be of value to teachers and learners of English in a wide range of professional contexts, both in the United Kingdom and internationally, because it addresses the development of ethical professionals.

The root of the English word 'ethics' is 'ethos' which was originally a Greek word meaning 'character'. An 'ethikos' is one who 'shows moral character' and the 'ethos' or the 'character' of a student, teacher or subject is derived from their foundational beliefs and values. *Ethical English* conceives the 'ethos' of learning and teaching English as a liberal art in the humanities. The 'liberal arts' or *artes liberales* (Cicero, 1942, 3. 7. 26) were the academic disciplines for freedom. The thesis of this book is clear: teaching English should 'free' learners; it should liberate them to live ethical and generous lives. As a *liberal* art English teaching and learning should be practiced in a spirit of generosity. For John Milton in *Of Education* a 'complete and generous education' is one that 'fits a man [sic] to perform . . . all the offices, both private and public' (Milton, 1895, p. xxiii). Such an education prepares its students to be good citizens, family members, neighbours, community members as well as employees and colleagues. To do so teaching and learning will be holistic as it will address the development of the whole person and prepare students for the whole of life (not just work).

In classical Greece, a liberal education was the schooling and education provided for the sons of wealthy citizens (boys who were not slaves) who did not need to be apprenticed to a trade. In other words, a liberal education was the education for those who would have a voice, deliberate the key issues for their society and express themselves well. Yet in ancient Athens very few experienced a liberal education. Many of the male population were slaves and women could not cast a vote or participate in debate. The freedom that the citizens experienced was at the expense of others, a large slave population in particular. It is sobering to note that if, in the twenty-first century, we replicate this situation where some have a voice and others are marginalized we will not be living in a 'free society' at all.

What we now term 'English' is a direct descendant of what Classical and Renaissance educators would have recognized as the liberal art of 'Rhetoric' that was used to persuade in political, legal and moral debate. English therefore has a special place in preparing people for participation in a liberal democratic society by enabling them to evaluate arguments, to make ethical choices and communicate their views well. In classical Rhetoric, a convincing or watertight argument had 'logos', 'pathos' and 'ethos'. A persuasive speaker needed to use *words* (the literal translation of 'logos' is 'word' but it is understood as 'speech' or 'account' and also has 'connotations of tale' or 'story'). He or she needed to gain the sympathy and interest of the audience at an emotional level ('pathos' might entail use of a 'hook' or analogy). But any speaker wishing to persuade an audience needed to establish 'ethos' or 'moral competence' from the very beginning.

In classical times 'ethos' or 'moral competence' in turn had its own three constituent elements. 'Ethos' was generated by a combination of 'phronesis', 'arête' and 'eunoia'. 'Phronesis' denotes practical wisdom in action or what we might term 'prudence' and is a key quality of any teacher. 'Arête', or virtue, is sometimes translated as 'excellence' in the sense of achieving a 'personal best' and being the best one can be by living up to one's full potential. 'Eunoia' is goodwill and there needs to be goodwill between students and teachers. The three parts of this book might be regarded as addressing the three elements of 'ethos'. The first part considers spirituality and well-being (eunoia); the second addresses morality or the achievement of a personal best in moral as well as academic terms (arête); the third concerns the practical wisdom (phronesis) required to teach an area of the curriculum that deals with beliefs and values. I believe that these three parts constitute an overlooked framework for evaluating the ethics of teaching and learning English.

PART ONE

Ethical English as spiritual education

1

Ethical English

In play after play, Shakespeare comes down on the side of the *ethos* or *spirit* rather than the letter of the law. Legalism (the rigid and inflexible adherence to laws and the literal interpretation of rules) can result in injustice unless it is tempered by attention to the 'ethos' or 'spirit' of the law. This is also true of the barren and unsympathetic implementation of a curriculum, a specification, a scheme of work or even a lesson plan in English. *The Merchant of Venice* is a paradigm case for learning about the teaching of English as well as life. When Antonio's case comes to court, it looks as if it will be straightforward. The facts of the case are uncontested. Antonio owes money to Shylock and because of his disastrous business failure he cannot repay the loan. The Judge (Portia in disguise) rejects the defendant's submission that the court should not enforce the terms of the contract (with its inhumane penalty clause of a pound of human flesh) for failure to repay by the specified date. The Judge rules that if the letter of the law is not strictly adhered to it will undermine the credibility of Venice as a centre in which to do business where contracts are legally binding. In other words, there will be *economic* consequences if the letter of the law is not followed.

The same sort of argument is still being rehearsed and applied to English. It is often assumed by policy-makers that *literacy* should be privileged over *literature*, business letters over imaginative writing, *accuracy* over *creativity*, or there will be economic consequences (Pike, 2003d). Shakespeare (who ended up being rather good for the English economy) would not have agreed with those who privilege the letter over the spirit or the ethos of the law. In *The Merchant of Venice* Shylock rejects Antonio's offer to settle the claim humanely and prepares to exact the penalty, according to the letter of the law. But as the penalty is to be exacted Shylock's literal interpretation of the contract, is brought up by the Judge.

'Tarry a little', the Judge tells Shylock, 'there is something else'. *Ethical English* is about the 'something else' in English; it addresses its 'spirit' or 'ethos'. Genuinely humane action and compassion often requires that the spirit rather than the letter of the law is followed, as Portia explains:

> The quality of mercy is not strain'd
> It droppeth as the gentle rain from heaven
> Upon the place beneath: it is twice bless'd;
> It blesseth him that gives and him that takes:
> 'Tis mightiest in the mightiest: it becomes
> The throned monarch better than his crown;
> His sceptre shows the force of temporal power,
> The attribute to awe and majesty,
> Wherein doth sit the dread and fear of kings;
> But mercy is above this sceptred sway;
> It is enthroned in the hearts of kings,
> It is an attribute to God himself;
> And earthly power doth then show likest God's
> When mercy seasons justice.
>
> (*The Merchant of Venice* Act 4 Scene 1)

Just as our humanity suffers and we are diminished if we ignore the spirit and insist on the letter of the law, children and young people will suffer if 'English' comes to be the acquisition of functional literacy rather than nurturing their personal growth through response to literature (Pike, 2007e, 2007f). This book is about the 'spirit' of English in schools and as such concerns its fundamental character. This is vital because, like Shylock, who was incapable of excising *exactly* a pound of flesh, none of us is able to keep the letter of the law. We are only human, after all.

Clearly, 'the letter kills but the spirit gives life' (2 Cor 3.6). On this view, how might English best meet the 'needs of learners'? We need to begin in the right way and conceive of 'needs' holistically as the education of the human spirit rather than seeing students as 'grade material' or economic assets (or costs). Having a sufficiently high view of learners is vital. In Hamlet's 'What a piece of work is a man' speech, Shakespeare unashamedly reminds us about the extraordinary nature of humanity. He asks the existential question:

> What a piece of work is a man, how noble in reason, how infinite in faculties, in form and moving how express and admirable, in action how like an angel, in apprehension how like a god: The beauty of the world, the paragon of animals – and yet, to me, what is this quintessence of dust?
> (*Hamlet* Act 2 Scene 2)

Shakespeare used the Geneva Bible (see Chapter 11) and its rendering of the verse to which Hamlet alludes is salient: 'The Lord God also made the man of the dust of the ground, and breathed in his face breath of life, and the man was a living soul' (Gen 2.7). In this account, humans were made from material that is the stuff of the arid and lifeless desert. The image of the 'desert' is also central to a well-known definition of the 'spiritual' that teachers of English may endorse:

> Were they [children and young people] not able to be moved by feelings of awe and wonder at the beauty of the world we live in, or the power of artists, musicians and writers to manipulate space, sound and language, they would live in *an inner spiritual and cultural desert*. (SCAA, 1995, p. 4, my italic)

According to C. S. Lewis in *The Abolition of Man – Reflections on education with special reference to the teaching of English in the upper forms of schools* 'the task of the modern educator' is 'to irrigate deserts' (rather than to cut down jungles) but this involves more than generating 'awe and wonder'. It is as teachers 'inculcate just sentiments' (Lewis, 1978/1943, p. 13) that they 'irrigate'. English, rightly conceived, will nurture the growth of feelings and emotions that support a commitment to social justice.

Engagement with a poem such as Shelley's 'Ozymandias', may help us to apprehend, in more than a rational or propositional way, something of the spiritual potential of English. The speaker in the poem meets a traveller who has a tale to tell:

> I met a traveller from an antique land
> Who said: "Two vast and trunkless legs of stone
> Stand in the desert. Near them on the sand,
> Half sunk, a shattered visage lies, whose frown
> And wrinkled lip and sneer of cold command
> Tell that its sculptor well those passions read
> Which yet survive, stamped on these lifeless things,
> The hand that mocked them and the heart that fed.
> And on the pedestal these words appear:
> 'My name is Ozymandias, King of Kings:
> Look on my works, ye mighty, and despair!'
> Nothing beside remains. Round the decay
> Of that colossal wreck, boundless and bare,
> The lone and level sands stretch far away.

This poem is a gift to teachers and students of English. What questions does the poem evoke? What might readers imagine when they read this sonnet?

We might think about the conversations the poor sculptor may have had with Ozymandias and what their dialogue was like (taking Browning's 'My Last Duchess' as an inspiration perhaps). What conversations did Ozymandias have with his consort, his friends and his courtiers? Can we remember seeing ancient columns or fragments on holiday or in books or films that feature the remains of ancient civilizations? What feelings are evoked by descriptions such as 'shattered visage' or 'colossal wreck'? What associations do 'these lifeless things' bring to life in us? What are the reverberations of the hubris and megalomania of: 'My name is Ozymandias, King of Kings: Look on my works, ye mighty, and despair!' Do we think about the enormous statues of more recent dictators being toppled in a desert land? Do we begin to think about freedom and democracy and how life would have been lived under such a tyrant?

Whether Shelley depicts the colossal statue of Ramesses II, the Egyptian Pharoah, inspired by news of its arrival at the British Museum in 1816 or by the temple at Thebes near Luxor in Upper Egypt is not as important as the capacity of the poem to allow readers to stand somewhere else, to experience vicariously another place, another world, and to inhabit a different culture and time. To imagine what it was like in that 'antique land' and how people lived is more important than historical accuracy. When a class reads about the 'wrinkled lip and sneer of cold command' what commands can they imagine Ozymandias issuing? Did the people he ruled really believe he was God or did they worship other gods? What did they believe about life after death? Do readers reflect on what is left of a great civilization and its people, now lying in the sand? Embalming and mummification aside, do they reflect on mortality and that everything human returns to dust? These are the kinds of questions that matter imaginatively and ethical English fosters the ability to ask such questions as well as to find answers.

In addressing the spiritual, moral and religious aspects of English this book seeks to discover something foundational in the human experience with which English teaching at its most fundamental, engages. The Hebrew creation narrative is set in the Fertile Crescent between the Tigris and Euphrates, the 'Cradle of Civilization'. Breathing life into dust or the desert recurs in the discourse on spirituality that seeks to depict what being human and humane is all about. Outside the Near East, there are striking similarities. In ancient Chinese accounts of creation the 'breath' of the cosmos is related to the *Tao* or 'the Way' (to which we return in Chapter 6). In Hebrew, the word for 'spirit' is *ruah* and denotes the movement of *air* or *breath*. To be alive we need to take our first breath. If we have ever witnessed the birth of a child and have waited intently for the cries of the baby when he or she first inhales, we will be acutely aware that *living* and *breathing* go together. If we have witnessed the final breath of someone we love we will be painfully aware of it. The Latin *spiritus* for 'soul or breath' is related to *spirare*, 'to breathe' and it is from

'*In-spirare*' that we get the modern English word: 'inspiration'. This literally means to *breathe life* into something and is related to the Old French *espirit*. This book concerns how teachers and learners can thrive and flourish, how they can inspire and be inspired. Living is spiritual but some English lessons help students to live more fully than others.

The thesis here is that English must nurture the human spirit. Yet English in schools in England is increasingly a subject with an identity crisis as questions are asked about whether its primary concern should be literature or literacy (Medway, 2010). Literature as an art form is so important because it can help us reassess and realign our lives. Vygotsky points out in *The Psychology of Art* that:

> from the most ancient times art has always been regarded as a means of education, that is as a long range programme for changing our behaviour and our organism. (Vygotsky, 1971, p. 253)

Arguably, for the sort of change Vygotsky describes to occur, where an individual's 'organism' as well as 'behaviour' is transformed, a 'spiritual' change is required. John Dewey argues in *Art as Experience* (1934), one of the twentieth century's most influential texts on aesthetic education, that we should recover 'the continuity of esthetic experience with normal processes of living' (p. 10). Just as early in human history 'the arts of the drama, music, painting and architecture' did not have a 'peculiar connection with theatres, galleries, museums' (Dewey, 1934, p. 7) the spiritual need not be confined to places of worship. In distancing aesthetic experience from institutions Dewey makes an analogous point to that of writers on spirituality and religious experience. For instance, Wordsworth's poetry often illustrates the nature of spiritual apprehension and one of the best-known descriptions of a 'spiritual state' occurs in his lyric 'Lines Composed a Few Miles above Tintern Abbey'. An inner spiritual journey, such as that described by Wordsworth in 'The Prelude' (1988/1799), can bring about a profound personal resolution, realignment and fresh vision where the individual's perspective is radically altered. He describes the way such insight: 'has revealed /The invisible world' and believes that striving for the infinite is essential as 'Our destiny, our being's heart and home/Is with infinitude'. In 'The Prelude' (1988/1799), Wordsworth writes that the individual mind:

> Doth, like an Agent of the one great Mind,
> Create, creator and receiver both,
> Working in alliance with the works
> Which it beholds.

Schleiermacher (1959), who can be seen as the 'theological expression of romanticism' unsurprisingly 'saw the artist and the poet as a mediator of spiritual reality to humans' (Long, 2000, p. 149) and at different points in their lives Blake, Coleridge, Shelley and Wordsworth all adopted the persona of the poet-prophet. The visionary activity of such Romantic poets demonstrates that they considered themselves to be performing a spiritual role and were united in their belief that the mind could gain access to the infinite through the faculty they termed Imagination. It should not surprise us that such views are still influential upon conceptions of the subject of 'English' in the twenty-first century (Stevens, 2011) but it is important to have some idea of how we arrived at this point.

Searching for the spirit of English

In the Victorian age the enormously influential Matthew Arnold, the son of Thomas Arnold, the Headmaster of Rugby School, brought to education the view he shared with the Romantics of the spiritual efficacy of the artist. Believing that great literature was the answer to society's ills, he asserted that, 'Good poetry does undoubtedly tend to form the soul and character; it tends to beget a love of beauty and truth in alliance' (Arnold, 1908). Arnold saw in literature and the arts the hope of spiritual redemption that he derived from the Romantics. It is important to trace developments since the Romantics and Arnold if we are to understand why 'spirituality' has come to be defined as it has in schools such as those in England and to appreciate the sources of educational policy concerning 'spiritual education'.

After the First World War, the commitment to the spiritual efficacy of literature was reasserted in the Newbolt Report, *The Teaching of English in England*, which declared:

> We claim that no personality can be complete, can see life steadily and see it whole, without that unifying influence, that purifying emotion which art and literature alone can bestow. It follows then, from what we have said above, that the bulk of our people are living starved existences, *that one of the richest fields of our spiritual being* is left uncultivated. (Newbolt, 1921, p. 257 italic for emphasis in original)

At a difficult time in the life of the nation, Sir Henry Newbolt and his well-regarded committee of educators put their faith in art and literature. The potential of literature was subsequently emphasized during the first half of the twentieth century through the efforts of a small circle of critics at Cambridge in the 1930s, of whom F. R. Leavis (1948), I. A. Richards (1929) and T. S. Eliot (1932) are the best known. According to this group, the purpose of reading great literature was to 'protect the *human spirit* against the cultural disintegration which Richards observed in contemporary society' (McGuinn, 2004, p. 53, my italic).

The 1944 Education Act made Local Education Authorities in England responsible for contributing towards the 'spiritual, moral, mental and physical development of the community'. The 1988 Education Reform Act retained the word 'spiritual', and the 1992 Act required OFSTED to inspect the 'spiritual, moral, social and cultural development' of children in schools. Subsequently the 1994 OFSTED inspection handbook pointed out that, ''Spiritual' is not synonymous with 'religious'; all areas of the curriculum may contribute to pupils' 'spiritual development' (p. 86). The following year the SCAA document *Spiritual and Moral Development* put it like this:

> The term [spiritual] needs to be seen as applying to something fundamental in the human condition which is not necessarily expressed through the physical senses and/or expressed through everyday language. It has to do with relationships with other people and, for believers, with God. It has to do with the universal search for individual identity, with our responses to challenging experiences, such as death, suffering, beauty, and encounters with good and evil. It is to do with the search for meaning and purpose in life and for values by which to live. (SCAA, 1995, p. 3)

In 1999, New Labour shifted the emphasis towards citizenship, personal, social and health education with the *Every Child Matters* (ECM) agenda, although 'spiritual education' remained a requirement in the National Curriculum. In 2004, OFSTED provided the following guidance:

> Spiritual development is the development of the non-material element of a human being which animates and sustains us and, depending on our point of view, either ends or continues in some form when we die. It is about the development of a sense of identity, self-worth, personal insight, meaning and purpose. It is about the development of a pupil's spirit. Some people may call it the development of a pupil's 'soul'; others as the development of 'personality' or 'character'. (p. 12)

The dangers of spirituality

The threats as well as the opportunities associated with defining spirituality in some of the ways noted above warrant careful consideration. If spirituality is 'typically defined as a form of experience or understanding which has to do with the realm of the transcendent' (Long, 2000, p. 147) this may be dangerous because 'it puts in question the fundamentals which underpin education' and can lead to spirituality being seen as 'an escape from, or at least a distancing from the very world of experience that education addresses or serves' (Blake, 1996, p. 454). Certainly, if 'spirituality is understood primarily in terms of withdrawal and transcendence, its relationship to much of what goes on in the classroom will likely be tenuous' (Smith and Shortt, 2001, p. 5). It has been argued that 'spirituality may operate within educational processes in ways which go beyond the inner, the mystical or the ineffable' (Smith, 2001, p. 65) and that Romantic conceptions of spirituality in particular need to be reconsidered. It is important to emphasize that, far from being an 'escape' or 'a distancing from the world of 'experience', spirituality is inextricably bound up in the everyday. Such a position necessarily means 'we are faced with the challenge of working out how spirituality penetrates the full extent of the mundane curriculum' (Smith and Shortt, 2001, p. 5). This book, which sees the integration of the spiritual with the everyday in English, seeks to contribute to such working out and reflects Dewey's call for such unity.

Arguably, the most dangerous fallacy in all of the definitions above, from the Romantics and Arnold to Newbolt and more recent curriculum documents, would be to always consider 'spirituality' to be beneficial. Such an undifferentiated and uncritical approach is unwarranted. We ought not to assume that every kind of spirituality will be good. The issue of spiritual well-being is taken up in the next chapter but for now it is worth considering the analogy that not all art is necessarily good or conducive to human well-being. For instance, the work of the German documentary-maker Leni Riefenstahl in *Triumph of the Will* is aesthetically remarkable (the subject is the Nuremberg rallies) but it is also Nazi propaganda. With regard to the 'spiritual', in one sense 'the most useful way of employing the word' is to denote that every human being is 'spiritual' (Lewis, 1960/1947, p. 175) but there was something deeply wrong, spiritually, with the Nazis. Nor are they alone in seeking to engage the deepest springs of human action for evil.

It would be quite wrong to assume that all aesthetic experience or any personal response is spiritually healthy. While nurturing children's non-material well-being, we have to be careful that we do not fall into the trap of assuming that the 'spiritual development' of young people will always be good for them. We should only accommodate spiritual awareness and growth that is conducive to *eunoia* and well-being. The danger of 'spirituality' is illustrated in *Perelandra*, the second novel in C. S. Lewis' science fiction trilogy for adults, where the megalomaniac scientist Weston, who is reminiscent of the Nazis, seeks 'spirituality', but is depraved and intent on rape. Weston sees himself tapping into the Life-force, and becoming one spirit with it. He tells Ransom that it is: 'A great, inscrutable Force, pouring up into us from the dark bases of being' (Lewis, 2005/1943, p. 83) and declares that 'to spread spirituality . . . is henceforth my mission' (Lewis, 2005/1943,

p. 81, my italic). There is something profoundly wrong here spiritually (not just morally) and Weston confesses that he would murder if he felt a 'spirit' told him to do so. This brings to mind Lady Macbeth praying to spirits that are the 'murdering ministers' that 'tend on mortal thought' (*Macbeth* I.v) to take away her feminine and human qualities such as compassion and guilt so she can see to it that Duncan is murdered. Evidently, the ambiguity of spirituality is a threat as well as an opportunity for 'what is "spiritual" is not necessarily good' because 'immaterial things may, like material things, be good or bad or indifferent' (Lewis, 2005/1943, p. 175). In English, only spirituality conducive to the well-being of students and teachers should be fostered.

Today, 'spiritual education' is firmly established in the current discourse on schooling and is considered to be vital in *all* schools, not just those schools that have a specifically religious foundation or ethos. In the United Kingdom, inspectors visiting all schools inspect and comment upon children's 'spiritual education'. We have books such as *Spirituality and Education* (2000) by Andrew Wright; *The Spirit of the Child* (2006) by David Hay and Rebecca Nye and more recently *The Spirit of the School* (2009) by Julian Stern, and we also have the well-established *International Journal of Children's Spirituality* which regularly explores the relation between the spiritual and aesthetic (Pike, 2004b).

Aesthetic response to literature

The 'increasing instability of English as a subject' (Ellis, 2011, p. 245) has significant implications for pedagogy as well as spirituality. Any approach to English which makes the nature of learning routine, relies on systematic questioning and gives learners the impression that paraphrasing, genre recognition or copying the conventions of certain types of text (at text, sentence and word level) are of central importance, is wholly inadequate. It fails to do justice to the 'spirit' of English. At the end of a profoundly moving first reading of *King Lear*, it is not unusual for a literature class to want to *be* rather than to explicate; attempts to rationalize such experiences may be futile as well as inappropriate. That literature so often resists paraphrasing and explication indicates the nature of knowing and the importance of 'being' when we experience a work of literature. In English, aesthetic experience should be central (Stevens, 2011) to 'being' and attempts to redefine the subject through an emphasis upon literacy (Pike, 2003c), should be resisted as they are not true to the spirit of English.

Faith in explicitness is still sometimes seen as a panacea for all perceived pedagogic ills. The prescribed treatment may have very grave side effects upon student's motivation and engagement. Heavy doses of explicitness, regularly administered, is sometimes still thought to be the cure. The National Literacy Strategy (NLS) promoted teaching that was 'direct and explicit' (DfEE, 2001, p. 16), and the simplicity of this ideology is apparent in the admission that the 'implications . . . for lesson organisation are few, but very significant: more explicit teaching' (p. 17). We were told that 'explicit attention to language learning' (p. 66) would be of great benefit. Further, the 'transfer of skills from one lesson to another' had to be 'part of the explicit teaching agenda in all lessons' (p. 15) as objectives 'benefit from being explicitly taught and from being identified' (p. 11). The concomitant of the emphasis upon explicitness is that its converse, the implicit, may be marginalized and neglected. This matters because, by definition, literary texts work implicitly rather than explicitly.

A distinctive feature of any literary work is that it has gaps (indeterminacy) in it that 'are a basic element for the aesthetic response' (Iser, 1971, p. 12). In much the same way, having the right sort of gaps or indeterminacy in an English lesson is a precondition for pupil participation and aesthetic response. Gaps need to exist that stimulate the learner to bring vision, creativity and imagination to the lesson. Negotiating such indeterminacy is vital to learning in English, and engendering expectations that learning in this area can always be rational, clear-cut and straightforward is deeply misguided. We must be wary of initiatives that seek to prescribe and make routine the nature of the text (the lesson) in which students participate. By increasing the degree of explicitness in the lesson, we radically alter the nature of the aesthetic and spiritual space inhabited by learners. The boundaries within which the learner thinks and responds are shifted. The aesthetic space for learners decreases as the degree of explicitness in the lesson increases. This is because the fewer the gaps (for independent learning and personal response) that the lesson supplies, or the more routine they become, the less personally involved the learner is likely to be.

Arguably, the questions young people are currently learning to ask in school do not often concern the 'ultimate meaning and purpose of life' (Wright, 2000, p. 16). Hence the spiritual value of teaching English derives from its *ontological* potential. The term 'ontology' refers to the being of beings (onta) or existence and to the account (logos) of this. The value of English teaching for students lies, to a great degree, in the questions it enables them to ask and in its potential to help them move towards an understanding of 'being'. The threat to both spiritual and literary education is that teaching, learning and appreciating literature and language are increasingly seen as a technology rather than having anything to do with ontology. This is especially important at a time when knowledge, skills, targets and measurement are privileged over being and the wonder of being. That there are beings like us at all, rather than dust, should prompt wonder (Pike, 2004c).

Aesthetic response to literature can involve learners in a reassessment of their existence and such a reassessment is often more spiritual than rational because the aesthetic 'demands an organ other than scientific thinking' (Hegel, 1997, p. 138). The aesthetic distance (between the world of the reader and that of the text) is valuable because it can lead readers to embark upon their own spiritual journeys (Pike, 2002a). Yet 'aesthetic distance' can also provide the stimulus or motivation to embark upon such a quest in the first place. Works that force 'no turn toward the horizon of yet unknown experience' (Jauss, 1982, p. 25) and merely fulfil expectations do not provide a sufficient spiritual challenge. Conversely, works of art that deal with 'challenging experiences, such as death, suffering, beauty, and encounters with good and evil' have the potential to lead readers to 'search for meaning and purpose and for values by which to live' (SCAA, 1995, p. 3).

Although in one sense 'aesthetic distance' provides the possibility of especially long distance travel whereby young learners encounter new horizons, the spiritual significance of such experiences can be found close to home in children's aesthetic responses to literature (Pike, 2000d). Response to a new work can augment or reconfigure the reader's experience and can result in a 'change of horizons' (Jauss, 1982, p. 25). The function of art as 'a central and essential human and social activity' (Stibbs, 1998, p. 202) involves its 'ability to shock and inspire, to change vision, ideas and feelings' (Stibbs, 1998, p. 210). This is so necessary in learners' lives because artistic activity can empower them to reassess their attitudes, values and expectations and also to enable them to confront their prejudices.

The importance of 'personal response' is emphasized in *Taking English Forward* (OFSTED, 2012) where introducing too much of a focus on literary critical skills at the expense of personal response is singled out for criticism. This document calls upon schools to develop policies to promote 'reading for enjoyment' and to 'refresh' Key Stage 3 (ages 11–14) schemes of work (OFSTED, 2012, p. 5). Inspectors documented instances of 'over-teaching' where too much is crammed in and lessons are assumed to be better the more activities they have. After extensive observation, the inspectors concluded:

> The quality of pupils' learning was hampered in weaker lessons by a number of 'myths' about what makes a good lesson. The factors that most commonly limited learning included: an excessive pace; an overloading of activities; inflexible planning; and limited time for pupils to work independently. Learning was also constrained in schools where teachers concentrated too much or too early on a narrow range of test or examination skills. (OFSTED, 2012, pp. 5–6)

In one lesson observed, after just a few pages of reading a novel, students were set the task of writing PEE (Point, Evidence, Explanation) paragraphs when there had been 'no opportunity for students to provide a personal response to the opening of the novel; to discuss its impact; whether it worked; what they liked/disliked; what might happen next, or what reaction they had to characters or events' (OFSTED, 2012, p. 10). In lessons where there was an inappropriate emphasis upon assessment, inspectors observed strategies that would have engaged students being neglected in favour of work on the skills required for the 'analytical, literary-critical essay' (OFSTED, 2012, p. 10).

Further research is now needed to elucidate the contribution of different texts to a range of readers' spiritual development. While some contemporary works undoubtedly foster ontological insight it is also the case that, in the attempt to motivate children to read, some trivial and superficial works are chosen which merely 'foreground the ephemeral preoccupations of the present' (Benton and Benton, 1998, p. vii). Certainly any over-emphasis upon non-fiction is likely to be to the detriment of the 'spirit' of English. The pleasure of language and the art of reading ought not 'to be described and discussed as if they were, like good manners and clean shoes, essential to the prospect of employment' (Hattersley, 1998, p. 50).

According to Halliday, 'language is as it is because of what it has to do' (1978, pp. 18–19) but since 'Proto Indo-European' (the earliest language known to linguists, spoken in the area of the Fertile Crescent 6,000 years ago), language has been concerned with more than getting things done. When literature is studied, if the reading of whole texts, and especially novels, is abandoned in favour of literacy instruction, we will all be the poorer spiritually. Thankfully, *Taking English Forward* (OFSTED, 2012, p. 43) calls for teachers of English to foster 'stamina' in reading that cannot be built up by focusing on short texts. If, instead of being captivated by a whole text (and then wanting to know how it works or what makes it especially effective), learners are encouraged to focus only on the mechanics of the 'parts', *education* will be diminished. Students should be encouraged to read in a way that 'allows them to enter and occupy the text' so that a 'common space is created in which students, teacher and subject can meet' (Palmer, 1993, p. 76). This meeting, the communal aesthetic encounter, is vital to the ethos of English and to students' spiritual well-being (Pike, 2002a, 2003b, 2004c).

Study questions

1 What ethos do you aim to create in your classroom?

2 Look at the key ingredients of 'ethos' in Rhetoric and identify which you are drawing upon in your classroom.

3 How would you describe the 'spirit' of English?

4 How spiritual is your teaching?

5 How might you nurture the spiritual development of your students?

6 How have your learners been inspired?

2

Well-being in English

In the last chapter we saw that the potency of English is linked to its ontological potential. Yet 'being in' English teaching is more like 'being married' than 'being in Washington D.C.'; it is more like 'being in love' than 'being in London'. It is *relational* rather than *situational*. Consequently, 'being *in* English teaching' should be more like 'being *with* a son' or 'being *with* a daughter' than 'managing' a class. It involves getting to know people rather than just knowing how to handle them. In this chapter it is suggested that 'English' provides a spiritual 'house' or even a 'home' for young people. Arguably, the ethos or spirit of this 'home', and how it is furnished by its spiritual parents, should provide both the security and the opportunities required for children to confidently make their way in the worlds they navigate.

English as a 'Spiritual Home'

In the thirteenth century, in the early stages of its life, the University of Paris accommodated its young students (some of whom were only 13-years old) in 'hospices' where they lived and learned in a communal setting. These hospices were referred to as 'pedagogies'. The use of the word is significant because *teaching and learning* go together with *living*:

> a pedagogy is a house, a holistic environment in which learners undergo both intellectual and spiritual formation according to a common rule. Being raised in a different house may . . . lead to developing a different character. (Smith, 2001, p. 8, my italic)

Taken literally, 'pedagogy' means to 'lead' a 'child' but mostly it is used as a synonym for 'teaching'. Pedagogy for ethical English provides a special sort of spiritual 'home'. Learners should always be provided with a non-threatening environment. In classrooms that are conducive to spiritual well-being learners are able to thrive and flourish (*eudaimonia*). Lessons will not be dull, barren, lifeless and repressed but will be characterized by enthusiasm and engagement. Teachers do not belong to the entertainment industry but their students should enjoy learning. There must be order and mutual respect but there will also need to be good rapport. Just as in a good home, learners will be keen to ask questions and not just to answer them. When children and young people feel secure at home and are inspired, they may feel adventurous enough to embark upon their own travels and to make their own discoveries. The ethos of English is, within ethical limits, to liberate rather than to restrict or constrain.

Studies indicate that English teachers in the United Kingdom who privilege the 'Personal Growth' model of English are especially interested in the life of the child (Goodwyn and Findlay, 1999; Marshall, 2000; Bousted, 2000). Ethical English focuses on the learner as an individual but also recognizes that aesthetic response can be enhanced through social interaction (Pike, 2003b). An English teacher, as a reader, is part of the communal aesthetic encounter and lives with other readers as they bring about a world of understanding. Involvement, engagement and close relationships characterize spiritual awareness in English teaching. The knowledge to emerge from the English classroom is often of a special sort (Pike, 2004d):

> a recurring tenet of the philosophy of personal growth through
> English affects English teachers' expectations of their relationship
> with their pupils which, they argue, must be based upon a special
> knowledge of the pupils as individuals and an awareness of their
> lives outside the classroom. (Bousted, 2000, p. 24)

For instance, an English teacher who collaborated on a research project was described by one of his pupils, in these terms: 'He gets on well with you. He knows what you're like so you don't have to put on an act with him. You can be yourself . . . he kind of understands how you feel' (Day, 1998, p. 262).

The spirit of ethical English teaching is typified by exchange and engagement because its pedagogy values students' views and experiences. The quality of one's teaching is contingent upon the quality of one's relationships. In order to be an inspirational teacher one has to get to know learners. Understanding what is important to them, what they value, what their priorities and aspirations are and what they enjoy, may be regarded as a prerequisite for inspiring them. In order to inspire one needs to engage with what matters to learners and not just what matters to oneself. Relational consciousness and empathy are key qualities of the inspirational teacher who will develop and nurture the gift of being able to see lessons (and life) from the perspective of the learner. English teaching that works from the 'outside-in', from curriculum to child, rather than from the 'inside-out', where 'responsive teaching' is engaged in (Pike, 2004a) may even be regarded as unethical because it pays insufficient attention to the needs of learners. In a classroom that is conducive to spiritual well-being relationships will bring out the best in people and enable them to experience amazement and excitement; the teacher will not be harsh. Under no circumstance should the human spirit be wounded, crushed or stifled. Instead, it will be nurtured. There will be respect for authority but not manipulation as relationships will be courteous and ethical. Ethical English provides a secure and stable spiritual 'home' characterized by trust.

Dewey's plea was for both the aesthetic and the spiritual aspects of human experience to be valued as 'part of the significant life of an organized community' (Dewey, 1934, p. 7) and he attributed the 'dislocations' and 'division of modern life' to their marginalization. We live in a social world and the responses, interpretations and experiences of others are required to augment our own (Pike, 2003b). John Donne's 'Meditation XVII' (1987/1627) is in this vein:

> No Man is an *Illand*, intire of it selfe; every man is a peece of the *Continent*, a part of the *maine*; if a *Clod* bee washed away by the *Sea*, *Europe* is the lesse, as well as if a *Promontorie* were, as well as if a *Mannor* of thy *friends*, or of *thine owne* were; Any Mans *death* diminishes *me*, because I am involved in *Mankinde;* And therefore never send to know for whom the *bell* tolls; It tolls for *thee*. (p. 87)

The emphasis on human relatedness is especially important in English because the learner can never be an island 'entire of itself'. Rebecca Nye has observed 'relational consciousness' to be characterized by an 'unusual level of perceptiveness' in the way children 'felt related to things, especially people, including themselves and God' (1998, p. 5) and Nye's concept of 'relational consciousness' has been seen as a 'relational orientation toward people or symbols at a spiritual level' (Reimer and Furrow, 2001, p. 15). The contrast between personal response to literature and merely knowing the conventions of different genres of non-fiction texts could not be greater ontologically; spiritual well-being is grounded in aesthetic response not linguistics. Most teachers of English might agree that 'it is either in art, or nowhere, that the dry bones are made to live again' (Lewis, 1980/1969, p. 305).

Well-being in other worlds

Entering other worlds is important to well-being for several reasons. For the poet W. H. Auden, each of us inhabits both a primary world of 'experience' and a secondary world of the 'imagination':

> Present in every human being are two desires, a desire to know the truth about the primary world, the given world outside ourselves in which we are born, live, love, hate and die, and the desire to make new secondary worlds of our own or, if we cannot make them ourselves, to share in the secondary worlds of those who can. (W. H. Auden, 1968, p. 49)

It is in this secondary world, as well as in the primary world, that significant spiritual education can occur (Pike, 2002a). The relation between the two worlds is critically important because we make sense of each world in the light of the other. According to Tolkien's theory of sub-creation:

> A Secondary World is one which the mind can enter. Because it contains this 'inner consistency of reality', what you find inside is 'true' in that it accords with the laws of that world. You therefore believe it, while you are, as it were, inside. The moment disbelief arises, the spell is broken; the magic, or rather art, has failed. You are then out in the primary Worlds again. (Hooper, 1996, p. 567)

In *On Stories*, C. S. Lewis writes that the state of being in a literary work is to be enjoyed and 'the atmosphere should be entered into so that it comprises our whole imaginative vision' (Ward, 2008, p. 17). Living inside a work imaginatively is central to well-being because the arts depend on '*connaitre* not *savoir*' (Lewis, 1971/1964, p. 109).

It is vital that children and young people are not confined to just one world. The image of the Pevensie children in *The Lion, The Witch and The Wardrobe* entering another world through the wardrobe door in Professor Digory Kirk's house is one of the most memorable and lasting images of the *Chronicles of Narnia* and all of children's literature. It seems unlikely that the image of the door of the wardrobe is coincidental. The 'cardinal' virtues (Prudence, Temperance, Justice, Fortitude) are so named because they come from the Latin word *cardo* denoting 'hinge' as in 'the hinge of a door'. In other words, they are 'pivotal' for everyone. Everything, in terms of human well-being, hangs or 'hinges' on these virtues (Chapter 8). An English pedagogic 'home' should always be furnished with such doorways to other worlds. What the Pevensie children acquire in the world of Narnia are not simply individual, internal virtues; they have significance for living together. The imaginative and spiritual cannot be divorced from the social and moral.

Two teachers and two homes

In *The Magician's Nephew* (C. S. Lewis, 1989/1955), the first in the sequence of the seven Narnia novels, Digory (as the boy who grows up to be the Professor in following novel, *The Lion, The Witch and the Wardrobe*) and his friend, Polly, the girl next door, are transported by his Uncle Andrew, a selfish and cowardly magician, by means of magic rings, to a World beyond their own World. The place is barren and lifeless. Interestingly, as we saw in Chapter 1, the novel's author declared that the task of the modern educator was to 'irrigate deserts'. In *The Magician's Nephew* the world to which the children are transported is the dead world of Charn, where they arouse a sleeping witch who is guilty of genocide and bent upon imposing her will and rule on everyone back in their world.

Ethical English teachers will not take Uncle Andrew, a manipulative magician, as a role model. He has scant regard for children's well-being, and coerces and emotionally blackmails them into otherworldly travel. The ethos of English, as understood in this book, never entails the use of 'magic rings'. We need to be realistic about the damage that teachers such as Uncle Andrew are capable of inflicting. In the end Digory and Polly come out of it rather well and prove to be resilient and enterprising but it is no thanks to Uncle Andrew.

In *The Magician's Nephew* (Lewis, 1989/1955), Uncle Andrew, a magician who is experimenting with powers too great for him to control, manages to trick Polly and sends her out of this world to another world where she could be in great danger. We pick the story up in Chapter 2, just after Polly has vanished, with Digory alone facing Uncle Andrew. He asks if Uncle Andrew is going to bring her back and is told that the green rings (as opposed to the yellow ring Polly had used to exit this world) draw you back:

> 'But Polly hasn't got a green ring.'
> 'No.' said Uncle Andrew with a cruel smile.
> 'Then she can't get back,' shouted Digory. 'And it's exactly the same as if you'd murdered her.'
> 'She can get back,' said Uncle Andrew, 'if someone else will go after her, wearing a yellow ring himself and taking two green rings, one to bring himself back and one to bring her back.'
> And now of course Digory saw the trap in which he was caught and he stared at Uncle Andrew, saying nothing with his mouth wide open. His cheeks had gone very pale.

Digory is manipulated by his Uncle who taunts him, and claims he lacks courage because women have brought him up. Digory's mother is dying, his father is in India and Uncle Andrew gets him to do what he wants:

> 'The sooner you go, the sooner you'll be back,' said Uncle Andrew cheerfully.
> 'But you don't really know whether I can get back.'
> Uncle Andrew shrugged his shoulders, walked across to the door, unlocked it, threw it open and said:
> 'Oh very well then. Just as you please. Go down and have your dinner. Leave the little girl to be eaten by wild animals or drowned or starved in the Otherworld or lost there for good, if that's what you prefer. It's all one to me. Perhaps before tea time you'd better drop in on Mrs Plummer and explain that she'll never see her daughter again; because you were afraid to put on a ring.'
> 'By gum,' said Digory, 'don't I just wish I was big enough to punch your head!'

Uncle Andrew is using the children to further his own career. He is vain, arrogant, self-centred and causes immense frustration in the children. Digory can barely stop himself from physically attacking Uncle Andrew who does not only annoy, but scares the children. They do not want to be in his presence and try to get away from him because he makes them feel uncomfortable. They know they are in danger when they are with him and prove to be good judges of character for he has no regard for their well-being. Uncle Andrew has his comeuppance and ends up looking ridiculous but it is a salutary tale that some teachers and some of the 'worlds' to which they wish to take children are unhealthy and can wound and harm the child's spirit.

Conversely, ethical teaching is always for the benefit of the child. English teachers committed to children's spiritual well-being should seek to emulate Digory as the teacher in whose house the Pevensie children live in the following novel *The Lion, The Witch and The Wardrobe*. Professor Digory Kirk is a remarkable teacher of children. In contrast to the depiction in the movie (Adamson, 2005), in the novel the kindly Professor meets the children at the front door and welcomes them to his home. Once settled, Lucy (the most spiritually sensitive of the children) and then Edmund and finally Peter and Susan enter the world of Narnia through the wardrobe door. Digory provides a wardrobe where children can 'step further in' than they ordinarily would. When Lucy feels snow, 'something soft and powdery and extremely cold' rather than 'the hard, smooth wood of the floor of the wardrobe' that she was expecting; she feels 'a little frightened' but also 'very inquisitive and excited as well' (Lewis, 1989/1950, p. 183). This is perhaps the way the spirituality of literature often works.

The wardrobe through which the children enter Narnia is part of the furniture of the Professor's house. Ethical English should provide such 'wardrobes' where children can experience more than they would by remaining in their primary world. Digory provides his guests with a means of especially significant, long distance, travel. Yet it is entirely their choice whether to open the door and to step inside. Their 'teacher' is not even present, let alone coercive, when they walk through the wardrobe door (Pike, 2013).

What is exceptional about Professor Digory Kirk as a teacher of children is that he helps them to understand their experiences and to relate well to each other. The children feel safe with him and respect him. The two older, and least spiritually aware of the Pevensie children, Peter and Susan, cannot understand Lucy's experience of Narnia at all. The kindly Professor helps them and reassures them by being a good listener:

> So they went and knocked at the study door, and the Professor said 'Come in', and got up and found chairs for them and said he was quite at their disposal. Then he sat listening to them with the tips of his fingers pressed together and never interrupting, till they had finished the whole story. After that he said nothing for quite a long time. Then he cleared his throat and said the last thing either of them expected:

> 'How do you know', he asked, 'that your sister's story is not true?'
> 'Oh, but – ' began Susan, and then stopped. Anyone could see from the old man's face that he was perfectly serious.

When the older children point out that all the events that Lucy claims to have experienced (meeting Mr Tumnus the fawn and having tea with him, for instance) could not have happened in the time she was gone, the Professor begins from the assumption that Lucy is truthful rather than vice versa. Yet he is not naïve or gullible and suggests that the discrepancy between the rate of time in England and time in the other world is not something Lucy would have been likely to fabricate. The dialogue between Professor Digory Kirk and Lucy's brother and sister are rich in pedagogic significance. The children go to him rather than the other way round. He listens to them tell him the whole story without interrupting and prompts them to consider an alternative interpretation.

Professor Digory Kirk does not talk in a monologue with the children passively listening and then perhaps writing. There is a real dialogue. This is significant because 'it is essentially in the discourse between the teacher and pupils that education is done, or fails to be done' (Edwards and Mercer, 1987, p. 101). The children take the initiative; they are the instigators and take responsibility for their learning. What we see in the dialogue between the Professor and the children is what cognitive psychologists and discourse experts term a series of IRF (Initiation–Response–Feedback) 'loops' which good English teachers use all the time, often quite intuitively. There is genuine dialogue and real questions are asked. 'Real' questions are those to which one does not already know the answer; they are used in real life and differ from those used in schools and classrooms when children often play 'guessing games' and try and come up with the answer they think the teacher wants to hear.

The Professor's first question is 'How do you know that your sister's story is not true?' He wants them to justify their assertion, to provide the evidence for the conclusion they have reached. He does not simply tell them that their conclusion is invalid or unsubstantiated or just plain wrong. And his question prompts them to do the thinking for themselves; it is a stimulus. He provides them with the exercise of verbal reasoning and guides their thought, gently 'scaffolding' their thinking. It is worth considering how this works with an expert teacher like Professor Kirk. According to Vygotsky, one of the most influential figures in Western developmental psychology, the reasoning we engage in with another person initially (*inter*mental reasoning) eventually becomes the reasoning we can engage in on our own (*intra*mental reasoning). If Peter and Susan had been issued with paper and pens and given the task of arguing the case for or against the proposition that their sister was lying, they would have been faced with a blank page and would not have had the chance to rehearse their ideas or try them out on an expert.

Expert teachers do precisely what Professor Digory Kirk does and ask for justification when a view is put forward. Put simply, this is an apprenticeship model of learning. It is also exactly the sort of conversation Jesus had with the woman at the well (who learned by *asking* questions not just *answering* them, just like the Pevensie children). For Vygotsky, 'Human learning presupposes a specific social nature and a process by which children grow into the intellectual life of those around them' (Vygotsky, 1978, p. 88). Through engaging in dialogue with a more able peer or a teacher or parent, the child's learning is 'scaffolded' until he or she has the strength to stand unaided. Another analogy is of the stabilizers (or training wheels) on a bicycle when a child is learning to ride. The parent holds the saddle (or seat) until it is not really being held at all and the child can balance on the bicycle without any support. In teaching the support is provided not by steel scaffolding or a reassuring parental hand but through language. The right words used in the right way are a combination of scaffold, stabilizers and stimulus.

The way the teacher uses language is extremely important. Some teachers' words can get the child 'riding the bicycle' (thinking and reasoning independently) far more effectively than others. Of course, like the parental hand when riding a bicycle the learner needs to trust the teacher. The Professor, as an expert teacher, asks very skilful follow-up or supplementary questions of just the right sort. He does not do lots of talking but does just enough to stimulate the right sort of thinking. Peter and Susan grow into the thought of their teacher. He also provides very clear explanations and instructions. Significantly, the children are in a pair and have engaged in dialogue before conversing with their teacher. This is very different to being a passive learner sitting at the back of a class of 30 others while the teacher talks but very little is going on inside one's head. Peter and Susan want to learn and their teacher provides a rigorous cognitive challenge for them.

Here, the teacher is rightly valued, not merely as a child-centred facilitator, but as an expert who should be listened to and respected. He pitches work at a challenging level which 'stretches' learners and is relevant. This helps children to develop intellectually but is quite different to the model in some classrooms where children are mainly quiet and attentive listeners and writers. This latter model can lead to some pupils being more passive than one might wish; some classrooms can lapse into transmission teaching on occasions when dialogue would be better (Pike, 2000b, 2001). This approach is prone to produce students who do not take the initiative, justify and negotiate. In developmental and cognitive psychology (how children grow and think) following the work of Vygotsky, the adult supports the learner until the learner can stand unaided; the construction of knowledge and understanding is a social activity and language is central.

What we witness the Pevensie children go through with Professor Digory Kirk is a ZPD (zone of proximal development). This is a zone of especially productive learning and represents a major leap forward in understanding. The classic definition of a ZPD is the: 'distance between the actual developmental level as determined by independent problem solving and the level of potential development as determined through problem solving under adult guidance or in collaboration with more capable peers' (Vygotsky, 1978, p. 88). In other words, it is the difference between what the learner can do unaided and what he or she can do with a little support or 'scaffolding' through *words*.

The result of engaging with the Professor is that real or 'principled' knowledge rather than 'ritual' knowledge is attained. Ritual knowledge is 'knowing how to do something' (Edwards and Mercer, 1987, p. 97) but not really grasping why it works. It is getting the answer right in school without really knowing why it is the right answer. For instance, it is 'possible to learn how to do many algebraic operations without understanding how or why they work' (Edwards and Mercer, 1987, p. 96). The problem with ritual knowledge is that it 'substitutes for an understanding of underlying principles' (Edwards and Mercer, 1987, p. 97). An important definition for all teachers is that:

> Principled knowledge is defined as essentially explanatory, oriented towards an understanding of how procedures and processes work, of why certain conclusions are necessary or valid, rather than being arbitrary things to say because they seem to please the teacher. (Edwards and Mercer, 1987, p. 97)

Professor Digory Kirk helps the children think logically and ruminates 'I wonder what they *do* teach them at these schools?' (Lewis, 1989/1950, p. 219) Yet he does not just teach for cognitive development. There is a moral dimension to his teaching and the learners reflect upon ultimate questions about the nature of reality. The teaching and learning encounter helps learners live better and enables them to understand other people (especially Lucy) better. This is not just about effective and efficient teaching informed by cognitive psychology, it is ethical and is in the interests of learners.

Professor Kirk treats the children with dignity and is honest about what he does not know:

> If there really is a door in this house that leads to some other world (and I should warn you that this is a very strange house, and even I know very little about it) – if, I say, she had got into another world, I should not be at all surprised to find out that the other world had a separate time of its own; so that however long you stayed there it would never take up any of *our* time.

When Susan asks him if he really means that 'there could be other worlds', he readily replies 'nothing is more probable' (Lewis, 1989/1950, p. 49).

Well-being through reading

Liberating students to experience other worlds through literature is central to English that should enable children and young people to travel to places they would not normally visit if they were left to their own devices. One example of this in English is the reading of classic, pre-twentieth-century works that 'transcend the restrictions of time and the written word' and enable 'people of all ages and backgrounds the opportunity to enter other worlds' (Iser, 1971, p. 30). Rather than simply allowing children and young people to read whatever they like, teachers of English have a moral responsibility to introduce them to high quality literature. Only reading about the world they already know well is inadequate; an ethical approach to English will introduce them to new worlds that are different to the one they currently inhabit. The difference (be it social, cultural, ethnic, religious, moral or linguistic) between the world of canonical texts and that of the modern reader can justify the inclusion of a 'canon' of pre-twentieth-century works in the curriculum for ethnically and socially heterogeneous schools in the twenty-first century. It is misguided, therefore, to assume that only texts written in the late-twentieth or early-twenty-first century can be relevant to today's adolescents; Blake and Donne 'can have a good deal more relevance to life today than contemporary poems that foreground the ephemeral preoccupations of the present' (Benton and Benton, 1998, p. vii).

A literary text differs from any other form of writing because it 'neither describes nor constitutes real objects', and by definition it 'diverges from the real experiences of the reader in that it offers views and opens up perspectives in which the empirically known world of one's own personal experience appears changed' (Iser 1971, p. 8). The literary work does not reside entirely with the reader's own experiences; if it did, it would not be indeterminate, and 'indeterminacy is the fundamental precondition for reader participation' (Iser, 1971, p. 14). In their indeterminacy, literary texts are resistant to the course of time, 'because their structure allows the reader to place himself [sic] within the world of fiction' (Iser, 1971, p. 44).

Many effective approaches to teaching such authors have been developed (e.g. Atkinson, 1995; Pike, 2000b, 2003a). A text's indeterminacy requires a reader to bring personal experience, cultural background, imagination, predisposition and even idiosyncratic knowledge with him or her so that a co-construction of meaning with its author is achieved. Consequently, although the relevance of pre-twentieth-century literature to the lives of young people growing up in a multi-cultural society is often considered to be limited (Grimes and Belote, 1994), it is important to recognize that relevance is not dependent upon writer and reader residing within the same culture or having similar backgrounds. In assessing the role of a reader's experience, Iser (1971, pp. 7–8) concludes that 'we recognize in literature so many elements that play a part in our own experience', and yet they are 'put together in a different way – in other words, they constitute a familiar world reproduced in an unfamiliar form'. The nature of a literary text is especially pertinent in considering some objections to classic literature being read in schools. Pre-twentieth-century literature, it has been suggested (Gabler and Gabler, 1982; Davis, 1992), can perpetuate anachronistic values and prejudice sponsored by governments wishing to engineer a certain sort of social cohesion. Yet, it is the very difference between today's experience and such texts that can result in the work 'transcending its historical position' (Iser, 1971, p. 44).

Subject knowledge and social justice

It is sometimes mistakenly argued that 'thinking skills' are more important than subject knowledge (100 academics in *The Telegraph*, 20 March 2013). The problem with this, of course, is that one needs knowledge to be able to think. In English if a student does not possess sufficient cultural literacy (Hirsch, 1987) comprehension of a text is impeded or prevented. If a child does not understand the metalanguage (grammar) of English he or she will not have the fuller vocabulary needed to critique a text well or comment with precision on its style and structure. As we have seen, English is more than a subject on the curriculum, it is important to our culture and if it ceases to emphasize works from the English literary canon (and especially those written pre-1900) we will all be the poorer. Children from the poorest backgrounds will continue to be poorest, though, as they are less likely to have highly educated parents who discuss Shakespeare or take them to the theatre or read classic novels, for instance.

If English teachers are to liberate, to provide a way out, it is vital that they provide children with an inspiring, imaginative and informed introduction to English literature and the language in which it is written. While there is a place for the study of the media and film this should not have an equivalent place alongside Shakespeare; it certainly should not receive more attention than high quality literature in English. If English is to liberate young people it must avoid 'dumbing down'. A prequisite of a culturally rich curriculum is having teachers who are both able and keen to teach it.

Yet many 'well-qualified' English graduates seem to have spent insufficient time studying the English literary heritage (or English language) to enable them to teach it well. Many 'English' degrees seem to have a majority of content devoted to more popular or fashionable areas than the English literary heritage. Having interviewed hundreds of applicants for places on a PGCE (Post Graduate Certificate in Education) English course over the last dozen or so years has been an eye-opener with regard to the content of many 'English' degrees and the subject knowledge of final year students or graduates. When asking which Shakespeare plays an English graduate has read it is not uncommon for just three or four plays to be listed (often *Romeo and Juliet* which they read in Year 9, *Macbeth* from GCSE (General Certificate in Secondary Education), one from A level and one at degree level).

I once asked a student with a First class honours degree in English to list the Shakespeare plays with which she was familiar. She listed just three, one of which was *King Lear*. I then thought to strike up an intelligent conversation about *King Lear* and happened to observe that it was remarkable how great an influence Cordelia has in the play given she has so few lines. The student (who did not appear to be phased by nerves) asked if Cordelia was 'one of the bad sisters or the good one'. Knowing *King Lear* is not a prerequisite for entry to initial teacher education in English; the point is that this was a Shakespeare play the graduate offered as one with which she was familiar. Of course, the problem with not knowing something can be that you don't know what you don't know. Consequently a subject knowledge audit is provided (Appendix 1), which lists the sort of knowledge a teacher of English should possess if he or she is to have at their command a repertoire of texts and terms with which to engage students through appropriate pedagogy. An English graduate entering nine months of Initial Teacher Education (ITE) in the United Kingdom should be able to focus on 'how to teach' rather than having to augment subject knowledge by reading what they might have read in their previous three or four years studying English at degree level.

The contrast between the student with a First (from a University that will remain nameless) and my own experience of English in the 1980s at the University of Leeds is striking. I showed my naivety in my second year as an undergraduate having commenced the mandatory Shakespeare course by asking for a list of plays I should read. I had anticipated a list of perhaps six plays (maybe the tragedies or the histories or the late plays) but I was kindly told that 'this is a *Shakespeare* finals paper'. It took a little while to sink in but after the shock had worn off I set about drawing up a timetable to read one play per week and got through 30 Shakespeare plays in the three ten week terms we then had (it was one course among many and just the sort of thing a student on an English degree might be expected to do). Today, many students of English at degree level at some universities appear to spend an equivalent amount of time, or more, on courses such as 'Popular Culture', 'Myths, Meaning and Movies' or 'Body, Media and Culture' (Pike, 2003).

This is not to suggest that all modern English degrees have gone the way of the one taken by the applicant with the First for many provide students of English at degree level with a comprehensive introduction to the literary heritage. Such knowledge of the canon of pre-twentieth-century literature is important in today's classroom as it can enable readers to acquire the cultural knowledge that supports citizenship in the West and England in particular (Hirsch, 1987). Reading the canon in English has many other advantages besides, especially if taught well (Pike, 2003), but many children and young people are unlikely to have their cultural literacy augmented and enhanced if their teachers believe this to be elitist or they do not have sufficiently wide knowledge themselves. Some of the best teachers of English have excellent subject knowledge upon which they can easily draw in a sequence of lessons in imaginative and intellectually stimulating ways. Teaching dramatic monologues by Browning (such as 'Porphyria's Lover' or 'My Last Duchess') perhaps using drama techniques when scripting one end of a telephone conversation may be natural if the teacher is familiar with these works but impossible if he or she does not have this subject knowledge (Pike, 2004). A prerequisite for enabling young people to enjoy John Donne's poetry (and to imaginatively create their own metaphysical conceits, for instance) is an appreciation of Donne's wit on the part of the teacher of English.

Yet many of the more academically able students in English may be insufficiently challenged by being set shorter, more accessible, works that elicit a more positive reaction initially than some more challenging works which might stretch them more. Some students who could be reading *To Kill a Mockingbird* are set *Of Mice and Men*; those who could be reading *A Man for all Seasons* (and learning about a different time to the one they live in) are reading *Blood Brothers*. Of course they may well read these less challenging works as well but if they are higher ability students they may benefit from being given a greater challenge (which may in the long run be more satisfying). Some more able 15- or 16-year-olds who could be reading George Eliot's *Silas Marner* or Jane Austen's *Northanger Abbey* are sometimes to be found studying *Heroes* by Cormier in their English lessons. It is not that Cormier does not write well but he is not as challenging as Eliot or Austen. If a student in set 1 in a comprehensive school is not challenged academically to the same degree that he or she would be if attending a grammar school, we need to ask questions about how well the comprehensive is serving them.

Some colleagues of mine in one state school looked sceptical when I chose two books of Milton's *Paradise Lost* for a Lower Sixth group to study as they thought this would be unpopular and inaccessible to modern 17-year-olds. I explained that in many respects this was an ideal text for students of that age as issues of authority, independence and rebellion were explored in Milton's epic poem. Acquiring the background knowledge to appreciate and enjoy the poem was a real education for many of them. For English to be ethical and to liberate students from the narrow, parochial and particular it will need to guard against 'dumbing down' among both teachers and students so that they are enabled to think.

A knowledge and appreciation of classic works is not just the preserve of the most academically able students in English (Grove, 1998). There are numerous activities and approaches to enable less academic students, including those with special educational needs (SEN) to access and enjoy their heritage. From the animated tales of Shakespeare on DVD (perhaps with cartoon strip tasks to follow) to syllable-clapping and chanting Blake's 'Tyger, Tyger, burning bright' (perhaps identifying rhyming patterns with highlighter pens), there are ways and means to include all students. *Including students with SEN and/ or disabilities in secondary English* (TDA, 2009) provides a valuable audit of classroom activities to ensure that barriers to learning are overcome. Apart from augmenting their experience, giving access to their literary and cultural heritage and being enjoyable (so long as appropriate pedagogy is adopted) there is a social justice argument for literature not becoming the preserve of the elite or the most able students in English (Pike, 2004, pp. 141–2).

When, at the age of 29, with eight years teaching experience, I was appointed as head of a large faculty including English in a 'flagship' comprehensive, I knew that this was the territory of an important battle I would have to fight. The English department, by time-honoured custom, only entered the top five classes (out of eight or nine) for GCSE English literature, as it was felt that the chance to gain the all-important C grade in GCSE English (language) would be jeopardized by spending time reading additional literature rather than focusing on improving writing (spelling, punctuation and grammar). I was told by my new colleagues (nearly all of whom were old enough to be my mother) that if I entered everyone for English literature the percentage of students gaining a C grade in English would drop dramatically and I (the new boy) would be held responsible by the Head teacher for presiding over a drastic fall in results. It was with a deep breath that the decision was taken. The English team, to their credit, worked hard to engage less able students in a wider experience of literature, so it was a relief when results went up not down (by around 20% over two years) in GCSE English. Often students do not lack the *skill* but the *will* to learn and reading more literature (while putting in place strategies to improve their language grade) did appear to offer significant benefits.

We need to reflect upon the purposes of studying literature. Davies, for example, maintains that:

> The fundamental aim of such an area of study is to help readers discover what texts are trying to reveal, in a spirit of good faith. This form of study aims to give young people access to what different generations and cultures are trying to tell each other about their lives; it aims to give them access to the excitement or amazement of hearing such things, and thus to enlarge the scope of their lives. (1996, p. 141)

This necessarily entails giving children and young people responsibility and fostering independent learning and personal response. Encouraging children to reflect upon their own perspective has been observed to have profound effects (Pike, 1999, 2000c). We are reminded in *The Magician's Nephew* 'what you see and hear depends a good deal on where you are standing' (Lewis, 1989/1955, p. 118). The spiritual and moral significance of teaching literature from other times is that it gives readers somewhere else to stand.

It is, of course, vital that those students with SEN or EAL (Cameron, 2003; DfES, 2005; DfES, 2002, Hawkins, 2006) who need help to improve their literacy receive it. It is disempowering if one cannot read textbooks at school or media items outside school. It may also be dangerous if one cannot read health and safety information or posters on the walls of a doctor's surgery.

It is often demoralizing if one cannot read stories. We need to ensure that our curriculum decisions are ethical, in that they must be taken for the right reasons and in students' best interests. A key tenet of ethical English is that students are not worth more than their peers if they can read Milton and get a top grade at A level. A child is not more valuable if they are more intelligent and decisions in school need to reflect this. Equally, too much emphasis has been placed on those students on the C/D border over the last 20 years in English when it should be just as important to help a child achieve a A rather than a B or an E instead of a F or G grade.

According to John Rawls in *A Theory of Justice* (1971) we should draw a 'veil of ignorance' over our eyes when making decisions. Applied to a school setting, if I do not know whether I am the most or least intelligent student, decisions made will be just for everyone. They will not discriminate against the least able as I may be one of them. Rawls did not invent this notion which has been known in different forms for centuries. In 1948, Mahatma Ghandi suggested that we look at the poorest and weakest man and consider if any decision to be taken would benefit him: 'Will he gain anything by it? Will it restore him to a control over his own life and destiny? In other words, will it lead to swaraj [freedom] for the hungry and spiritually starving millions?' In the Gospel of Matthew, Christ tells a parable where the King declares: 'I was hungry and you gave Me food; I was thirsty and you gave Me drink; I was a stranger and you took Me in; I was naked and you clothed Me; I was sick and you visited Me; I was in prison and you came to Me.' (Matt 25. 35–6). Those being addressed then ask the King when they had performed any of these acts and the King tells them 'when you have done it unto one of the least of these, my brethren, ye have done it unto me' (Matt 25.40). A hallmark of a humane, liberal, compassionate society is that those who may appear to be 'least' are accorded dignity and respect. They are spiritually significant.

Study questions

1 What sort of 'house' are you building?

2 How does your role *in loco parentis* promote positive attitudes and responsibility in learners?

3 How can you be more benevolent while maintaining good order in the classroom?

4 How can we gauge if something is spiritually healthy?

5 What are your relationships with students like?

6 Which cardinal virtues have you promoted through English?

7 How can English foster well-being?

8 How have you helped learners to enter other worlds?

9 Why is diachronic reading important?

10 What do you see as the ontological potential of English?

11 How can you engage learners?

12 What ultimate questions have learners asked in your lessons?

13 When have you reached the spirit of the child?

3

The art of planning and assessing English

This chapter considers the art of planning teaching and assessing learning that is true to the spirit of ethical English. As we saw in the last chapter English should challenge and include everyone but we need to think a little more about the character of English in order to understand how it may meet diverse needs. Arguably, 'English belongs more in the arts than in the linguistic disciplines' (Goodwyn, 2011, p. 96) and here we consider how that might apply to the planning, teaching and assessment of English. If 'art and works of art, by springing from and being created by the spirit, are themselves of a spiritual kind' (Hegel, 1997, pp. 138, 145) then English teaching is spiritually significant. Important work (Stevens and McGuinn, 2004) has been done in this area but the present chapter develops the notion of teaching English as an art by recognizing that spiritual and aesthetic experience often go together.

The art of planning English

In 1876 in a letter to her friend, Frederic Harrison, George Eliot observed that teaching could be compared to the 'picture' or the 'diagram'. Both are visible but in strikingly different ways. According to George Eliot 'aesthetic teaching' is more akin to the 'picture' than the 'diagram':

> I think aesthetic teaching is the highest of all teaching because it deals with life in its highest complexity. But if it ceases to be purely aesthetic – if it lapses anywhere from the picture to the diagram – it becomes the most offensive of all teaching.

Here Eliot observes that 'aesthetic teaching deals with life in its highest complexity' and likens this to a picture rather than a diagram; this is central to the way English enables learners to explore ultimate questions as they respond personally to challenging works and topics.

Arguably, the planning of inspirational teaching and learning in English rarely arises from rational, mechanistic planning for attainment of 'targets'. Certain craft of the classroom skills and technical proficiency are important (as they are to artists such as painters because they *underpin* the art) but there is more to the creation of the 'picture' that is English than technical skills. To understand and work in a way that is true to the 'ethos' or 'spirit' of English we need to appreciate that:

> teaching is an art in that teachers, like painters, composers, actresses, and dancers, make judgements based largely on qualities that unfold during the course of the action. (Eisner, 2002, p. 155)

It is important to acknowledge that 'teaching is a form of human action in which many of the ends achieved are emergent' because they are 'found in the course of interaction with students rather than preconceived' (Eisner, 2002, pp. 155–6). The experience of teaching tells us that what is learned is not always planned before the lesson. This is not necessarily due to laziness or a lack of diligence; it simply recognizes that teaching and learning in English is not always predictable, nor should it be so. Excellent teachers take opportunities and 'teachable moments' as they arise with students. How young people respond on a particular day is not always predictable: they are, after all, only *human*.

In the previous chapter we saw that 'being' in English teaching was not straightforward in the sense that 'being in London' is; it is more like 'being in love' or 'being with a son or a daughter'. Being in English teaching requires the teacher to 'live with the intricacies, absurdities, and dissonances of life, without seeking to reduce them to neat formulae or *maps*' (Huebner, 1999/1962, p. 24 my italic), or as George Eliot put it, the 'diagram'. The aesthetic, imaginative and creative activities of pupils cannot be divorced from the 'aesthetic teaching' (Pike, 2004d) of their teachers and we need to appreciate that one does not tend to foster creativity in pupils by focusing too much on assessments. English teaching can only reach the spirit of the child if it is aesthetic and has the features of the 'picture' rather than the 'diagram'. To put it another way, the 'picture' of English pedagogy must not be reduced to the 'diagram' of 'painting-by-numbers'. A few years ago I worked on the latter type of painting with my daughter. We both knew that as long as we followed the instructions we would have a rather plump looking puffin in the 'right' colours sooner or later. We did not need to discuss the shade of blue for the sea or the shape of the puffin. As the 'teacher' I did not have to be imaginative; I just had to follow the numbers. The implication will not be lost on teachers of English.

Allowing 'for the creation of ends in process' requires a 'model of teaching akin to other arts' (Eisner, 2002, p. 156) and lessons in creativity do not always follow a formula where learning objectives are always precisely defined and efficiently communicated to learners at the start of a lesson. Looking to other arts can be helpful to those seeking to understand the ethos and the art of English: the 'picture is made by deploying pigments on a piece of canvass, but the picture is not a pigment and canvass structure' (Langer, 1957, p. 28). Analogously, the art of both teaching and learning English transcends the sum of its parts. English teachers need to be encouraged to practice their art not to suppress it.

If notions of teaching as an art 'result in attention being devoted to personal factors and qualities' (Muijs and Reynolds, 2001, p. vii), which are portrayed as difficult or troublesome, this is especially harmful to ethical English. Evidently, 'the significance of implicit and intuitive elements in human action' (McLaughlin, 1999, p. 12) alerts us to the inadequacy of 'technical rationality' as a means of understanding the ethos of English. The mnemonic 'Operational' is a way of remembering the key elements of a lesson plan, especially for newly qualified teachers or those wishing for guidance in planning (Pike, 2004a, pp. 12–21). The stem of the mnemonic is readily identified as the word 'opera' (Objectives; Plenary; En1, 2, 3, Resources; Assessment) which as an art-form, is a multi-media event. As a dramatic composition its performance requires the co-ordination of different people and especially their movement and speech; various participants play different roles. Likewise, students in English learn through their response to the art of the lesson. Planning an English lesson is planning for the 'opera' to begin.

Ethical teachers will necessarily be concerned with more than technical proficiency, as they will seek to nurture the spiritual and moral development of their students. Arguably, when excellent teachers go about planning, they are thinking, 'what powerful learning experiences can I generate that will also provide me with ways of enabling student progress?' They are thinking 'what is an exciting and challenging task for my students?' 'How can it be differentiated so that all students can succeed and learn something about both the content and also their own development?' (Goodwyn, 2011, pp. 102–3). Reference to 'powerful learning experiences' reminds us of the spiritual and moral potential of English.

The ethics of planning English

Let us consider one instance of the process a teacher of English might go through when planning to teach and employing Assessment for Learning (AfL). The teacher decides that, after teaching transactional writing and the form of business letters (making sure everyone in the class writes 'Yours sincerely,' correctly at the end of their letters with a capital 'Y', lower case 's' and comma after the final 'y') some engagement with imaginative literature is due. He or she wants to foster children's spiritual and moral development too and feels that the time is right for these 13- and 14-year-olds to ask some 'big questions' about human life. The *Frankenstein* playscript by Philip Pullman is chosen for this Year 9 class and exciting roleplays and prediction exercises at key moments come to mind alongside more reflective work on the theme of whether human beings should 'play God' and engage in genetic engineering or cloning, for instance. The teacher also feels that the opportunity should be taken for students to engage in their own creative writing on the 'playing God' theme.

Arguably, it might only be after this creative and imaginative phase that the teacher will look at the requirements of specific Assessment Focii or AFs for En1 (Speaking and Listening), En2 (Reading) and En3 (Writing). An integrated approach where all the modes of language use are employed is preferred and the acronym 'OPERA' is used to check that plans evince the techniques that underpin the teacher's creative art. First, though, the teacher looks at the AFs for En1 (Speaking and Listening) and En2 (Reading) because the oracy will be textually based (DfE, 2011):

Reading

AF2 – understand, describe, select or retrieve information, events or ideas from texts and use quotation and reference to text.

AF3 – deduce, infer or interpret information, events or ideas from texts.

AF4 – identify and comment on the structure and organization of texts, including grammatical and presentational features at text level.

AF5 – explain and comment on writers' use of language, including grammatical and literary features at word and sentence level.

AF6 – identify and comment on writers' purposes and viewpoints, and the overall effect of the text on the reader.

After reading the whole play discussion will be in pairs and then students will concentrate on the last of these, AF6, after performing short scenes in small groups. Before finalizing what to do the teacher checks the AFs (Assessment Focii) for Speaking and Listening and realizes that AF1, AF2 and AF3 are automatically (and painlessly) going to be covered. It is not an onerous process:

AF1 Talking to others
Talk in purposeful and imaginative ways to explore ideas and feelings, adapting and varying structure and vocabulary according to purpose, listeners, and content.

AF2 Talking with others
Listen and respond to others, including in pairs and groups, shaping meanings through suggestions, comments and questions.

AF3 Talking within role-play and drama
Create and sustain different roles and scenarios, adapting techniques in a range of dramatic activities to explore texts, ideas and issues.

The teacher will follow role-play and performance by students scripting a dialogue about the monster they have created. They will then do some small group discussion work where they will debate the rights and wrongs of 'playing God' and of scientists cloning or engaging in genetic engineering. When it comes to planning the small group work the teacher looks at AF2 within Speaking and Listening and then finds the levels at which the children were working the last time they did small group discussion work. The teacher sees that most of the children were achieving level 5 although some were achieving level 4 and two in the class were achieving level 3. Looking down the column, AF2, the teacher finds the following level descriptors:

L6 Across a range of contexts
engage with complex material making perceptive responses, showing awareness of the speaker's aims and extending meanings, adopt group roles and responsibilities independently, drawing ideas together and promoting effective discussion.

L5 Across a range of contexts
recognize significant details and implicit meanings, developing the speaker's ideas in different ways, sustain roles and responsibilities with independence in pairs or groups, sometimes shaping overall direction of talk with effective contributions.

L4 Across a range of contexts
show generally clear understanding of content and how it is presented, sometimes introducing new material or ideas, take on straightforward roles and responsibilities in pairs and groups

L3 Across most contexts
respond to the speaker's main ideas, developing them through generally relevant comments and suggestions, attempt different roles and responsibilities in pairs or groups.

The teacher then designs the speaking and listening activity to allow children to make progress and to work towards the next level. Differentiation that enables a learner to achieve a personal best academically is a vital aspect of ethical teaching (see Pike, 2004a and 2013, Chapter 9). Adopting a 'one-size-fits-all' approach generally fails to sufficiently extend and challenge the most able or to offer adequate support for the least able in a particular class. By pitching work at an individual level we can avoid causing frustration or boredom in learners. Here the teacher shows the children the criteria before they start the speaking and listening activity so they know exactly what they have to do to make personal progress. The teacher also explains that following the activity they will peer assess each other and set targets based on the levels within this AF. However, the right balance is kept; children are aware of the criteria but are engaged with the literary work. The tail is not wagging the dog (if the tail is assessment and the dog is teaching and learning).

The same approach is taken to writing a range of texts (and even creative writing). Once the children have had their imaginations stimulated and are enthusiastic to begin writing they look at the different AFs to remind themselves of the technicalities that underpin their imaginative writing and help it to have the effect they want:

AF1 – write imaginative, interesting and thoughtful texts

AF2 – produce texts which are appropriate to task, reader and purpose

AF3 – organize and present whole texts effectively, sequencing and structuring information, ideas and events

AF4 – construct paragraphs and use cohesion within and between paragraphs

AF5 – vary sentences for clarity, purpose and effect

AF6 – write with technical accuracy of syntax and punctuation in phrases, clauses and sentences

AF7 – select appropriate and effective vocabulary

AF8 – use correct spelling.

Especially when it comes to creative writing, we need to be aware that 'correct spelling' or producing a text that is 'appropriate' to 'reader and purpose' does not get to the 'spirit' or 'ethos' of the whole *Frankenstein* experience. Certain skills and accuracy need to develop over time but imaginative composition is not defined by having 'cohesion within and between paragraphs' (AF4) any more than Shelley's *Frankenstein* is just about technology or the physiology of a 'monster'.

Although what has just been sketched might be regarded as ideal and illustrates what is possible, this approach may be regarded in certain respects as both ambitious and unrealistic in some schools. Some English departments might not wish to assess En1, 2 and 3 in one unit and might prefer to focus on one of these for the main assessment and perhaps one in a mini assessment during the unit. More importantly, many schools might not have such a 'relaxed' or 'responsive' approach to planning assessment because one or more year's work (and often the whole key stage of three years) may be planned in advance in terms of what AFs will be covered in which unit of work. This would also include specifying which texts and topics were to be covered. Further, for many, AfL would be regarded as working 'best' when the teacher looks at what AFs will be assessed and how, and only then plans the unit of work to build up those skills for final assessment. We might even think of this as 'planning backwards' so that first the teacher plans the assessment and then puts in place how to meet the criteria by designing teaching and learning accordingly. The point here is that this might really be a retrograde step in terms of the teacher's creativity, imagination, flexibility and his or her capacity to be responsive and ensure work is tailor-made to meet the needs of a particular class.

The art of assessing English

For Goodwyn (2011), in *The Expert Teacher of English*, assessment must evince four qualities (authenticity, integrity, interest and satisfaction) if it is to be developmental for the teacher. As soon as terms such as these (especially 'authenticity') are used, the need for assessment to be ethical comes into focus. Goodwyn defines 'interest' (p. 108) as generating 'work of interest to the teacher's understanding of the student' (p. 105) and explains that, 'the teacher is interested in the feedback that the students' outcomes provide about the teaching'. He further suggests that the teacher needs to believe that the task was worth doing (for it to have integrity) and states that teachers should evaluate whether the quality of the task design was really effective (p. 105). For Goodwyn:

> Good assessment allows students to demonstrate what they 'can do' and also to experience some sense of achievement. It also reveals what they are struggling to do and what they need to try next to continue to improve; in that way all assessment tasks can be diagnostic. (p. 105)

We need to be sensitive here though; the emphasis on the 'can do' should not be lost in the precision of a diagnostic assessment that only identifies what a student needs to do better. The challenge for teachers committed to developing the spiritual, moral and ethical potential of young people is to 'design a task that has a real context and a longer-term purpose than a "test"' (Goodwyn, 2011, p. 104).

The fulfilment of human potential should not be seen only in narrow, academic terms. Fostering arête (or a personal best) is a key element in ethical English. It is especially important therefore to 'reflect on assessment in English at the level of its deepest purpose' (Goodwyn, 2011, p. 102) and to ask when assessment is 'good' in its arêtaic sense, in terms of the fulfilment of human potential. If the deepest purpose of assessment is to help human beings gain self-knowledge in the broadest sense, it might be considered to have decidedly spiritual qualities. If it is to manage and manipulate it is likely to be spiritually unhealthy as well as unethical.

Arguably, AfL *properly understood and practiced* is about the quality of relationships and development of understanding between the student and the teacher. Certainly, for Black and Wiliam it is 'the quality of the interaction [between pupil and teacher] which is at the heart of the pedagogy' (1998, p. 16). Marshall and Wiliam give an example of communication with eight pairs of students in an English lesson and comment that the teacher has 'created sufficient trust within the class that she is able to tell pupils, in pairs 1 and 4, that they are going in the wrong direction' (Marshall and Wiliam, 2006, p. 12). This trust or goodwill is an example of *eunoia* and is integral to ethical English:

> How pupils come to trust teachers in this way is a complex process, but an important element is that Catherine's [the teacher's] interventions suggest to the pupils that she is genuinely listening and interested in what they have to say, rather than simply telling them what to think. Her interventions are all focussed on the task of improving the pupils' work rather than on judging them, and they can see how her questions are designed to make them think further. In this way the dialogue in her classroom has the flavour of what might be called authentic conversation, as opposed to the ritualised ping-pong match of so much classroom exchange. Indeed, one feature of effective teacher-student talk is that one can imagine the same sort of dialogue occurring outside an educational setting, which is rarely the case with traditional teacher-pupil exchanges. (Marshall and Wiliam, 2006, p. 12)

AfL, properly understood, is concerned with 'improving the communication links between teachers and students about the assessment aspects of their work' (Black et al., 2003, p. 31). In this way students may become 'active learners who are able to, and expected to, take responsibility for their own learning' (Black et al., 2003, p. 7). Taking responsibility is ethical as is seeing students as individuals. The focus in AfL on each student, not just those who put their hands up (because each child participates in the assessment) may be regarded as respecting the dignity of child and ensuring a focus on individuality. Ideally, 'where it gives each pupil specific guidance on strengths and weaknesses' (Black and Wiliam, 1998, p. 12) this will 'help students take *active responsibility* for their own learning' (Black and Wiliam, 1998, p. 15 my italic). Clearly, the ethos of AfL is participatory as it enables students to 'develop their understanding of themselves as learners' (Tanner and Jones 2006, p. 60) and aims to yield the information needed 'to provide personalised and targeted instruction to learners' (Clarke et al., 2010, p. 54).

There is also the potential for such engagement and involvement to boost intrinsic motivation where judgements are not simply made in relation to a level or grade but where the focus is on what makes a more skilfully crafted or satisfying piece of work. Marshall and Wiliam refer to Sadler's notion of 'guild knowledge' (2006, p. 5) whereby pupils are 'apprenticed into the guild through the assessment process' (2006, p. 5). The development of such a community is integral to the ethos of English. As soon as one thinks about assessment in terms of the quality of relationships and interaction one can see the significance of the spiritual as 'relational consciousness' (Hay and Nye, 2006). If 'formative assessment cannot be done to the pupils but must be done with them' (2006, p. 4), this is clearly redolent of the spirituality of English that has 'being-with' learners at its heart (Chapter 2). Rightly conceived, AfL is open, honest and transparent and as it is 'criterion-referenced' rather than 'norm referenced' it is the most defensible form of assessment (because the goal posts do not move). In 'criterion referenced' assessment if one fulfils the criteria for a particular grade, one is awarded that grade. In 'norm referenced' assessment grade boundaries shift according to the performance of the population taking the assessment and what the 'norm' or average is for that population. The view that 'excellence is measured not by what level is achieved but by what progress is made' (Black et al., 2003, p. 76) is also congruent with the classical ethical view that arête (excellence) concerns the fulfilment of potential and striving for a personal best.

The strength and the weakness of Assessment for Learning (AfL) is that it does focus on the 'parts' or 'ingredients' of work to a considerable degree – and as we saw at the beginning of this chapter, the art of teaching English transcends the sum of its parts. AfL places emphasis upon giving feedback to students so that the teacher makes progress 'stepped, divisible into sub-skills' (Clarke et al., 2010, p. 55) but this approach, based on atomization, can be problematic. If we think in terms of spirituality and English teaching, one has to question whether any of the AFs or level descriptors do justice to the most important lesson one might take as a human being living in the twenty-first century from *Frankenstein* (Shelley, 1818). The aesthetic dimension of English (its imaginative and creative scope) does not lend itself easily to neat formulae and prediction:

This does, however, make any discussion of progression difficult in that it is hard to be precise about what the trajectory of the development of the imagination might be, or why one way of expressing something works better than another. It is sometimes possible to offer a retrospective explanatory analysis when comparing two pieces of work but the complexity of any given piece of writing means it is hard to itemise or predict in advance the features that might make it good except in the most general terms. (Marshall and Wiliam, 2006, p. 3)

Despite everything that has been said in praise of AfL, rightly conceived, (and the emphasis in the classroom and different ways of implementing AfL make a significant difference) it is very much about being precise about the 'trajectory' of a child and his or her progression and it is certainly concerned with itemizing features of work in advance and not just retrospectively. Progression can only occur 'if classroom discussion develops beyond a series of rapid-fire closed questions – which seem pacey but often include a few pupils and allow little time for reflection – towards an atmosphere where the activities are so scaffolded that they offer real opportunities for thinking' (Marshall and Wiliam, 2006, p. 6).

Yet there are still a number of problems with conceiving English teachers as skilled technicians that 'scaffold' learning. Such a reduction betrays the assumption that the world can be known in a rational, analytic and scientific way. While this might be sufficient for the more technical aspects of the subject of English (such as teaching grammar or spelling) it fails to do justice to the experience of teaching literature or of imaginative composition in the English classroom. According to Raymond O'Malley, 'the intrusion of marking or grading on whatever plane will always favour the substitution of the measurable and the technical for the unmeasurable and essential' (1950, p. 25). O'Malley wrote of the students he taught:

Each of them has spent fourteen years finding his way through his own particular tangle of problems, not always very successfully. *To grade him [sic] for anything at all would seem plain cruelty*; to choose the power of imaginative composition as the criterion for the grading would seem doubly cruel. (1950, p. 23)

In 'Measuring the Inner Light' Raymond O'Malley memorably compared the process of grading imaginative work in English with the attempt to measure a spiritual event. He suggested that we should view such assessment 'with the same suspicion that a Quaker Meeting would show towards a supposed means of measuring the Inner Light' (1950, p. 25). What Quakers mean by the Inner Light is the potential for good in everyone or an inward source of inspiration. Some Quakers interpret this in more humanistic terms and others more religiously but according to their founder, George Fox, we should walk in this 'Light' (Pike, 2006a). It seems fitting to reflect upon George Fox's account of the 'Inner Light' written in 1664. In the extract below, the specifically Christian references have been omitted. The full title refers to the doctrine of the 'Light of God and Christ' but the passage below has the capacity to resonate with English teachers (of all faiths and none) in the twenty-first century that acknowledge they are engaged in a spiritual activity. The description of the 'Inner Light' is applicable to both teachers who craft creative lessons and the students who are creative in those lessons:

> This Light which shows you these things is within you . . . It will show you how you have spent your time and what you have acted and whom you have wronged, and all your evil thoughts and vain words and all your ungodly deeds that ever you have done . . . This Light will teach you if you love it and obey it. It is present with you in all places and in all companies when you are about your labours and occasions . . . Therefore all you that love the Light within you, stand *still* in it, *out* of all your own thought and carnal reasonings, conceivings and imaginations . . . If you love it and obey it, it will lead you out of darkness and out of your evil deeds into the light of life, and into the way of Peace, and into the life and power of Truth. (Fox, 1993/1664 *with specifically Christian references omitted*)

O'Malley's title is so provocative because it refers to measuring the immeasurable and seeking to quantify the spiritual in English. In referring to the 'Inner Light' he drew attention to the spirituality and creativity of our subject and the way it eludes statistical measurement (Pike, 2006a). O'Malley believed that a piece of 'imaginative composition, unlike work that is merely technical, is its own justification' (O'Malley, 1950, p. 20) and considered that imaginative composition was the 'summit' of English teaching arguing that 'here, if anywhere, will arise notions of *what finally matters in life and what doesn't*' (O'Malley, 1950, p. 20 my italic). When we consider what does and does not matter in life, we are on spiritual territory. For an assessment to be genuinely 'good' at the deepest level it needs to be spiritually healthy.

The ethics of assessing English

AfL and other forms of formative assessment are ethical when they are committed to achieving excellence for each individual. AfL might also show us it is mistaken to assume that 'every student cannot be excellent' or that one cannot excel unless one is better than another. Ethical English defines excellence as a 'personal best' and problematizes statements such as this one:

> By definition, one cannot expect everyone to attain the highest level of achievement. If they all achieve it, it can no longer be the highest level. The very idea of the highest level presumes that there are lower levels. If everyone gets there, then the concept of the highest level vanishes. (Philips, 2002/1996, p. 333)

In arêtaic terms, one hardworking student's D grade can be more of an achievement than a lazy student's B grade. However, we know that the B is 'worth more' in the qualifications marketplace. While teachers may encourage the student with a D grade who has done their best, it has been claimed that there is 'a chasm between the liberal positions of our pedagogy and the coercive positions of our assessment' (Harrison, 2004, p. 18).

For Foucault, schools, examinations and assessments wield power over students and the examination provides an example of 'disciplinary' power. We need to consider the spirit of human beings. There are senior citizens today (50 or 60 years after their school days) who feel that they are unintelligent and inferior to others because they were labelled as such when they were at school. Reading *English for the Rejected* (1964) by David Holbrook is instructive in this regard. As English teachers we need to think about the impact of our assessment long after our students have left school. For one human being (employed as a teacher) to make judgements about another human being (a student in compulsory education) is a significant responsibility and we need to discharge it ethically. If ethical English is to liberate and free students we need to consider how it can be reconciled with notions of assessment as activity that constrains and takes away the freedom and liberty of human beings by reducing them to a grade or number. It is not difficult to see why assessment in English that marks out success and failure and discriminates between students might well be viewed as antithetical to spiritual flourishing. Schrag's view is that:

> Whereas, in earlier times, the masses of people remained invisible, now each of us becomes visible as an individual, but only along dimensions that apply to all. Thanks to the exam, each of us can be put in his or her place on a finely graded hierarchy – one that is organized around the concept of the norm. (1999, p. 377)

Evidently a larger population than ever is now to be schooled and 'sorted' for the job market. It has been argued that the problem is that 'as the scale goes up, an institution must concentrate on common characteristics – similarities – and not on things that tend to differentiate' so that the movement is from 'more to less variation, toward simplicity and legibility' and therefore school and curriculum planners, 'must adopt standardized rules and methods of production' (Loomis and Rodriguez, 2009, p. 51). In other words, the individual has been subordinated to the technical measurement of the performance of the group. The individual is only visible in relation to the whole population. If the guiding principle of the assessment is to place people in relation to a supposed 'norm' this sends a powerful message to young people.

The problem is especially acute when it comes to English as a school subject as it is at the sharp end of what some would regard as social engineering. The economic value attached to the grade C in England at GCSE (and its equivalent in other education systems across the world) can lead to an obsession with summative assessment rather than progress (although in the United Kingdom, OFSTED are now focusing far more on progress not simply attainment). Nevertheless, in such a brave new world 'summative assessment' still trumps 'spirituality' so that:

> The noumenal world of meaning, value, and liberty is traded off for the phenomenal world of the technical model. (Loomis and Rodriguez, 2009, p. 72)

The commitment of English teachers to the intrinsic or inherent worth of both their students and subject (evidenced by their support of the 'personal growth' model) has led to some, not unfounded, scepticism regarding the current obsession with grades and assessment in schools, exacerbated by the high value of a GCSE in English as a commodity.

Another consequence of assessment that would appear to be antithetical to spirituality is the risk that it will foster 'extrinsic' rather than 'intrinsic' motivation (a decidedly unhealthy state of affairs for human beings). Comparison with one's peers according to a predetermined standard of attainment (the grade or level) with less credit given for value added and little acknowledgement of individual progress may be unethical as well as demotivating. The sort of motivation a student (or teacher) possess is very important indeed. Human beings are not designed to be motivated only when a 'carrot' is dangled before them. Caring about marks or grades rather than the quality of work for its own sake is a symptom of ill health, spiritually, and leads to the commodification of what is human. We need to encourage children to enjoy English for its own sake, unlike Eustace who early in *The Voyage of the 'Dawn Treader'* is spiritually troubled:

> He always had this notebook with him and kept a record of his marks in it, for though he didn't care much about any subject for its own sake, he

cared a great deal about marks and would even go to people and say, 'I got so much. What did you get?' (Lewis, 1989/1952, p. 27)

When Eustace becomes a dragon he thinks how he will be able to lord it over his cousins but soon realizes that all he really wants is to be 'friends'; this is the first important step in the development of his 'relational consciousness'. Eustace needs to be spiritually cleansed (his undragoning) and to go through a painful transformation before he appreciates that friendship matters more than being 'better' than others.

Equally, there are problems with students not doing their best and not striving to excel, for fear that this will single them out as different from their peer group. If our classrooms communicate the message that it is acceptable for a student to be the same as others but not to have done *better* than others, this denies a student the opportunity to be different and to be an individual. If the collective level or average militates against individual excellence this will certainly curtail freedom. A myth will illustrate:

> You remember how one of the Greek Dictators (they called them 'tyrants' then) sent an envoy to another Dictator to ask his advice about the principles of government. The second Dictator led the envoy into a field of corn, and there he snicked off with his cane the top of every stalk that rose an inch or so above the general level. The moral was plain. Allow no pre-eminence among your subjects. . . . Cut them all down to a level . . . All equals. Thus Tyrants could practice, in a sense, 'democracy'. But now 'democracy' can do the same work without any other tyranny than her own. No one need now go through the field with a cane. The little stalks will now of themselves bite the tops off the big ones. The big ones are beginning to bite off their own in their desire to Be Like Stalks. (Lewis, 2001/1965, pp. 201–2)

Students should not be embarrassed about excellence (whether academic, vocational, sporting or artistic) and yet some adolescents are so concerned about their success that they stop trying to succeed simply because they want to fit in and be like everyone else. It would be better for everyone in our democratic society (which has to compete in the global marketplace) if we encouraged children to strive for excellence and to celebrate the success of their friends.

In evaluating how ethical assessment is, much depends upon the motives for it, how it is valued and whether human beings are treated as a means to an end or as an end in themselves. Virtue ethics (Aristotle, 1987) may be considered to be more appropriate for an ethics of English teaching than the consequentialist ethics associated with the utilitarianism of Jeremy Bentham and John Stuart Mill where the end justifies the means. A disadvantage of 'benefit maximisation' (doing what is considered best for the greatest number) is that insufficient respect may be paid to individuals. Equally, it is not always wrong for learners to know about their attainment in relation to others. The ethical context matters here; there are certainly problems associated with not knowing where one's gifts and talents lie. It is important to be honest with young people so they strive for a 'personal best'.

Clearly, it should not be the case that those from the poorest homes living in the poorest areas get the worst results at school. Children from social priority areas should not have the least chance of gaining a place at University. It should not only be those who live in the most affluent areas whose parents can afford it that benefit from a high quality education. A school serving a social priority area in which research was recently carried out (Pike, 2009b, 2010d, 2012b) sought to raise the attainment of its students. The school succeeded in its social justice mission but it did so by placing an emphasis upon the development of the character and virtues of each young person it educated. One virtue this school promoted was humility as it sought to enable students to be ethical in their attitudes towards assessment and it defined this core value for students in the following terms:

> We seek to do our personal best without bragging and to encourage others to achieve their best without being critical or jealous of their efforts. (Pike, 2010d)

This is important because we do not just need social mobility but the development of good character. If assessment is handled well and is concerned with enabling a student to be the best they can be and with helping them fulfil their potential this might even be regarded as bringing about the spiritual quality of 'hope'.

Study questions

1   What is the most challenging area for you to assess in English?

2   How is it possible to achieve excellence for everyone?

3   What are the advantages and disadvantages of summative assessment in English?

4   What are the advantages and disadvantages of formative assessment in English?

5 How can you ensure you engage in ethical assessment?

6 When have you taught a lesson where you sensed that something really significant happened, perhaps something you might describe as 'spiritual'?

7 When have you drawn from the 'Inner Light' in your teaching?

8 Can you sense the difference in your teaching between those times when are you simply being rational and others when you are being intuitive and spiritual?

9 When are you most authentic and spiritually true to yourself?

10 So far, these questions have just focused on the teacher but there is more. Have you ever felt that you have touched the *spirit* of a child?

11 When have you *inspired* learners?

4

The spirit of professional learning in English

In the last chapter we looked at the art and ethics, of planning teaching and assessing learning. Every time teachers assess their students' learning this generally leads to reflection upon how they can plan and teach better so that learners learn better. Many teachers of English go further though and undertake 'action research', which has been defined as 'the study of a social situation with a view to improving the quality of action within it' (Elliott, 1991, p. 69). Many courses of Initial Teacher Education (ITE) and Continuing Professional Development (CPD) seek to equip educators with the action research skills needed to investigate their practice and improve it, a key aspect of professional learning at Masters level and beyond in education. Teachers in England have an obligation to 'take responsibility for improving teaching through appropriate professional development' (DfE, 2012, TS8) and schools that are 'teaching schools' akin to 'teaching hospitals' will wish to build their capacity to conduct their own research to provide local research-led, evidence-based, professional development for their teachers (Pike, 2002b).

Teachers of English deal with complex problems to which ready-made or 'off the peg' answers are often unavailable. They are professionals who think critically about the best course of action to take when teaching particular students in particular groups in particular situations at particular times. If teachers are to develop as ethical professionals they cannot function as technicians who are only efficient and effective implementers of the latest strategy or curriculum. Reflective teaching and learning are essential to professional practice. Technical proficiency and knowing the craft of the classroom are essential but so too are professional judgement and critical analysis. For Aristotle *techne* denotes technical skill and may be concerned with effectively and efficiently achieving a particular end but *phronesis*, or wisdom in action, denotes the use of critical judgement which action research has the capacity to facilitate.

Teacher research: 'Going the Extra Mile'

One of my student teachers recently referred to action research as 'going the extra mile' as the aim is not just to teach but to improve teaching. The research skills of the teacher are an integral part of his or her professionalism not least because, 'When teachers engage in enquiry in their classrooms, they gain a better understanding of their practice and ways to improve it' (Wilson, 2009, p. 198). Another way of putting it is that, 'Action research is a form of enquiry that enables practitioners everywhere to investigate and evaluate their work. They ask 'What am I doing? What do I need to improve? How do I improve it?' (McNiff and Whitehead, 2006, p. 7). Good teachers routinely reflect on their practice to modify it and make adjustments but to qualify as 'action *research*' this needs to be rigorous and systematic. If a teacher seeks 'to make changes to their practice and at the same time *systematically collects evidence* of the effects of these changes, then they are engaging in action research' (Wilson, 2009, p. 198, my italic).

Although there are variations on a theme, professional enquiry employing action research generally follows the same sequence or cycle (Somekh, 1989). First, identify a need, problem to be solved or area to be improved. Second, collect evidence of the issue or problem; describe the situation now and how you want it to be different. Third, reflect upon how the situation can be improved by drawing upon research evidence, scholarship and theory (this is vital for work at Masters level and beyond). Fourth, deliberate and design your intervention in the light of your study. Fifth, act in accordance with the plan. Sixth, evaluate how successful the intervention has been (this must be evidence-based). Seventh, consider what strategy should be adopted next.

If all this sounds rather obvious it is important to acknowledge that even as professional educators we may find it harder than we might think to reflect perceptively and accurately on a situation in which we are immersed and therefore we need specific tools to help us do so. Improving learning and teaching is often far from straightforward; hence the need for systematic and evidence-based research. In social situations such as classrooms and schools it is all too easy to rely on anecdotal evidence or subjective perceptions that are unreliable. For instance, sometimes as a teacher you may feel you have talked for about a quarter of an hour when your students have been sitting listening for half an hour. Alternatively you might feel that the boys did not contribute much when a tally by an observer will reveal exactly how many boys responded and will give a much more accurate, evidence-based picture of the level of engagement according to gender in a mixed class. The following two examples of action research into English teaching will illustrate this.

Action research case study 1 (Helen, PGCE student teacher)

The problem Helen observed was that in one of her groups a few students would dominate class discussion and quieter members of the group appeared to be deterred from participating as a result. Individually or in small groups the quieter students seemed to have the ability to engage verbally. She did not want to discourage her students that were keener to contribute to class discussion but she did want more equal participation and for her classroom to be more inclusive. Helen wanted to break down barriers to non-participation. Having identified an area for improvement, Helen needed a second opinion about the state of affairs she perceived and asked her mentor in school to observe the class. Unprompted, and without knowing the issue Helen had identified, her mentor noted that there were strikingly uneven levels of participation across the members of the class. Especially with issues of engagement or participation, subjective perceptions are notoriously unreliable and it was important to have the professional judgement and experience of the mentor confirm that this was an issue. Nevertheless, as data and hard evidence rather than just a second opinion was required, Helen asked her mentor to record which students volunteered to ask a question and which students spontaneously asked questions. Helen did not use 'named questions' where she chose particular students to answer but relied on volunteers to put their hands up. The data collected was revealing. Of the 25 students in the class, 8 did not volunteer to answer a question during the lesson. At the other end of the participation spectrum, 3 students dominated with the most vociferous student seeking to answer 33 questions, the second most vocal answering 20 and the third most vocal student answering 15 questions.

Helen had to do some reading about research into questioning (and supplied these references at the end of her assignment). She found out that taking volunteers to answer questions is generally the method of questioning that has the most uneven participation rate because it encourages the same confident individuals who wish to answer. The method of random questioning, for instance, (where a computer program is used and a student's name is displayed on the whiteboard) greatly increases the level of participation and can ensure a more even spread of respondents. However, the disadvantage of random questioning is that this method detracts from the autonomy and professional judgement of the teacher and his or her ability to pitch questions at particular students (a key differentiation strategy). Helen also felt that another disadvantage of random questioning was that some students would be embarrassed if they were called upon to answer a question in front of their peers to which they did not know the answer. She preferred to choose pupils to answer and to target her questions based on ability as she not only wanted to exercise her professional discretion but also wanted to create a more inclusive classroom. Helen read that classroom discussion of this sort actually hinders high levels of participation because 'only one person speaking at a time leaves thirty others in a state of utter passivity' (Beadle, 2010, p. 110). It should be added that strategically chosen pairs can be especially helpful in this regard as they have the benefit of propelling everyone into mental activity so long as an ordered and task-focused environment is maintained.

In order to involve the whole class, Helen introduced more group work where pupils had to discuss the answers to questions in a small group before contributing to a whole class discussion. She also took the step of sharing her aims with the class about needing to see more participation from the quieter members of the group. Pupils' names were ticked on the board when they answered a question so the distribution was displayed. This was an overt step that illustrates how different this sort of research is to more conventional notions of research. By using a combination of group work and displaying ticks next to names class participation became much more equal and data was collected to provide evidence of the improvement. The change appeared to be sustained, as it seemed to have the effect of prompting the quieter students to choose to involve themselves in answering questions once they had 'broken the ice'. The task had highlighted to these members of the class that Helen wanted to hear from them in her lessons. In evaluating though Helen was critical of some of her earlier assumptions. She wondered if she would demotivate those who had been keen previously and had contributed the most. She also wondered if increases in 'participation' would lead to a rise in attainment as some students seemed happier to be quiet and attentive and others wanted to be more vocal and different learners have different learning styles. She concluded what she termed her 'foray into action research' by reflecting that only time (and further research) would tell whether encouraging vocal participation in lessons was necessarily good for all learners. Finally Helen related her professional learning and development to the *Teachers' Standards* (DfE, 2012) she had to meet to gain QTS (Qualified Teacher Status) in the United Kingdom (Appendix 2).

Action research case study 2
(Mark, Head of English)

Action research can range from the sort undertaken during ITE, to larger scale, more extensive research, undertaken by more experienced members of staff as part of Masters or Doctoral programmes. This can be published and used by other schools and may be what is increasingly expected of 'teaching schools' that have an obligation to carry out research as well as providing ITE and CPD. While I was Head of a Faculty comprising English, Communications and Drama with responsibility for whole school literacy in a large comprehensive school, I undertook some action research into a particular aspect of the teaching of English. The findings from the 'Keen Readers' project was published in *Journal of Curriculum Studies* and elsewhere (Pike, 2002b, 2003a) and may serve as a useful example of action research undertaken over a longer period of time that is possible for a full-time member of staff in a school. A necessarily condensed version is given here of the work carried out with a group of students across Years 9, 10 and 11 (from the ages of 14 to 16).

My reading of students' work and data collection (surveys of attitudes and reading journal entries) confirmed that certain adolescent readers were less 'keen' on reading poetry than other genres. In general, they preferred novels and short stories, plays or drama scripts, to reading most poems, which they encountered in secondary school. It seemed as though once children left primary school where poetry for pleasure such as limericks were the staple diet, and had to tackle poetry with serious themes, their enthusiasm waned and they lacked the confidence to develop insights and interpretations of their own. The problem was exacerbated when they were faced with pre-twentieth-century poetry. Consequently, the 'Keen Readers' project sought to cultivate keen readers in both senses (motivationally and intellectually) of classic poetry. In short, I selected the least keen readers I could find and developed a range of strategies for helping them to engage both intellectually and emotionally, with such poetry. This was important because response to such poems counted towards a large part of their final grade for GCSE English literature (There are certainly other 'black spots' that would benefit from special attention and action research by teachers of English).

The aim of the research project was to examine how to foster motivated and intellectually acute readers and ameliorate negative attitudes to poetry. Students were closely observed during 400 hours of English lessons. Teaching strategies were developed throughout this time in response to students' learning needs by means of action research. The students were interviewed, kept journals, answered questionnaires and recorded their discussions of a wide range of canonical literature throughout their course. The writing students produced during lessons and in the terminal examination was analysed, with the general focus of attention being their responses to texts and teaching methods. Significant improvement in both the motivation and attainment of all the students was evident between the ages of 14 and 16. For instance, one boy Peter, who had a particular loathing of poetry in Year 9 and gained a very modest level 5 at the end of that year, gained an A* (the highest possible grade) in GCSE English literature at the end of Year 11. He had also become an enthusiastic and appreciative reader of several challenging pre-twentieth-century poems.

Responsive teaching (Pike, 2004a) strategies were developed whereby students were encouraged to relate texts to their own experiences by reading them as a 'stimulus'. A simple explanation of this concept is that 'the text is a stimulus activating elements of the reader's past experience' (Rosenblatt, 1978, p. 11). Consequently, when students made their first annotations around a poem or wrote their initial journal entries and discussed the poems, any memory stimulated by the text, however seemingly irrelevant, was encouraged. When two girls, Anna and Josie came to the line, 'But tradition approves all forms of competition', in 'The Latest Decalogue' by Arthur Hugh Clough, it prompted them to discuss how they competed with each other in music and dance. Although Anna felt that they were digressing, Josie, quite rightly, reminded her friend of the instructions in their journals: 'it says if a poem triggers off a memory or something, talk about it'. This initial emphasis on 'stimulus' was not at the expense of Rosenblatt's (1978, p. 11) other dimension, text as 'blueprint', where the focus is upon the text, but it did ensure that teenagers perceived the relevance of pre-twentieth-century texts to their own lives. This was the foundation upon which teaching and learning (about the literary, linguistic, social and cultural features of texts) was built.

Extensive reading about the teaching of poetry and also of teaching for engagement was embarked upon, especially over summer and Easter holidays. Special attention was paid to the responses of students and significant periods of time were devoted to reflection about how they learned best. Analysis of transcripts of recordings of paired discussion and whole class discussion was undertaken to identify the sort of teacher talk and dialogue that challenged and stimulated students' thinking. It helped that I was a keen reader of poetry myself and believed my students could respond personally, aesthetically and imaginatively to works considered difficult or obscure. I wanted my students to share an acquired pleasure and believed their reading and aesthetic response was a vital part of their spiritual and moral development.

The 'Poetic' in professional learning

Reading poetry (imaginative literature) can also aid reflection in teacher education (Pike, 2011f). The importance, in English teachers' professional learning, of writing and responding to poetry has been asserted (Dymoke, 2003; Dymoke and Hughes, 2009) and it has recently been argued that teachers who are 'readers' are likely to be good teachers of reading (Cremin, 2011). Yet we can go further than this and plausibly argue that reading literature would seem to be likely to help teachers to *read people* and situations, which is central to their vocation. The link between reading literature and reading people is illustrated rather well in *The Voyage of the 'Dawn Treader'* (Lewis, 1989/1952), where the odious Eustace has read only non-fiction (about factories and methods of production) and has failed to have his spiritual or aesthetic sensibilities honed. He gets into serious trouble (becoming a dragon) because he has not read the right books (imaginative stories about dragons would have come in handy). He fails to read people well and his diary is an amusing example of misreading because he has only read non-fiction and has yet to develop the virtues underpinning good character that will allow him to 'read' wisely and well.

It is ironic that most of the books on teacher education and development also happen to fall into the non-fiction category (no doubt because so many are still labouring under the misapprehension that teaching is a technology rather than an art). Even in the development of teachers of English, comparatively little work has been done on the value of *literature* itself informing or contributing to reflection in professional learning. This might be regarded as especially surprising in view of the fact that as:

> the great literary and artistic products of human culture have precisely sought to explore the roots and springs of virtue and vice, a special role may be claimed for the arts in helping us to understand human character. (Carr, 2007, p. 385)

Clearly, the subject matter of English (literature) may be especially conducive to fostering the professional learning of its teachers. That so little attention has been devoted to what we might term the 'poetic' in professional learning is an indication that teaching itself is regarded by so many as a series of skills to learn rather than a humane art where character and the quality of relationships is central. For teachers of English, approaches that draw upon the poetic in professional learning may well have much to offer to augment the more prosaic and didactic texts that are most often employed in professional learning, even when these focus on teachers' experiences in the classroom.

In order to 'test' this 'hypothesis' my student teachers read a number of poems (from GCSE anthologies) during a university-based session devoted to professional learning. This had the advantage of familiarizing them with the range of poems they would need to teach but I asked them, in the first instance, not to think of how they would teach the poems but to reflect upon the significance of the poems for their own professional learning. It should be noted that these student teachers were familiar with reader response approaches to poetry that encourage readers to see the relevance of poetry and literature to present preoccupations and concerns (Benton et al., 1988; Pike, 2000a, 2000c, 2003a). It was therefore an easy step to adopt a similar approach to professional learning. I asked my student teachers to reflect upon how these poems were relevant to their personal and professional lives as teachers.

Their comments indicated the relevance of a range of different poems to their professional practice. When one read 'What has happened to Lulu' it brought home to her 'the impact the home environment might have on a child' and the importance of 'being sensitive to what may be going on with a pupil outside your classroom and how this might impact on their behaviour'; another was struck by the 'importance of communication and teachers knowing situations away from school'. As communicating with parents is so important the responses to this poem were directly relevant to satisfying the *Teachers' Standards* (2012) which state that one needs to 'communicate effectively with parents with regard to pupils' achievements and well-being' (DfE, 2012, TS8).

After reading 'Leisure' by W. H. Davies one student teacher remarked, 'I should not be constantly thinking about school and will probably be a better teacher if I put time aside in the week for myself . . . this poem reminds me of the need to stop and stand back for a while sometimes'. Another student teacher explained that it 'teaches how important it is to stand back and take stock – it reminds me how important it is to sometimes stop and reflect'. Another commented upon the way it stressed the 'importance of the bigger picture and the validity of the individual Romantic experience' within English (cf. Stevens, 2010b).

Student teachers also commented on the value of poetry in reflecting upon and dealing with behaviour management in the classroom. After reading 'Human Interest' by Carol Ann Duffy one teacher observed that it 'helps me to understand that some people can react inappropriately and immediately to certain situations'. This is certainly relevant to the requirement for teachers to 'have high expectations of behaviour, and establish a framework for discipline with a range of strategies' (DfE, 2012, TS7) and to 'demonstrate consistently the positive attitudes, values and behaviour which are expected of pupils'

(DfE, 2012, TS1). Shakespeare's Sonnet 130 informed professional learning for another teacher for whom it emphasized 'the importance of looking below the surface; of realizing that what we should do as teachers is bring out the best in the individual whatever their circumstances/barriers might be'. Removing or overcoming barriers to learning is a key factor in raising attainment and teachers need to 'have a secure understanding of how a range of factors can inhibit pupils' ability to learn, and how best to overcome these' (DfE, 2012, TS5).

Perhaps the most important comments were that poetry *in general* contributed to professional learning. For Aristotle, poetry was superior to history because it dealt with the universal rather than just the particular. One male student teacher commented that the value of poetry in this context lay in enabling him 'to think about why I want to teach ensuring I don't lose sight of what's most important' and observed that 'Poetry can open your eyes to things that you may not otherwise experience and this can build sensitivity towards students'. Unsurprisingly, the capacity of poetry to inform the professional learning of teachers of English was acknowledged by each of the student teachers in the group. The capacity of poetry to inform professional learning is likely to be due to it possessing greater 'indeterminacy' (Iser, 1978) or 'aesthetic space' for teachers to inhabit. These responses certainly lend credence to the view that aesthetic response underpins 'aesthetic teaching' (Pike, 2004d). Reflecting upon the human condition is central to ethical English and in concluding Part One it would be remiss not to acknowledge the inner life of the teacher.

The spirit of professional learning: The inner life of the teacher

English teachers may be increasingly aware that one 'does not develop a new pedagogy simply by choosing from a 'grab bag of teaching tricks' and may be increasingly 'ready to look beyond technique for whatever guidance may come from spiritual traditions' (Palmer, 1993, pp. 30, x). Teaching from within, out of *who* we are as human beings (a notion developed in Chapter 8), is often neglected in the literature on professional development. One exception is the now well-known book, *The Courage to Teach – Exploring the Inner Landscape of a Teacher's Life* (Palmer, 1998). The acknowledgement of the inner life of the teacher is likely to strike a chord with many teachers of English. According to Palmer, 'teaching holds a mirror to the soul' and 'If I am willing to look in that mirror and not run from what I see, I have a chance to gain self-knowledge – and knowing myself is as crucial to good teaching as knowing my subjects and my students' (Palmer, 1998, p. 2). With regard to teaching, Palmer puts it like this:

> In fact, knowing my students and my subject depends heavily on self-knowledge. When I do not know myself, I cannot know who my students are. I will see them through a glass darkly, in the shadows of my unexamined life – and when I cannot see them clearly, I cannot teach them well. . . . The work required to 'know thyself' is neither selfish nor narcissistic. Whatever self-knowledge we attain as teachers will serve our students and our scholarship well. Good teaching requires self-knowledge: it is a secret hidden in plain sight. (Palmer, 1998, p. 3)

Palmer sees the search for self-knowledge requiring deeper questions than those that are normally asked in teacher development. He suggests the most common question we tend to ask ourselves as teachers is the 'What' question – what shall we teach? We also ask the 'How' question with regard to pedagogy and method and deliberate how should we teach? Yet only occasionally do we ask the 'Why' question and think seriously about the purpose of teaching English or the ends to which we teach it. We tend to ask the 'Who' question concerning the selfhood of the teacher even less (Palmer, 1998, p. 4). The progress depicted is of going deeper as one progresses from asking 'What' to 'How' to Why' to 'Who' questions. The last of these questions pertains to the spiritual development of the teacher. The ancient inscription on the Temple of Delphi read, 'Know thyself' and much philosophy and theology since has sought to follow this injunction. To 'know thyself' is essential for the teacher and is further explored in Chapters 8 and 12 which focus on the character and beliefs of the teacher respectively.

Great philosophers and theologians have addressed the need to 'know thyself'. Many English teachers will be familiar with Socratic teaching and Plato has the character of Socrates use the term 'know thyself' to refer to ancient wisdom and to motivate his dialogues. Clement of Alexandria believed that, 'If one knows himself, he will know God' and Calvin stated that 'Nearly all wisdom we possess . . . consists of two parts: the knowledge of God and of ourselves'. For both 'believers' and 'non-believers', knowing oneself is vital. To be both authentic and ethical, teaching will be congruent with a teacher's beliefs and values (his or her worldview) and will be underpinned by a commitment to enhance social justice. For believers, spiritual disciplines (such as study, meditation, reflection, solitude, simplicity and prayer) can aid reflection and sustain our souls. Those who do not share the theological presuppositions of 'believers' may still be uneasy with models of teacher development that pay little or no heed to what we might term the 'spirit' of the teacher. On this view, it might be worth attempting to re-write the action research cycle in terms that acknowledge the spirit of ethical English:

The spirit of action research

1   *Respond to a call (identify what should improve or develop).* This may begin with a sense of unease, a feeling of dissatisfaction or dissonance, intuitively knowing that something is wrong. There may be recognition of equilibrium being disturbed and a lack of authenticity or peace. It is important that an area for investigation is not decided upon out of frustration, anger or emotion (although a passionate commitment to improve a situation and enhance social justice should underpin action). The vocation or 'calling' of the action researcher is to seek change for the better. The diligent searcher after greater truth and justice ('researcher') will ask questions about the terms in which a situation needs to be 'better' that transcend effectiveness and efficiency.

2   *Seek truth (collect data).* This should be done ethically with the full consent of those with whom one is working. Research should be a collaborative activity *with* children and young people, not something done *to* them. It should augment 'relational consciousness'. Generally 'mixed methods' (qualitative and quantitative) will be drawn upon to depict the situation with honesty and integrity, free from bias, prejudice or uncritical subjectivity.

3   *Read and interpret well (analyse data/generate hypotheses).* The spiritual discipline of study should be practised (and respected by colleagues as real work). It is important to use 'respondent validation' to ensure that one's interpretation of data is approved as accurate by participants. As well as explicit rational analysis, a period of contemplation, meditation and peace at a distance from the action may be appropriate. This may well be aided by aesthetic encounter and experience. For citizens of faith it may be authentic to seek guidance from sacred texts, a community of believers or through prayer. Any analysis will be informed by evidence and data and will be ethically grounded.

4   *Meditate and study (plan action).* Questions will be asked about what action may bring greater peace, authenticity and well-being. It should be possible to 'view the movie' in one's mind of what will be done. Visualize oneself acting well. See other participants responding, as

one would want them to respond, being better than they are now. Read well (both fiction and non-fiction).

5 *Act authentically and ethically (implement action).* Action will be true to beliefs and fundamental convictions that are ethical and in the best interests of students. Inner peace may be an indicator of authenticity and being true to one's convictions. Moral courage and resolve may be required as change for the better is not always easily achieved.

6 *Perceive growth (collect data to monitor change).* Attend to the fruits of action. Data collection must be respectful, non-coercive, open rather than covert, socially just and ethical. Reflection, contemplation, prayer, meditation, listening to learners and others, evaluating their views in the light of one's 'mission' and 'vision' will follow.

7 *Reflect authentically and ethically (analysis and evaluation).* Reflect in the light of fundamental convictions and social justice. Distance, space, quiet, solitude as well as rational cognitive faculties may aid reflection. Gratefulness and appreciation should be shown to participants, colleagues, friends, mentors and all from whom one has received help.

Study questions

1 What is action research?

2 Why is action research especially suited to the continuing professional development of teachers of English?

3 Think of three possible projects you could engage in using action research to improve your practice?

4 Which is the most important of the three and why?

5 How might spiritual disciplines aid action research?

6 How might action research be both authentic and ethical?

7 Why is it vital to 'know thyself' as an action researcher?

8 Why is the 'inner life' of the teacher so important?

PART TWO

Ethical English as moral and character education

Part Two of this book addresses the ethics of teaching and learning English with a particular focus on moral and character education. In Chapter 5, educational foundations are evaluated. In contrast to Enlightenment values (Medway, 2010), or even critically enlightened Romantic values (Stevens, 2011), as a basis for teaching and learning in English, *educational* values are advocated. Chapter 6 gives examples of such educational values, drawn from a range of cultures and traditions and the concept of the *Tao* is introduced as a moral code which might underpin teaching and learning in English. Chapter 6 also considers the importance of working with young people on the development of their character and we look at how this can be engaged in with reference to examples from English. Chapter 7 explores the similarities between critical literacy and education for democratic citizenship and shows how good readers make good citizens. Finally, in Chapter 8, the character of the teacher (his or her personal moral qualities) is examined in the context of professional and personal development.

There is a long and respected tradition within English of attending to moral and ethical matters. Here a broad definition of 'moral' as 'how to live' following Arnold (1879), is taken. Arguably, 'literature has more potential than almost any other subject for expanding the moral imagination and helping students to understand moral possibilities' (Halstead, 2011, p. 340). Part Two considers the contribution made to the teaching of English by both contemporary and classical moral and character education. From the United States, Karen Bohlin's *Teaching Character through Literature* is drawn upon, as is the work of Thomas Lickona on essential virtues and Marvin Berkowitz (2004) on character education supporting academic attainment. This work is influential in public (state) schools in the United States and has much to offer.

In the United Kingdom, there is renewed interest in character education and the work of James Arthur (2003, 2010) and colleagues at the Jubilee Centre for Character and Values at Birmingham University is making a significant contribution. For instance, a number of myths about character, virtue and virtue education have recently been exposed (Kristjánsson, 2013) and a number of projects have been undertaken including valuable work on the 'Knightly Virtues' where character is taught through classic literature. In addition to these sources, recent work (Pike, 2013, 2014) applying key themes from C. S. Lewis' *The Abolition of Man – Reflections on Education with Special Reference to the Teaching of English in the Upper Forms of Schools* underpins the analysis here. Part Two draws upon Aristotle's virtue ethics which emphasize excellence of character so that a teacher 'perceives what is good or fine or right to do in any given situation' (Slote, 1997, p. 240) and two key principles of Kant's deontology (1785), 1) the Golden Rule 'Do to others what you would have them do to you' and 2) 'never treat people as a means to an end'. The values taught by the literatures of a range of cultures and traditions are seen to provide an educational foundation that enables English teachers to do justice to the diversity of the texts and the students they teach.

5

Educational foundations for English teaching

In Part One of this book we considered the importance of spiritual and aesthetic experience in English, which is a major strand in the DNA of our subject due to the influence of Romanticism. Yet there is the need for any spiritual and aesthetic experience to be ethically underpinned by humane moral values. The way English can seem to be concerned with subjective inner experience rather than knowledge and truth, needs to be addressed if it is to be ethical. The Enlightenment conviction that truth matters, must not be lost from English classrooms where there is a risk of relativism concerning both literature and life (Medway, 2010).

We have probably all heard English teachers tell students, 'It's your opinion, it's only your interpretation that matters; there's no right or wrong answer' and we understand what they mean when they are seeking to foster personal creativity or response to a literary work. Yet, taken more literally, this presents serious problems on both literary and moral grounds. If a student believed that it was acceptable to persecute people on the basis of their religion, sexuality or ethnicity we should have no hesitation in seeking to correct them. Equally, it is patently absurd to suggest that any personal response to a literary work is as *valid* as any other.

It is argued in this chapter that ethical English deals with both myths and truths; it may help to lead students to acquire humane and tolerant values as they experience, vicariously, through aesthetic encounters, the ways others have lived in different times or places to their own. Studying English is both rational and affective and draws upon Enlightenment and Romantic traditions. The two are by no means mutually exclusive and, at its best, we see in English 'the trees of knowledge and life growing together' (Lewis,

1978/1943, p. 10). It will be argued in this chapter that *educational* values are necessary to augment both Enlightenment values (Medway, 2010) and critically enlightened Romantic values (Stevens, 2011) if teaching and learning in English is to do justice to the diversity of both the texts and the students they teach (Pike, 2011b).

Enlightenment values in English

Peter Medway privileges humane Enlightenment values as a basis for English teaching. He emphasizes reason and argues that:

> An insistence on English as a development of mind as well as soul, of knowledge and cognitive capability as well as emotional and aesthetic response, is necessary to counteract the anti-intellectualism that has at times dominated English . . . ultimately deriving . . . from Wordsworth's Romanticism. (Medway, 2010, p. 11)

For Medway, the central aims of education should be 'drawn from Enlightenment values' (Medway, 2010, p. 3). The *philosophes* of the Enlightenment claimed that *reason* shed the same light the world over. Certainly, the importance of truth in English teaching should not be ignored in favour of creativity and imagination. (The contesting of truth claims is discussed in Part Three.) The Enlightenment's central concern might be considered to be *truth* rather than people's subjective feelings or beliefs; the notion is that truth claims cannot be verified on the basis of how the observer feels. Put simply, for instance, water does not boil at a different temperature depending on the observer's feelings. But if a Science teacher leads children to believe that science is the sole arbiter of truth, or that humanity is on a path of inexorable progress, he or she may well have 'indoctrinated' them in Enlightenment thinking (this is explored in Chapter 12 on 'materialism'). Yet Medway also acknowledges the importance of 'the sorts of knowledge that can't be expressed propositionally' (Medway, 2010, p. 3). Poetry in particular raises challenging issues for an account of English aligned with Enlightenment reason:

> A discourse, after all, that uses what we might call musical effects to aid persuasion smacks of the magic, spells and incantations that belong to the superstition so vigorously combated by the Enlightenment and judged so hostile to the critical rationality that education should be about. (Medway, 2010, p. 8)

Interestingly, using 'musical effects' to 'aid persuasion', was included in the original meaning of the Greek word 'ethos'. Of course, reason is important but as teachers of English know only too well there are also spiritual, relational, intuitive and affective ways of knowing. These often seek to take account of the complexity and depth of human experiences and respect knowledge gained through imagination, emotion, belief and tradition.

Medway himself, although he does not use the word 'spiritual', gives especially good examples of a 'spiritual' sort of knowing (Medway, 2010). In Dicken's *Hard Times* Sissy Jupe demonstrates 'relational consciousness' (an important aspect of spirituality) rather than detached, objective, scientific reasoning. Sissy understands horses differently to a veterinary surgeon: 'As a sick horse, if you might want a scientist for your vet, you'd certainly prefer Sissy for your nurse, not just because of her kindness but because she understands' (Medway, 2010, p. 4). Yet Medway argues for the importance of Enlightenment knowledge by showing that Sissy's folk knowledge and intuition would not save the horse population from a serious infection which would be best treated with 'science-based veterinary procedures' (Medway, 2010, p. 4). While the importance of Sissy's sort of 'spiritual' understanding is affirmed, it has its limitations. Equally, we have to be wary of putting too much faith in the Enlightenment project.

The *philosophes* of the Enlightenment were critical of parochial prejudices and often considered that they belonged to what they thought of as an international republic of letters. In the twenty-first century, however, the core project of the Enlightenment as the displacement of local, customary or traditional moralities, and all forms of transcendental faith, might also be considered to lack respect for diversity; a critical and rational morality as the basis of civilization might well be regarded as insufficiently inclusive.

David Stevens's analysis of Enlightenment values deserves careful attention for he advocates *critically enlightened* Romantic values as the basis of English pedagogy and states:

> Enlightenment values are by themselves, I believe, insufficient as a basis for this project: such values may give us the potential for the language of critique, an essentially rationalist discourse; but without the dialectical relation with the language of possibility, predicated on a critically Romantic outlook, they remain partial at best, lacking the affective, celebratory characteristics of a truly holistic English pedagogy. (Stevens, 2011, p. 55)

Enlightenment values might be considered by many English teachers to privilege scientific ways of knowing and to marginalize more intuitive, relational, aesthetic or spiritual ways of apprehending reality. We might even regard Enlightenment values as aggressively secular and incapable of accommodating the perspectives of different religious traditions and cultures or of appreciating spiritual insight. We are not solely rational beings. When I respond to *The Boy in Striped Pyjamas*, which John Boyne terms a 'fable',

I care less about its historical accuracy and more about the moral lesson it teaches and the power it has to engage a class of students with a subject of immense importance. I care about historical accuracy, especially when it concerns the Holocaust and think it important for students to be aware of Boyne's inaccuracies, but only after they have engaged emotionally with its most important lesson. Issues of truth are unavoidable in English teaching, which cannot be reduced to personal feelings; equally, feelings matter rather a lot.

Romantic values in English

As an underpinning or foundation for English teaching David Stevens posits Romanticism arguing that:

> the core of effective English teaching could be construed as the centrally Romantic idea of wonder as the essence of art. (Stevens, 2011, p. 46)

Stevens is a powerful advocate of Romanticism and many English teachers will find such a view resonates with their vocation and has much to commend it. Yet Stevens himself acknowledges that 'the context of values, within which any radically Romantic creativity must operate, is notably missing' (Stevens, 2011, p. 48) and this is a concern that many educators will share. Stevens recognizes the 'uncomfortable ambivalence about the nature of Romanticism' especially in its early German form which could be seen as 'a precursor to emotional nationalism and all the evils that arose from this: facism and Nazism especially' (Stevens, 2011, p. 47). Stevens advocates 'valuable, value-laden and challenging insight', in the English classroom, 'through the creative use of all texts, in a spirit of celebratory intertextuality and critical questioning' (Stevens, 2011, p. 55). There are difficulties here too, though. Should we really celebrate *all* texts? We might recall the example in Chapter 1 of the documentaries of the German film-maker Leni Riefenstahl that are not only aesthetically remarkable but also Nazi propaganda. In the twenty-first century, ethical English is vital especially when analysing texts:

> Through much of the last century most critics either ignored or condemned ethical questions, as if they were no better than crude intrusions on the 'aesthetic' or 'beautiful'. Only recently have more and more critics acknowledged that authors and readers cannot – indeed must not – avoid engaging in ethical discourse, as an essential part of their joining in any serious narrative encounter. (Booth, 2005, p. ix)

Clearly teachers are in a position of authority and with their greater knowledge, experience and position comes 'ethical responsibility' (Albright, 2002, p. 289). Stevens (2011) draws upon Romanticism, following Freire, to support an education of questions rather than of answers. Yet, on their own, Romantic values that privilege the 'spontaneous overflow of powerful feelings' (Wordsworth) are inadequate for the *education* of the young. Stevens therefore seeks 'a repositioning of Romanticism on radical and reflectively critical grounds' (Stevens, 2011, p. 47). Clearly, the *telos* or purpose of English in education cannot be ignored. Schooling necessarily influences the moral perspective of the young person. Education concerns 'changing minds' (Medway, 2010, p. 8). What is sought is a change in the hearts as well as the minds of learners. As beliefs and values, as well as knowledge and skills, are acquired through schooling, 'changing minds' is far more than an academic endeavour; it concerns ethics. Critically enlightened Romantic values have serious limitations.

Ethical 'Behaviour Management'

It is not just Romanticism that is implicated in morally iniquitous results (Barnes and Wright, 2007). Figures such as Goebbels, who was Minister for Enlightenment (Volksaufklärung) and Propaganda in the Third Reich, used their exceptional critical ability in order to manipulate people rather than to enhance their freedom. They were skilled social scientists and knew all about the power of behaviourism which can be traced to John B. Watson's work in America that appeared in 1924 and which exerts a powerful influence upon the behaviour management systems of many schools in the twenty-first century. Behaviourism was developed and popularized by B. F. Skinner who was Professor of Psychology at Harvard (1958–74) and the father of Operant and Behavioural Conditioning. Skinner placed rats in what has come to be known as a Skinner Box where food pellets were released if they pushed a lever; the right behaviour was rewarded as the rats came to associate an action with a particular result. The influence of behaviourism might be seen in schools where clear consequences (rewards and sanctions) are enforced in order to manage behaviour and produce a compliant student body that is well trained. This is not, by any means, to decry or detract from the importance of good and fair discipline in a school but simply to point out that there is more to ethical learning and leadership than effectively and efficiently knowing the social science of managing and manipulating behaviour. For Skinner 'the problem is to induce people not to be good but to behave well' (1971, p. 70).

By contrast, an ethical educator will seek to cultivate virtue and moral character and the right motives for behaving well rather than just 'scientifically' manipulating and 'managing' student behaviour (see Chapter 6). This makes all the difference to our humanity and to the sort of education children and young people receive. In a radio interview, B. F. Skinner was asked about the influence of behaviourism on upon the Nazis. The interviewer, Richard Evans, asked if behaviourist principles could be a threat employed by a hostile government and Skinner replied:

> There's no doubt about it . . . a science of behavior is just as dangerous as the atom bomb. It has the potential of being horribly misused. (Evans, 1968, p. 54)

The interviewer commented that 'Goebbels' diary' outlined the 'formula of communications control in Nazi Germany' and that 'many of the techniques' he describes 'reflect the principles of reinforcement that you [Skinner] have written about' to which Skinner replied, 'Oh, yes. The Nazis made good use of the social sciences' (Evans, 1968, p. 55). Arguably, by 'good' Skinner here meant ruthlessly 'skilled' or mercilessly 'efficient' but this illustrates the point that skill and efficiency are not accurate synonyms for the 'good' with which ethical teaching is concerned.

We return to Skinner's behaviourism and early twenty-first-century behaviour management in schools in Chapter 7 but it is worth pointing out here that much of Skinner's work was done on animals yet many of its conclusions were applied to humans. The thesis of this book is that ethical English has the potential to help us become more humane. To teach English ethically requires more than a technology of teaching; at its core is the cultivation of good character. We shall see in the following chapter that the *basis* or *values* upon which character is to be cultivated may be found in what Skinner cynically called the 'literatures of dignity and freedom' rather than Enlightenment science and technology. In fact, Skinner attacked C. S. Lewis (see Chapter 7) who defended the 'literatures of dignity and freedom' as sources of foundational values. There is a sharp contrast between the development of good character (founded upon educational values anchored in objective truth) and 'what works' or 'behaviour management' founded upon the science of behaviourism (discussed further in Chapters 7 and 12):

> A dogmatic belief in objective value is necessary to the very idea of a rule which is not tyranny or an obedience which is not slavery. I am not here thinking solely, perhaps not even chiefly, of those who are our public enemies at the moment. . . . But many a mild-eyed scientist in pince-nez . . . means in the long run just the same as the Nazi rulers of Germany. Traditional values are to be 'debunked' and mankind to be cut out into some fresh shape at the will (which must, by hypothesis, be an arbitrary

will) of some few lucky people in one lucky generation which has learned how to do it. (Lewis, 1978/1943, p. 44)

Ethical behaviour management that seeks to foster core values and good character (rather than simply gaining compliance) is described in the next chapter.

Ethics and ethnicity in English teaching

The Enlightenment certainly has a dark side. For instance, the Enlightenment encyclopaedists used the term 'civilization' for the 'progress' they believed reason would bring. The Enlightenment view was that a civilized person was rational and secular in contrast to the 'superstitions' of 'less developed' people. The juxtaposition of 'civilized' and 'savage' indicates the Enlightenment hubris which later provided a 'justification' for slavery and colonialism.

In the nineteenth century, evolutionary ideas depicted 'progress' in terms of a movement from 'savage' to 'civilized'. Darwin believed 'savage' people would become extinct and *On the Origin of Species by Means of Natural Selection* was subtitled *The Preservation of Favoured Races in the Struggle for Life*. Darwin expressed the view that 'superior' races would displace 'savage' or 'lower' ones. Such ideas influenced the Nazis who regarded Jewish and African peoples in particular to be lower races. The Nazis also killed many disabled people. Social Darwinism has no place in ethical English teaching. We seek to include everyone rather than eliminate the weakest. Consequently, both the positivist and the Romantic wings of the Enlightenment are problematic for a subject such as English that has a moral duty to promote social justice and inclusion.

Stevens' emphasis on critically enlightened Romantic values is vital (although these are insufficiently *educational* as an underpinning for ethical English). Criticality and the ability to see through common assumptions and propaganda are central educational values we might even apply to the Enlightenment itself:

To suggest that the Enlightenment offered, not science in place of myth, but new myths for old, is not to debunk it. But it means that we must not take Enlightenment claims at face value, but treat them as highly effective propaganda. (Porter, 2001, p. 19)

The notion of the 'scientific myth' is helpful for English teachers who find that dominant conceptions of pedagogy (of what teaching is and how it should be planned) are underpinned by a belief in technical rationality. Clearly, 'what the *philosophes* essentially did was to replace a *Christian* myth with a *scientific* myth' (Porter, 2001, p. 19) (see Part One). We must be careful not to argue that English should be based on Enlightenment values because its pedagogy cannot be reduced to a merely rational process. It requires intuition, sensitivity and relational consciousness.

Notions of the teacher as technician who plans and executes lessons in logical and rational ways rather than imaginative, artistic, creative, intuitive or spiritual ways (see notions of 'aesthetic teaching' in Chapter 3) can be problematized on the basis that science does not only concern objective 'facts' but assumptions, perceptions and interpretations about how the world is best understood (see Chapter 12). Further, if science is the key to progress the rationale for studying literature and other arts subjects may become increasingly tenuous. In the twenty-first century, Western civilization remains imprisoned by a (sometimes aggressively) secular quest for economic, scientific, technological and material advancement. Ethical English should play an important role in countering such a vision by focusing on humane qualities.

Cultural and critical literacy and analysis depend upon understanding the intellectual climate. Hermeneutics and literary theory are central to the ethos of our subject. English should enable students to evaluate myths, the cultural stories, that are influential in our time and to see how interpretations vary in a plural society:

> Far from being cast-iron 'facts', the notions of the noble savage and of progress are just as speculative, symbolic, and dependent upon preconceptions – faith even, one might argue – as the Christian formulations they succeeded. (Porter, 2001, p. 19)

The *philosophes* might even be said to have founded (or at least re-founded) a new 'religion', that of Humanism (see Part Three). If this leads to a tyranny of secularism then it will become increasingly difficult to respect 'faith-based' positions and this in turn make a cosmopolitan society harder to sustain.

The myth of the 'noble savage' is a case in point and is interesting because it persists in both the Romantic and Positivist wings of the Enlightenment. A brief examination of the background is fascinating (Barnes, 2010). In 1768 Louis Bouganville visited the recently discovered Pacific island of Tahiti and published an account of his visit. The French *philosophe*, Denis Diderot, who was something of an armchair anthropologist penned a *Supplement* to the *Voyage* in which he presented Tahitian society as an island paradise, free from despotism where men shared everything (including sexual relations with women) and goods were held in common. Diderot called these people 'noble savages'. Captain Cook, a down-to-earth Yorkshireman, was quite dismissive of the Romantic notion of the 'noble savage' and observed that there was not so much difference between the way sailors were greeted in Tahiti and the way certain women at English ports greeted men after months at sea.

Enlightenment visions of 'civilization' and 'progress' inspired colonial activity and were supported by faith in Darwinism that had social consequences. The French encyclopaedists used the term 'civilization' to describe the 'progress' reason would bring. Yet, as we have seen, reason has significant limitations in governing human action. Love or courage are just two examples of virtues that are not exclusively rational. Colonial expansion was supported ideologically by the appeal to Western 'civilization', evolutionary notions of 'progress' and the 'scientific' perspective that 'superior' races would supplant 'savage' ones. As Darwin put it in a letter of 1881:

> Looking to the world at no very distant date, what an endless number of the lower races will have been eliminated by the civilized races throughout the world. (Darwin, 1887)

When Darwin visited Tierra del Fuego on *The Beagle* he considered the native people to be 'much closer to wild animals than to civilized human beings' (Moorhead, 1969, p. 90). (As an aside, however stressful teaching is and however feral some groups can seem, we always need to be aware that human beings are not animals and are to be accorded dignity.)

The Romantic or Enlightenment stereotype of the 'noble savage' can also have the effect of marginalizing non-Western perspectives because the 'civilized' person is considered to be rational and secular while the person with a faith-based perspective is deemed primitive or irrational. Bertrand Russell's distinctly Enlightenment perspective that religion belongs to the infancy of human reason is entirely unhelpful when it comes to issues of inclusion and respect in a plural society. Notions of pastoral innocence have the same origins as that of the 'noble savage' and it is important to be sufficiently discriminating. Some of the practices of non-liberal and non-secular, people groups (such as commitment to community typified by Ubuntu culture in Africa) can put the fierce individualism and materialism of the West to shame. But just as in 'progressive' Western societies, cruel and inhumane practices exist in non-Western socities. Although the 'noble savage' stereotype of Romanticism can be seen as promoting cosmopolitanism and humane values there are problems here too and we need to recognize that not all cultural or religious practices will contribute to human flourishing. There is much to be learned from those non-Western ways of living where respect is accorded to elders and children and where hospitality and generosity are practiced but some practices are indefensible. Human sacrifice, especially infanticide, sati (widow burning), clitoredectomy (female genital mutilation) or 'honour' killings, are practices which should be eradicated rather than permitted out of respect for different traditions, cultures or religions. Not all spiritual, religious or cultural practices will be benevolent or inspire *eunoia* (well-being) and contribute to *eudaimonia* (thriving and flourishing). Rather than romanticizing or condemning anything 'ethnic' that is from 'different cultures and traditions' we have the opportunity in English to facilitate a balanced and critical appraisal of a range of beliefs and practices. But we must be prepared to exercise judgement and differentiate.

In the short story 'Anil' by Ridjal Noor in *Moon on the Tides* (2011), we would not condone the murder of Marimuthu's wife or the cover up orchestrated by the village headman that culminates in Anil's (the 7-year-old boy who witnesses the hanging) separation from his parents. We would not approve of the way, Ragunathan, is complicit in his son being sent away or the way he treats his family. The abuse of basic human rights (of a child and a woman) in this story is deeply disturbing as is the seemingly unassailable male hierarchy of power which supports and condones this abuse. Equally, the harrowing separation of Anil from his Appa and Amma helps us to appreciate the bonds of family and community that exist in many non-Western communities. Families and members of families do not always behave in rational ways. We might have thought that the fawning, weak, bullying Ragunathan was not much of a father and that Anil would be better off away from him but at the end of the story, Anil is crying for his Appa.

Clearly, there are problems with both Enlightenment and Romantic values as a basis for the teaching of English, not least because neither rationality nor emotion are sufficient to support an education that seeks to inculcate essential humane moral values. Both lack moral legitimacy (a key element of 'ethos' described in the Introduction) to provide a foundation for *education*. The emphasis on emotion in Romanticism is inadequate as more than feelings are required in moral education. We should not do whatever we feel like doing. *Educating* pupils entails helping them to acquire and to develop 'just sentiments' (Lewis, 1978/1943, p. 15). Enlightenment reason is inadequate because it cannot do justice to the rich diversity of human cultural experience. Reason is more redolent of the cold legalism or rational logic than the 'spirit' of English discussed in Chapter 1. Perhaps in English the best response is an agonistic liberalism. The term 'agonistic' comes from 'agon', a contest between rivals in a Greek tragic drama. To be 'agonistic' is to feel things deeply as we strive to be fair.

Study questions

1   What do you believe to be the best ethical foundation for the teaching of English?

2 What do you perceive as the greatest needs of children and young people?

3 How important are Romantic and Enlightenment values as a foundation for English?

4 What are the limitations or dangers of either Romantic or Enlightenment values as an ethical foundation for English in schools?

5 What is the purpose of your role as an *educator* of children?

6 Why are values important?

7 How do values help you make decisions as a teacher of English?

8 How do your values inform your lesson planning?

9 How do your values inform how you teach?

6

English as moral and character education

In this chapter we continue to explore both the contribution of the Romantics and the importance of truth and return to ancient notions of the cosmos explored in Chapter 1. Arguably, 'the values behind British education at present remain largely unknown, unscrutinized and undebated' (Copley, 2005, p. 111). We cannot presume to educate children and young people well if we cannot agree common values and this is especially important as the new *Teachers' Standards* (2012) in the United Kingdom require teachers to promote British values to deter extremism.

Subjective or objective?

We will begin by turning to the incident of Coleridge at the waterfall, Cora Linn, recounted by Dorothy Wordsworth in her *Recollections of a Tour in Scotland*:

> The waterfall Cora Linn is composed of two falls, with a sloping space, which appears to be about twenty yards between . . . A lady and gentleman, more expeditious tourists than ourselves, came to the spot . . . Coleridge, who is always good-natured enough to enter into conversation with anybody whom he meets in his way, began to talk with the gentleman, who observed that it was a *majestic* waterfall. Coleridge was delighted with the accuracy of the epithet, particularly as he had been settling in his own mind the precise meaning of the words grand, majestic, sublime, etc., and had discussed the subject with William at some length the day

before. 'Yes, sir', says Coleridge, 'it is a majestic waterfall'. 'Sublime and beautiful', replied his friend. Poor Coleridge could make no answer, and, not very desirous to continue the conversation, came to us and related the story, laughing heartily. (Dorothy Wordsworth, 1897/1803)

Coleridge endorses the judgement that the waterfall is 'sublime' but not that it is 'beautiful' for the 'sublime' and the 'beautiful' are not the same thing at all. He might come across as something of an intellectual snob 'laughing heartily', but Coleridge is right (at least according to Longinus, Burke, Kant and others). According to Longinus, the 'sublime' is generally regarded as that which inspires awe; for Burke, the sublime is likely to inspire terror as well as awe and for Kant, what is so terrifying about the 'sublime' is that it has no boundaries.

Dorothy Wordsworth's account of Coleridge's reaction appeared in *The Control of Language* (King and Ketley, 1939) and C. S. Lewis (as a teacher of English undergraduates at Oxford who took a keen interest in the teaching of English in the 'upper forms' of schools) turned to it to make an important point about values in English. For Lewis, as for Coleridge, the waterfall really is sublime and this is not simply a result of the projection of the perceiver's views. According to Lewis, who referred to King and Ketley's book as *The Green Book* (it has a light green cover) to preserve their anonymity, too great an emphasis upon the subjectivity of the reader was problematic in English (Lewis, 1978/1943). This is the point made by Peter Medway (2010). Yet Lewis goes further and notes that 'emotions and sentiments . . . can be reasonable or unreasonable as they conform to Reason or fail to conform' (Lewis, 1978/1943, p. 16). The problem with *The Green Book* as a textbook for secondary schools was the overemphasis upon the subjectivity of the reader. According to King and Ketley's book:

> When the man said *This is sublime*, he appeared to be making a remark about the waterfall . . . Actually . . . he was not making a remark about the waterfall, but a remark about his own feelings. (King and Ketley 1939 quoted in Lewis, 1978/1943, p. 7)

What Lewis objects to so strongly is an English textbook for schools, that is ostensibly about language, promoting the specific philosophical theory that all values are subjective. This has direct relevance to English today. Jean Bethke Elshtain gives as an example her daughter being taught in the fifth grade in a New England college town that values were simply 'subjective opinions'; when she asked her daughter if slavery was 'wrong' the response was 'I think slavery is wrong . . . but that is just my opinion' (Elshtain, 2008, p. 88). It is a serious matter 'in an age of human rights par excellence' that there are such 'forces at work in our world that undermine the ontological claims of human dignity' (Elshtain, 2008, p. 91). Moral relativism and subjectivism make it impossible to evaluate different moral codes and to provide meaningful moral education for children and young people. In English, teachers and learners who address the difference between 'fact' and 'opinion', will also need to appreciate that 'no knowledge is neutral but rather is always based on some group's perception of reality and on some group's perspective of what is important to know' (Hall, 2003, p. 176).

Today many school texts still offer a 'portrayal of the world from a mainstream perspective' (Hall, 2003, p. 179) and Western culture has its own, increasingly influential texts that perpetuate specific values. In our time 'a deluge of texts now claim the authority to instruct children on how to participate in childhood and consumer culture' (Luke et al., 2003, p. 254). These texts transmit messages about how children should behave, what they should like, what they should dislike, what is normal and acceptable and what is not. If 'the very premise of the modern textbook' is that it should be 'designed on the basis of psychological theories of instruction' (Luke et al., 2003, p. 251) such a premise might betray the assumption that modern textbooks are somehow neutral. Today, it is asserted that 'the designers of modern textbooks' focus on instruction 'qua scientific method rather than ideological and moral training' (Luke et al., 2003, p. 251) yet what appears to be a 'neutral' focus on skills is the result of specific beliefs about the nature and purpose of English. What masquerades as scientific 'fact', as we saw with the hubris of the Enlightenment, is necessarily based on assumptions and presuppositions.

In reviewing *The Green Book* Lewis showed that even though the student is not overtly or explicitly being taught a theory about life or the nature of the world, certain worldview assumptions of the authors are implicit in the text and exert an unseen but profound influence. He argues that the values in the text are so potent because they are latent. The influence of this textbook is immensely subtle and yet Lewis discerns clear 'Disapprovals' and 'Approvals' in the 'real (perhaps unconscious) philosophy' of the authors who reflect 'the whole system of values which happened to be in vogue' in their circles at the time of writing (Lewis, 1978/1943, p. 61). The student who thinks that he or she is doing a straightforward 'English prep' or as we might say 'assignment' or 'homework' has no notion that 'ethics, theology, and politics are all at stake' (Lewis, 1978/1943, p. 9). For Lewis the abuse of power by the textbook's authors rests upon the disturbing truth that 'they are dealing with a boy' who 'cannot know what is being done to him' (Lewis, 1978/1943, p. 9). If ever there was a description of indoctrination (in the pejorative sense) this is it. All too often students are unaware of the influence their schooling has upon them (Pike, 2006b, 2007a). Ethical English is conceived here as a collaborative venture and a partnership between teachers and learners characterized by transparency and trust (especially concerning values).

What Lewis objects to is subjectivity being encouraged rather than the acknowledgement that certain values are objectively good to hold. Lewis's damning verdict concerning the impact on a young boy is that the authors, 'while teaching him nothing about letters, have cut out his soul, long before he is old enough to choose' (Lewis, 1978/1943, p. 11). The key phrase here is 'before he is old enough to choose' or before he has the maturity to make a conscious choice. Even if we do not focus on value-laden textbooks such as *The Green Book*, the lessons, the curriculum, the ethos of schools, as well as the attitudes and interactions of people within them, all communicate powerful messages to children about what is worth worshipping and what is worthless, what is more valuable and what is less valuable. Lewis counters the position of King and Ketley and argues:

> The man who called the cataract sublime was not intending simply to describe his own emotions about it: he was also claiming that the object was one which *merited* those emotions. (Lewis, 1978/1943, p. 14)

Lewis, like Medway (2010), believed that truth and reason matter. Ethical English teachers should therefore encourage responses that are congruent with the 'First Principles of Practical Reason' (Lewis, 1978/1943, p. 29) summed up as:

> the doctrine of objective value, the belief that certain attitudes are really true, and others really false, to the kind of thing the universe is and the kind of things we are.' (Lewis, 1978/1943, p. 16)

The reason Coleridge agreed that the cataract was 'sublime' and disagreed with the tourist who called it beautiful was that he believed inanimate nature to be such that certain responses could be more 'just' or 'ordinate' or 'appropriate' to it than others' (Lewis, 1978/1943, p. 14). This is not just the view of Lewis 'the Christian':

> In early Hinduism that conduct in men which can be called good consists in conformity to, or almost participation in, the *Rta* – that great ritual or pattern of nature and supernature which is revealed alike in the cosmic order, the moral virtues . . . Righteousness, correctness, order, the *Rta*, is constantly identified with satya or truth, correspondence to reality . . . The Chinese also speak of a great thing (the greatest thing) called the *Tao*. . . . It is Nature, it is the Way, the Road.' (Lewis, 1978/1943, p. 15)

In a similar vein, Charles Taylor reminds us that for the ancient Greeks, 'the good we love is in the order of things, as well as in the wise soul, aligned with nature' (Taylor, 1989, p. 255). This ancient view is in sharp contrast to some misguided modern values talk:

> We moderns are apt to say that something is good because we value it, a crucial and highly problematic reversal of the idea found in the ancients that we cherish something because of its goodness. *In classical ethics, the good is importantly outside and independent of our will, and it is this very independence that compels our allegiance and helps shape our lives.* (Higgins, 2010, p. 221, my italic)

In other words, certain responses, to literature and life, really are better than others. In Latin, *educatio* signifies what we now refer to as 'bringing up' children and Lewis recalls Aristotle, for whom, 'only those who have been *well brought up* can usefully study ethics: to the corrupted man, the man who stands outside the *Tao*, the very starting point for this science is invisible. He may be hostile but *he cannot be critical*' (Lewis, 1978/1943, p. 31, my italic). This latter point certainly chimes with David Stevens's emphasis on criticality. Yet according to Lewis, if you do not accept the *Tao* you will 'destroy the bases of your own criticism as well as the thing being criticized' (Lewis, 1978/1943, p. 31). We need to be clear about the moral or ethical basis of our criticism.

The Moral Law (Natural Law)

In *The Abolition of Man*, C. S. Lewis refers to the *Tao* because it is the Chinese term for 'the Way' or 'the Road' of harmony:

> It is the reality beyond all predicates . . . It is the Way in which the universe goes on, the way in which things everlastingly emerge . . . It is also the Way which every man should tread in imitation of that cosmic and supercosmic progression, conforming all activities to that great exemplar. (Lewis, 1978/1943, pp. 15–16)

Lewis gives 'Illustrations of *The Tao*' drawn from different cultures and traditions such as the ancient Egyptian, Babylonian, Old Norse, Chinese, Indian, Jewish, Roman, Greek, Australian Aboriginal or American Indian. There are fewer ethical differences between cultures than we might at first think and terms such as 'order' and 'truth' denote the *Tao*, which is a 'law' in the sense that certain actions *merit* certain responses. Unlike the law of gravity we choose whether to follow it and whether to have harmonious lives or not. A summary of the Appendix to *The Abolition of Man* 'Illustrations of the *Tao*' follows; in the original as many as 30 quotations follow each principle or value or 'law' drawn from the great texts of different cultures and traditions. Here just a few of the sources used to justify and substantiate the *universality* of the given moral principle or value are given to provide an indication of the range of sources drawn upon:

1 The law of general benificence
In negative form, this includes refraining from murder or bringing any sort of misery and suffering upon one's fellows. It includes not being greedy, cruel or telling lies. In positive form, this includes showing kindness and goodwill, doing one another good not evil, enjoying society and human companionship and loving others as oneself.

> 'Utter not a word by which anyone could be wounded.' (Hindu, *Janet*)
>
> 'Never do to others what you would not like them to do to you.' (Chinese, *Analects of Confucius*)
>
> 'Love thy neighbour as thyself.' (Jewish, *Leviticus*)
>
> 'Do to others what you would have them do to you.' (Christian, *Gospel of Matthew*)

2 The law of special benificence
While similar to the first law, this second law is 'special' as it refers to the duties of brothers, sisters, wives, husbands, children as well as rulers. As human beings we have special obligations and owe particular duties of care to those of our closer and wider family.

> 'It is upon the trunk that a gentleman works. When that is firmly set up, the Way grows. And surely proper behaviour to parents and elder brothers is the trunk of goodness.' (Chinese, *Analects of Confucius*)
>
> 'This first I rede thee: Be blameless to thy kindred. Take no vengeance even though they do thee wrong.' (Old Norse, *Sigrdrifumál*)
>
> 'Is it only the sons of Atreus who love their wives? For every good man, who is right-minded, loves and cherishes his own.' (Greek, Homer, *Iliad*, ix. 340)
>
> 'If any provide not for his own, and specially for those of his own house, he hath denied the faith.' (Christian, *New Testament*, 1 Timothy 5:8)

3 Duties to parents, elders, ancestors
Honouring one's father and mother by supporting them, caring for them and fulfilling one's obligations to them by showing proper respect, even when they are dead, is prescribed.

'Your father is an image of the Lord of Creation, your mother an image of the Earth. For him who fails to honour them, every work of piety is in vain. This is the first duty.' (Hindu, *Janet*, i.9)

'You will see them take care . . . of old men.' (American Indian, *Le Jeune*)

'Honour thy Father and thy Mother.' (Jewish, *Exodus*, 20:12)

'To care for parents.' (Greek, *List of duties* in *Epictetus*, 111.vii)

4 Duties to children and posterity
Providing for the education of the young and respecting children are key requirements.

'Children, the old, the poor, etc. should be considered as lords of the atmosphere.' (Hindu, *Janet*, i.8)

'The Master said, Respect the young.' (Chinese, *Analects of Confucius*, ix.22)

'Can you conceive an Epicurean commonwealth? . . . What will happen? Whence is the population to be kept up? Who will educate them? Who will be Director of Adolescents?' (Greek, Epictetus, III.vii)

'The killing of . . . the young boys and girls who are to go to make up the future strength of the people, is the saddest part . . . .we feel it very sorely.' (American Indian, *Account of the Battle of Wounded Knee*)

5 The law of justice
Sexual justice, honesty and justice in court are singled out here. One must be faithful to one's spouse and not commit adultery. One should not steal and should render to each person his rights. The legal system should not be partial and treat the poor worse than the rich.

'Thou shalt not commit adultery . . . thou shalt not steal.' (Jewish, *Exodus*, 20.14,15)

'Choose loss rather than shameful gains.' (Greek, Chilon)

'If the native made a 'find' of any kind (e.g. a honey tree) and marked it, it was thereafter safe for him, as far as his own tribesmen were concerned, no matter how long he left it.' (Australian Aboriginal)

'Justice is the settled and permanent intention of rendering to each man his rights.' (Roman, Justinian, *Institutions*, 1.i)

6 The law of good faith and veracity
Fraud, lying, falsehoods are prohibited. Perjury is condemned as is saying one thing and doing another. Keeping good faith and keeping promises are essential elements of this law.

'I sought no trickery, nor swore false oaths.' (Anglo-Saxon, *Beowulf*)

'Hateful to me as are the gates of Hades is that man who says one thing, and hides another in his heart.' (Greek, Homer, *Iliad*, ix.312)

'The foundation of justice is good faith.' (Roman, Cicero, *De Officiis* I.vii)

'A sacrifice is obliterated by a lie and the merit of alms by an act of fraud.' (Hindu, *Janet*, i.6)

7　The law of mercy

The poor, the sick, the disabled, the weak should be cared for. It should be possible for a prisoner to be set free. Widows, orphans and old men should be looked after. We must always be tender enough to weep.

'In the Dalebura tribe a woman, a cripple from birth, was carried about by the tribespeople in turns until her death at the age of sixty-six . . . They never desert the sick.' (Australian Aboriginal)

'You will see them take care of . . . widows, orphans, and old men, never reproaching them.' (American Indian)

'I have given bread to the hungry, water to the thirsty, clothes to the naked, a ferry boat to the boatless.' (Ancient Egyptian)

'Has he failed to set a prisoner free?' (Babylonian, *List of Sins*)

'When thou cutest down thine harvest . . . and hast forgot a sheaf . . . thou shalt not go again to fetch it: it shall be for the stranger, for the fatherless, and for the widow.' (Ancient Jewish, Deuteronomy 24.19)

8　The law of magnanimity

Not only should we not injure, but we should protect others from being injured – death is not to be feared.

There are two kinds of injustice: 'The first is found in those who do an injury, the second in those who fail to protect another from injury when they can.' (Roman, Cicero, *De Officiis* I.vii)

'He who is unmoved, who has restrained his senses . . . is said to be devoted. As a flame in a windless place that flickers not, so is the devoted.' (Ancient Indian, *Bhagavad Gita*)

'The Master said, Love learning and if attacked be ready to die for the Good Way' (Ancient Chinese, *Analects*)

'Verily, verily I say to you unless a grain of wheat falls into the earth and dies, it remains alone, but if it dies it bears much fruit. He who loves his life loses it.' (Christian, John 12.24,25)

Teaching universal virtues

It is this concept, whether Greek, Roman, Aboriginal, Indian, Jewish, Christian or Confucian, that Lewis refers to as 'the *Tao*'. The universality of such core values was brought home to me sitting in the staffroom (as a newly qualified teacher) after a week in the classroom. The Head of English, Halima, and I played a kind of 'values snap' despite our different backgrounds. She had grown up on the Indian subcontinent and was actively involved with Amnesty International; I had grown up in England and had spent the summer working for the Salvation Army with disadvantaged teenagers. Yet we had core values in common including a passionate commitment to social justice. Terms such as 'righteousness', 'correctness', 'order' and 'truth' denote the *Tao* and one's relation to the *Tao* are of determining significance educationally:

> Hence the educational problem is wholly different according as you stand within or without the *Tao*. For those within, the task is to train in the pupil those responses which are in themselves appropriate. (Lewis, 1978/1943, p. 17)

Arguably, the *Tao* offers a more universally ethical basis for English teaching than either the rationality of the Enlightenment (Medway, 2010) or the emotion of Romanticism, however critically enlightened (Stevens, 2011). The *Tao* transcends democratic values and appears altogether more foundational for human ethical life being drawn as it is from the *literature and religions* of different cultures and traditions (Pike, 2011). Central to the *Tao* (Moral Law or Natural Law) is the understanding that certain actions '*merit*, our approval or disapproval' (Lewis, 1978/1943, p. 14). It is certainly hard to imagine a completely different sort of morality:

> If we did all that Plato or Aristotle or Confucius told us, we should get on a great deal better than we do. And so what? We have never followed the advice of the great teachers . . . . There has been no lack of good advice for the last four thousand years. (Lewis, 1981/1952, p. 133)

In the New Testament St Paul acknowledges that those outside the Jewish or Christian traditions 'show that what the Law requires is written on their hearts, while their conscience also bears witness' (Rom. 2.15). At the same time St Paul was writing these words the Roman, Cicero, was writing that there is a 'true law' that is 'unchangeable and eternal' (De Republica, 11.33). Arguably, the *Tao* 'is not one among a series of possible systems of value' but is 'the sole source of all value judgments' (Lewis, 1978/1943, p. 29). Consequently, this moral code provides a better foundation for educational values that underpin ethical English in schools than either Romantic or Enlightenment values (Pike, 2012a). What is especially interesting, given our discussion in the last chapter about the 'noble savage' is that the values given in the *Tao* are not a modern invention but have been around for thousands of years. Again though, we need to be sufficiently respectful of diversity for the seductive idea that different religions and cultures are reducible to a common set of beliefs or morality (which is an Enlightenment idea) would not be appreciated by many of those belonging to those different religious and cultural groups who might well see this as the imposition of liberal thinking. We also need to be especially clear that here we are referring to core values and not truth claims or religious doctrines which necessarily differ between groups.

Such universal core values are of the utmost value in a plural society not least because they originate in the literature and religious writings of different cultures and traditions. They are invaluable when we are asked whose values should be taught in a diverse, plural society. They provide a vital 'centre' which can 'hold' and support social cohesion rather than its converse:

> Things fall apart; the centre cannot hold;
> Mere anarchy is loosed upon the world,
> The blood-dimmed tide is loosed, and everywhere
> The ceremony of innocence is drowned;
> The best lack all conviction, while the worst
> Are full of passionate intensity.
>
> (from 'The Second Coming' by W. B. Yeats, 1919)

We need to consider if the doomsday scenario of a fractured society in which 'the centre cannot hold' is justified. A *medias res* between 'lacking conviction' and the sort of 'passionate intensity' we should all rather avoid, might only be possible if the 'centre' holds. Consequently, children and young people are not well served by the time-honoured custom in schooling of avoiding consideration of 'what lies at the centre of the system – its core value or values' (Copley, 2005, p. 107). A leading authority on character education in a plural society, has noted that:

> Despite this diversity, we can identify basic, shared values that allow us to engage in public moral education in a pluralistic society. Indeed, pluralism itself is not possible without agreement on values such as justice, honesty, civility, democratic process, and a respect for truth. (Lickona, 1991, p. 20)

Significantly, like the *Tao*, Lickona's 'Ten Essential Virtues' are 'found in cultures and religions around the world' (Lickona, 2004, p. 8) and might be regarded as 'ethical truths that have been intuited over millennia in virtually every culture' (Clouser, 1999, p. 105). Some truths 'need to be seized in an intuition rather than built up out of concepts; we need to know them, not to know about them' (Lewis, 1971/1964, p. 109). A brief summary of each of these virtues, which are used in many American public (state) schools, will enable the similarities to be seen between them and the *Tao*:

Lickona's Ten Essential Virtues summarized

1 **Wisdom or good judgement**: knowing when to act, how to act and how to balance the virtues when they conflict – like telling the truth when it will cause hurt.

2 **Justice**: includes interpersonal virtues such as civility, honesty, respect, responsibility and tolerance – moral indignation in the face of injustice.

3 **Fortitude**: courage, resilience, patience, perseverance, endurance and self confidence are part of fortitude – we develop our character more through sufferings than successes – setbacks make us stronger so long as we don't feel sorry for ourselves.

4 **Temperance**: self control and the ability to govern ourselves, to regulate our sensual appetites – pursue legitimate pleasures even in moderation – the power to resist temptation.

5 **Love**: goes beyond fairness and justice – love is selfless – willingness to sacrifice oneself for the sake of another – best summed up in 'love your neighbour as yourself'.

6 **A positive attitude**: our happiness or misery depends on our dispositions and not on our circumstances – we're as happy as we make up our minds to be.

7 **Hard work**: includes initiative, diligence, goal setting and resourcefulness – an old-fashioned virtue.

8 **Integrity**: being faithful to moral conscience, keeping our word, standing up for what we believe – to have integrity is to be 'whole' so that what we say and do in different situations is consistent.

9 **Gratitude**: chosing to be thankful is the secret of a happy life – we all drink from wells we did not dig – counting our everyday blessings.

10 **Humility**: avoiding pride, taking responsibility, apologizing, making amends – not causing harm because we want to feel important.

Such core values are a rich resource for teachers and students of English. Studying and responding to works of literature, offers one of the richest ways of learning the *Tao* or fostering essential virtues. In *Moral Education through English* the bold (but justified) claim is made that:

> Literature, more than any other subject in the curriculum, offers the fullest possible picture both of the complexities of the moral situation and the consequences of action. (McCulloch and Mathieson, 1995, p. 30)

This brings us onto the question of how English might foster such 'essential virtues'.

Teaching character in English

The values described so far (depicted in the *Tao* and Lickona's 'essential virtues') are helpful because many teachers 'have found subscribing to any set of values deeply problematic in a pluralistic society' and often therefore 'commit themselves to nothing in particular – or to a sort of undefined humanism where the only question is one of personal feeling' (Arthur, 2005, p. 249). The view taken here is that ethical English should help young people in their growth towards autonomy, where they become justly discriminating in life as well as in response to literature. For Aristotle 'the aim of education is to make the pupil like and dislike what he ought' (Lewis, 1978/1943, p. 15). This is the real *educational* task. Teachers have a moral obligation to seek to nurture children so that their responses are appropriate. If we were to hear children being racist or sexist or homophobic or disparaging of someone's religious beliefs in the classroom we would assert the absolute rightness of tolerant, humane and respectful values being expressed. There are, however, some misconceptions that need to be dispelled before teachers of English can be liberated to carry out that ethical task with ethical integrity. Kristjánsson (2013) has identified ten myths about character, virtue and virtue education suggesting these are perceived as notions that are unclear, redundant, old-fashioned, religious, paternalistic, anti-democratic, anti-intellectual, conservative, individualistic, relative and entirely situation-specific.

'Character Education' has, on occasion, been viewed with suspicion, especially by the educational establishment in the United Kingdom and in some Commonwealth countries, where teachers have had reservations about seeking to influence the character of students. It has been noted, however, that 'there is now a growing interest in Character Education in England' with teachers and policy-makers 'taking an interest in aspects of character development, social literacy and emotional intelligence' (Davison, 2005, p. xi). Clearly, 'character' is a major aspect of studying literature and 'the power of literature in the character development of adolescent readers' (Davison,

2005, p. xii) is undeniable. The approach that is congruent with the ethos of English as defined in this book is to work, collaboratively, with students so that 'we engage young people in their own character development' (Davison, 2005, p. xii).

If one of the reasons for the reluctance to teach specific values is that English teachers do not want to be accused of indoctrination we need to appreciate that, taken literally, all teachers are 'indoctrinators' (although not in the pejorative sense). Teachers routinely 'indoctrinate' children in 'tolerance' for instance. Schooling is an instrumental practice that seeks, for good or ill, to change children in specific ways. Clearly, 'every teacher indoctrinates to some extent, as children do not always understand the reasons why they should believe and act in certain ways even while teachers insist that they should do so' (Arthur, 2003, p. 37). In *Teaching Character Through Literature* an important point is made:

> Our temptation as educators of adolescents in an increasingly pluralistic society is to remain hands-off and assume a non-interference policy when it comes to the topic of moral choices and commitments. We are sometimes inclined to leave older students free to discover for themselves what is best and right and to avoid 'indoctrinating' young people with certain moral values. Indoctrination is precisely what many educators fear falling into. (Bohlin, 2005, p. 4)

Too many teachers feel forced to adopt a 'hands off' approach but we should be aware that when educators focus on academic progress and decide that morality should be relegated to the private realm, the 'pushers of pornography' and other anti-social vices 'proselytize them in a much larger, much more pervasive scale' and businesses that exploit young people 'are unrelenting in their efforts to pump their messages into the mainstream via internet, billboards and television' (Bohlin, 2005, p. 4). Aptly, Bohlin quotes a Head teacher who makes the case passionately and with eloquence:

> Is it a crime for us to try to influence or persuade them that love is better than violence, gentleness better than force, that it is better to love someone wholly than to use his or her body selfishly. In a society in which rock stars and professional athletes purvey their existential and ethical views, shall educators keep silence? (Jarvis, 1993, pp. 65–6)

Whether English in schools is sufficiently addressing the moral needs of students is open to debate.

To those who see English as the provision of skills or tools, it might be pointed out that 'embedded in every tool is an ideological bias, a predisposition to construct the world as one thing rather than another, to value one thing over another, to amplify one sense or skill or attitude more loudly than another' (Postman, 1992, p. 13). Even when literacy is regarded as a tool we should be aware that tools are never neutral in human hands. A tool is always put to some uses rather than others and serves particular ends and purposes. Teaching and learning in English has the capacity to help us to thrive, to act in socially just ways, to make ethical decisions and to enable us to participate in a fair and vibrant society. The view of literacy as a neutral, skills-based and value-free area of education rather than a value-laden and deeply ideological intervention in children's lives may be a product of our time. It would seem to parallel views of education that see the function of schooling itself in terms of the acquisition of knowledge and skills rather than values. Yet, even the focus on skills is the result of a value-position. While claiming to focus on acquiring skills and knowledge rather than cultivating values, values are inculcated.

Much moral education occurs in English especially when discussing issues in texts and evaluating the behaviour and motivation of characters. From the initial regicide in Shakespeare's *Macbeth* to Tom Robinson's unjust trial in Harper Lee's *To Kill a Mockingbird* to the destruction of Piggy's spectacles in Golding's *Lord of the Flies*, young people witness injustice and cruelty. These novels (and the teachers that teach them) promote justice and kindness by showing us the iniquity of injustice and unkindness. Many of the didactic elements in the Narnia novels are 'part of the great moral tradition of humankind that Lewis in *The Abolition of Man* calls the *Tao*' (Tankard, 2007, p. 72). The question is not *whether* we teach children how to live but *how* we will do so and *what* values we will teach.

A young person who wants to become a professional tennis player works together with their coach to become the best they can be. I was privileged to be in China (speaking on the *Tao*) when the British player Andy Murray beat Spain's David Ferrer to win the Shanghai Masters. Yet Murray had to work hard to become so good. Arguably:

> What you mean by a good tennis player is the man whose eye and muscles and nerves have been so trained by making innumerable good shots that they can now be relied on. (Lewis, 1981/1952, p. 73)

It is significant that Lewis refers to 'trained habit' as character education 'has long relied upon an Aristotelian principle that character is formed in large part through habitual behaviour that eventually becomes internalized into virtues (character)' (Berkowitz and Bier, 2004, p. 80). Players such as Federer and Murray do not play the odd good shot: they *are* good tennis players; they have trained themselves to be consistent through repeated practice. Analogously 'a man who perseveres in doing just actions gets in the end a certain quality of character' (Lewis, 1981/1952, p. 74).

We should be aware though that there is a great difference between practicing justice or temperance and being a just and temperate person. As we saw in Chapters 2 and 3 the difference between *doing* and *being* is significant. In fact:

> right actions done for the wrong reason do not help to build the internal quality or character called a 'virtue', and it is this quality or character that really matters. (Lewis, 1981/1952, p. 74)

It is possible that a bad tennis player could hit the ball in anger and that this shot might by chance actually cause him to win the game 'but it will not be helping him to become a reliable player' (Lewis, 1981/1952, p. 74). Character education as conceived here is congruent with ethical English because it is not something that is done to students, it is working with them to help them become the best they can be.

This emphasis on character also needs to be tempered with realism. Even the shots of the best Wimbledon or US Open champion, have at some time or other fallen short. Everyone's shots in life fail to hit the mark at some point. There will have been times when even the most consistent, stable and virtuous of English teachers have known what the right action was but have failed to do. Or we have known that an action was wrong but have done it anyway (the character of the teacher is discussed further in Chapter 8). For C. S. Lewis this means we need redemption but whether or not one believes the central truth claim of the Christian faith that this is through Christ there is an important point here. We can help children and young people strive towards consistency but we can guarantee that they will, like us, not act virtuously all the time (however well we work with them to develop their character through English). How we promote virtue while offering opportunities for rehabilitation, restoration and forgiveness when students (and teachers) fail to be the best they can be is of central importance to ethical English.

Too often schools educate the head, or the mind, for academic success or vocational proficiency while paying scant regard to moral education and the teaching of right and wrong. When teachers and school leaders speak of the 'mean' or average in schools we automatically assume that this refers to the monitoring and assessment of academic performance but it is worth remembering that, for Aristotle, the 'mean' refers to the place between excess and insufficiency in moral terms. The first chapter of *The Abolition of Man* is entitled 'Men without Chests' because the heads of the people depicted (who have completed the system of schooling) look bigger than their chests. For Lewis the chest is the seat 'of emotions organized by trained habit into stable sentiments' but students suffered from an 'atrophy of the chest' (Lewis, 1978/1943, p. 19). It is a grotesque and disturbing image. When Lewis depicts the hideously disproportionate size of the head in relation to the chest he is not suggesting that we have spent too much time on the head but that we have spent too little time on the chest. Describing students, he observes: 'It is not excess of thought but defect of fertile and generous emotion that marks them out' (1978/1943, p. 9). This is graphically illustrated in the third novel of Lewis's science fiction trilogy *That Hideous Strength* where the 'Head' of a supposedly scientific institute, the NICE, is literally just that, a guillotined head, bracketed to a wall and kept alive by pumps and tubes. Here, literally, the 'chest', and anything else from the head down, has been done away with. This fictional work is especially important because it is the literary partner to *The Abolition of Man*, Lewis's treatise on English in schooling.

If we are focusing on what is most easily measured (knowledge and skills) we are unlikely to be giving our attention to what is most important. Each of us is more than an intellect (head) and more than an animal with appetite (stomach) for each has a moral sense and character (chest). Our moral sense (the chest) acts as an indispensable 'liaison officer' between the cerebral and visceral aspects of our make-up and it 'may even be said that it is by this middle element that man is man' (Lewis, 1978/1943, p. 9). Our moral character and 'just sentiments' make us fully human and humane.

It is as teachers help students to develop 'just sentiments' that they thrive and flourish. A good example of this is 'stock responses' which might be regarded as 'the correct symbols, the organized and willed responses, the conventional reactions we assume when writing or talking about important matters' (Hooper, 1996, p. 610). Whereas I. A. Richards saw stock responses as one of the 'chief difficulties of criticism', C. S. Lewis saw these responses as invaluable to human flourishing. I. A. Richards refers to a poem that evokes 'views and emotions already fully prepared in the reader's mind' so that what happens during the reading is 'more of the reader's doing than the poet's' because once the 'button is pressed' then 'the author's work is done, for immediately the record starts playing in quasi (or total) independence of the poem' (Hooper, 1996, p. 610). However, Lewis suggests that stock responses such as finding death bitter, virtue lovely or love sweet are vital because 'such deliberate organization is one of the first necessities of human life, and one of the main functions of art is to assist it' (Hooper, 1996, p. 611).

Character education on the playing fields of England

In the United States, character education is virtually a synonym for 'Moral education' in public (state) schools. In the field of English in education, works such as *Teaching Character through English* (Bohlin, 2005) are influential.

Character education is not, however, an American invention and was an integral part of schooling in Britain in the nineteenth century. Of course, it was not a British invention either and its roots lie in classical conceptions of character and virtue. Yet much schooling now settles for *techne* (technical proficiency) rather than educating for what Aristotle termed *phronesis* (moral deliberation).

A famous remark, attributed to the Duke of Wellington, is that 'The Battle of Waterloo was won on the playing fields of Eton'. The connotations of the phrase the 'playing fields of Eton' are that the British under Wellington defeated the French under Napoleon because of the character, discipline and ethos that the officers had learned while boys at public school. The same could be said of many of the other 'public' schools that in England refer to old, established, private schools attended by the Elite. In Part One of this book we looked at the claim made in Sir Henry Newbolt's report *The Teaching of English in England* (1921) that literature is 'one of the richest fields of our spiritual being' and provides a 'unifying influence' (Newbolt, 1921, p. 257). Although the Newbolt Report (1921) sits on a shelf in my study it is not read as widely as the famous poem 'Vitaï Lampada' (Carry the Torch of Life) which Newbolt also wrote and for which he is remembered. In this poem the virtues of sportsmanship and chivalry in the service of the British Empire are valorized. The poem 'Vitaï Lampada' made his reputation in 1897 and is about a schoolboy cricketer who fights for the British Empire in Africa. In the carnage and panic of the battle with the 'colonel dead' and the Gatling gun jammed, the memory of schooldays stirs the men to heroic action: 'his Captain's hand on his shoulder smote/ Play up! Play up! And play the game!'. The poem depicts exactly what character education *once meant*:

Vitaï Lampada

There's a breathless hush in the Close to-night
Ten to make and the match to win
A bumping pitch and a blinding light,
An hour to play and the last man in.
And it's not for the sake of a ribboned coat,
Or the selfish hope of a season's fame,
But his Captain's hand on his shoulder smote
'Play up! play up! and play the game!'

The sand of the desert is sodden red,
Red with the wreck of a square that broke;
The Gatling's jammed and the colonel dead,
And the regiment blind with dust and smoke.
The river of death has brimmed his banks,
And England's far, and Honour a name,

But the voice of a schoolboy rallies the ranks,
'Play up! Play up! and play the game!'

This is the word that year by year
While in her place the School is set
Every one of her sons must hear,
And none that hears it dare forget.
This they all with a joyful mind
Bear through life like a torch in flame,
And falling fling to the host behind
'Play up! play up! and play the game!'

It is unsurprising that when war was declared Newbolt was recruited by the
WPB (War Propaganda Bureau) to help maintain public opinion in its favour.
Arguably, the tradition of promoting service in the British Empire in school
may be one reason for the suspicion of character education in many schools
today that seek to distance Britain from its imperial past. Many character
educators today would also wish to distance themselves from Newbolt's
propaganda.

The poem 'Vitaï Lampada' always evokes memories for me of schooldays
at Bishop Wordsworth's School in Salisbury Cathedral Close (although I was
never picked to play cricket for the school). The school was still very much
in the tradition of the British 'stiff upper lip' where notions of service were
promoted. Times have changed but not all of this change is for the better.
Character education (such as that based on Lickona's 'essential virtues')
is often marginalized in favour of an emphasis on the academic (narrowly
focused on tests, targets, grades and criteria) even though the provision of high
quality character education is associated with improved academic attainment
(Berkowitz and Bier, 2004; Pike 2010d). Educational organizations such as the
Centre for Character and Citizenship at the University of Missouri-St Louis
which publishes the *Journal of Character Education*, the Jubilee Centre at
Birmingham University in the United Kingdom and the Centre for the 4th and
5th Rs (Respect and Responsibility), part of the State University of New York
in the United States are leading research into character education which is
seeing a resurgence in the early twenty-first century.

There is significant potential for the development of character in English.
A recent ESRC (Economic and Social Research Council) and AHRC (Arts and
Humanities Research Council) funded case study of a school serving a social
priority area focused on the character of students, especially within English
lessons (Pike, 2009b, 2010b, 2011a). In one of these an English teacher was
observed engaging in the sort of practice advocated in *Teaching Character
Education through Literature* (Bohlin, 2005). The English teacher encouraged

students to undertake a character analysis task employing the students' understanding of the school's core values:

Determination
We know that hard work and the refusal to give up are essential if we are to achieve anything worthwhile.

Integrity
We can be trusted to be honest and truthful, to say what we mean and to do what we say.

Accountability
We recognize that having the freedom to express ourselves means we must also accept responsibility for our words, thoughts and actions.

Courage
We aim to do what is right, whatever the cost; we stand up for the weak, whatever the danger; we face our fears and find ways of defeating them.

Compassion
We care for those who are in difficulty and who are hurting, recognizing that the world does not exist for us alone.

Honourable purpose
We aim to be positive in everything, doing what is good and aiming to benefit others as well as ourselves.

Humility
We seek to do our personal best without bragging and to encourage others to achieve their best without being critical or jealous of their efforts.

The use of the core values did not occur in every lesson by any means for this teacher was observed making no reference to the school's core values on two previous occasions. The fact that the school's core values were employed in English *at all* would, however, seem to be innovative and ethical practice:

Teacher: Think about our core values because we've been looking at all the different qualities of these characters. Think about the core values that we at Trinity live by or try to live by. I want you please to write down which core value you think Beatrice and Benedick either embody or break. Okay, what do I mean by embody?

Sarah: Stick to

Teacher: Stick to – so which one do they either stick to or break? And I'd like a brief explanation. You've got 3 minutes to do that . . . Which of the core values? . . .

(Children discuss task)

Teacher: Just bob your pens down for me please. Very quickly, hands up if you have a core value that you think Beatrice embodies? Bethany?

Bethany: Determination

Teacher: Why determination?

Bethany: Cos um she stands up for what she believes in like when Hero is getting um slandered and like the shame of it, she believes him

Teacher: Good yeah determination – could also be seen as courage. How about a core value that she breaks? Anyone got a core value that she breaks? Christina?

Christina: Humility

Teacher: Why humilty?

Christina: She can be quite boastful

Teacher: She can be quite boastful, I do agree. Very quickly, has anyone got a core value that Benedick embodies?

Ellis: Courage because he fought in a war

Teacher: Absolutely courage because he fought in a war and the big one, the one that he breaks?

Guy: Integrity

Teacher: Why Integrity?

Guy: Because he lies about his feelings towards Beatrice.

What we need now are more studies of character education in English. Further research could take inspiration from work such as Bohlin's or it could look at students' character development in different contexts through English. A valuable exercise for an English department or teacher would be to see which values might be explored in work on different texts or topics. Certain texts, such as the *Narnia* novels by C. S. Lewis, Shakespeare's *Macbeth* or *To Kill a Mockingbird* by Harper Lee (and many others besides) offer especially powerful opportunities for character education. Documenting how one works together with students on their character development through the use of literature would create an important and valuable resource for the educational community (Pike, 2007d).

Study questions

1   How might you promote the *Tao* or 'Essential Virtues' through English?

2   How universal do you believe the *Tao* to be?

3   How important is moral education in English?

4   Where do you derive your foundations for moral education in English?

5   Why is English *par excellence* the place for moral education on the curriculum?

6   What are the unique features of English as far as moral education is concerned?

7   What are your core values? What are the core values of your classroom?

8   How well do you educate and exercise the 'chest' as well the 'head' of a student?

9   How can you educate both through a particular lesson or scheme of work?

10 How would you introduce your students to the importance of core values?

11 How good a character educator are you?

12 How can you be a better character educator in English?

7

Learning citizenship and character in English

In the last chapter we considered the cultivation of the virtues and character of the learner. In this chapter we turn our attention to the development of virtuous, ethical, moral behaviour between learners and the character or ethos of the community of learners in English. As individuals live in communities this is an area to which ethical English may make a significant contribution.

English: Liberal art for liberal society

The potential for English to inform citizenship education is extensive as there are many concerns both areas have in common (Pike, 2010d, 2011b). It is unsurprising that, in the United Kingdom:

> Citizenship Education tends to be located within existing subject areas in secondary schools, predominantly but not exclusively in the English/ Humanities cluster. (Davison, 2005, p. xi)

While work on charities such as Shelter in citizenship lessons is valuable, reading *Stone Cold* by Robert Swindell's followed by good classroom discussion in English might be more effective. Arguably, the best of *Literacy in Citizenship* (DfES, 2004) draws upon literature. For instance, the approach to rules in society and how they are enforced is taught with reference to the leadership qualities of Jack and Ralph in William Golding's *Lord of the Flies* and this novel is used to provide a 'stimulus on what constitutes the basics of organizing a society' (DfES, 2004, p. 27).

English is a liberal art that prepares citizens for participation and service in a liberal democracy. The sort of liberal values that English may legitimately promote are politically liberal, in the sense that they are the values of liberal democracy (although, even here, the role of English is to promote critical reflection upon liberal democracy rather than blind allegiance to it). It is important that educators should communicate with learners concerning the values they are seeking to inculcate so that students are treated with dignity as 'citizens' rather than 'subjects' (Pike, 2007a).

A brief analysis of what is generally meant by liberal society follows but first it may be useful to consider what the other options are in terms of governing society. Most of us would not swap living in a liberal democracy for life in a nation run as a personal dictatorship or one-party state. Nor would we want to live in a state run by the military (for instance, following a coup where a military leader becomes president and retains control of the armed forces) or in a police state. These nations are often characterized by human rights abuses and a lack of personal freedom where arbitrary arrest and imprisonment are common and where there is no guarantee of justice unless one bribes officials. Other alternatives are the anarchic, lawless, failed state or the theocratic state.

Having defined what a liberal state is not, we should turn our attention to its key qualities. Although far from perfect, in liberal societies, personal liberty is generally protected by liberal institutions. If one looks at where people want to live it is not a coincidence that there is mass emigration *to* liberal countries where there is personal freedom and *away from* nations that do not protect personal freedom. I recently observed that most of the taxi drivers in New York City seemed to be from non-liberal, non-democratic, states. People from the West are not emigrating to live in dictatorships where personal rights are unprotected. Fundamentally, ethical English promotes liberty and the freedom of the individual; it therefore exhibits a high degree of congruence with liberal society and is ideologically well placed to prepare children and young people for life in such a society.

Liberal societies are fully democratic. The United Kingdom is a liberal democracy and so too are, for instance, the United States, Canada, Australia, New Zealand, Israel, The Netherlands, Germany and France. Generally, in liberal societies there is the tolerance of difference so long as it does not harm others. According to J. S. Mill in *On Liberty*:

The sole end for which mankind are warranted, individually or collectively, in interfering with the liberty of action of any of their number is self-protection . . . The only part of the conduct of anyone, for which he is amenable to society, is that which concerns others . . . Over himself, over his own body and mind, the individual is sovereign. (1914/1859, p. 73)

Consequently, liberal societies are characterized by personal freedom and liberty. The emphasis in English (and in English society) is on the freedom of the individual, and freedom to express oneself. A liberal country will have a 'free press' that is not controlled by the government.

It is important, however, to stress that we are referring to *politically* liberal rather than *comprehensively* liberal values. While it has been suggested that 'the liberal educator has to promote the values that are necessary to living in a liberal society' there is general agreement that educators should 'stop short of promoting a liberal set of moral beliefs or lifestyle' (Haydon, 1997, p. 128). One can be a *political* liberal and believe in personal freedom while not being a *comprehensive* or *social* liberal who believes a wide range of ways of living are just as good as another. Freedom of religion and freedom of conscience and belief are hallmarks of a liberal society. One does not necessarily have to agree with other people's choices but, in general, their right to hold different views is respected. The core values of a politically liberal society are liberty, equality and rationality. The third of these values mediates between the first two and is necessary because the more freedom people have the less equal they tend to become.

Liberty, equality and rationality in a free society

Ethical English should enhance personal freedom. This freedom is to express oneself (although one is to be responsible for one's words and actions) and to interpret the world in a different way to another person. In other words, there is a sense that rigid conformity is unhealthy both in English and in liberal society where an original and individual contribution is valued. Creativity depends upon being liberated to be oneself and not to do as everyone else does. There is the freedom for a range of opinions in English where personal expression is privileged. The original Greek word for 'free' was 'Eleutheros' and denoted one who was not a slave. Yet the word is not simply used to describe the status of an individual. If a community was 'eleutheros' it was autonomous. If a community is free it is independent. It is not ruled by another state. Much of the debate around UK membership of the European Union centres upon just this issue, the extent to which the United Kingdom has autonomy and independence.

Talking is the mode of language that is used most often in a free society and is also, on occasion, too free and lacking in restraint as in *The Merchant of Venice* where the talk among strangers 'show something *too liberal*' (II.ii. 187, my italic). Today, in a liberal society, one still has to be able to speak and listen well or one's freedom is limited. Having a 'voice' (including well-developed speaking and listening skills) is critically important in a liberal democracy.

Learning to speak English well

A key theme in this book is that English should liberate learners. Yet simply being fluent or literate in English may not be enough for a young person to do all the travelling they may need to do in a twenty-first century where English is the language of the global village. If speaking English well enables a person to go further in life than they otherwise would we should consider what it means to speak English well. In the Introduction we saw how English was the passport to travelling 'without let or hindrance' as it is put on the first page of my British passport, which it is worth quoting in full:

Her Britannic Majesty's
Secretary of State
Requests and requires in the
Name of Her Majesty
all those whom it may concern
to allow the bearer to pass freely
without let or hindrance,
and to afford the bearer
such assistance and protection
as may be necessary.

We might say that very often the better one speaks English, the further one can travel both geographically and socially. Although learners in school may not be taught to speak the 'Queen's English' (in the sense of the dialect of English spoken by Her Majesty, which is known as 'RP' or 'Received Pronounciation' and would be described by some as 'plummy'), it is vital that they have the ability to speak Standard English confidently and clearly. Acquiring the ability to communicate well in Standard English is vital because speakers of English outside the United Kingdom (which outnumber those within the United Kingdom many times over) have learned this dialect, often referred to as 'BBC English'. Throughout the Cox report (DES, 1986) emphasis was placed upon English as an international language. This influential report stated that 'If pupils do not have access to Standard English, then many important opportunities are closed to them' (4.5) but there tends to be less emphasis upon this now in many schools.

Teachers of English (and school leaders) have a moral responsibility to help to liberate those they educate and to enable them to travel, to experience new places and people and make the most of new opportunities. It is therefore crucial that students acquire Standard English in its spoken and written forms. While not every child will benefit from the sort of elocution lessons experienced by Eliza Doolittle in *Pygmalion*, if pupils from state schools in disadvantaged and economically depressed regions far removed from London and the South-East are to compete with those from elite private schools and experience social mobility, then clarity and confidence in Standard English is vital. According to a recent article in *The Independent*, 'Many fear they are being hindered in their search for jobs or held back in their careers because of their regional accents, or because they struggle to speak clearly' (Sutcliffe, 2012) and consequently many adults are employing private tutors to teach them to speak in the way they desire. Those who can afford it often send their children to a 'public' (private) school where their children acquire a certain accent, which may be a social advantage in particular circles, as well as a Standard English dialect; we need to think carefully about the linguistic aspects of social mobility if we are to achieve greater social justice for students from state schools.

The way we speak is part and parcel of our identity and it is important to distinguish between accent and dialect here. Put simply we might say that accent concerns the way words are pronounced and dialect concerns the actual words and grammar used. The BBC presenter Huw Edwards has a Welsh accent but reads the news in Standard English (using standard vocabulary and grammar). To speak with a Yorkshire accent is different to using non-Standard English grammatical constructions, such as 'I were' rather than 'I was'. Pupils may or may not wish to cultivate the ability to speak in a certain accent but there is a moral obligation to enable students to develop the ability to speak and write in the dialect linguists call Standard English (with its standard vocabulary and grammar). This may, of course, be in addition to their regional dialect. Being bi-dialectal is socially advantageous and avoids denigrating a non-standard dialect with all the sense of identity, belonging and richness of vocabulary and grammar that it provides.

But how many state schools in disadvantaged areas in England provide their students with lessons in speaking well? It might take courageous leadership in addition careful and sensitive teaching to make certain linguistic opportunities available to young people in schools in disadvantaged areas. It would require trust and goodwill (*eunoia*) because it can lead to bad feeling between pupil and teacher if the child or young person believes his or her home background or region is being criticized and viewed as inferior. This can be implicit in a home or regional dialect being 'corrected'. There can be considerable resistance among pupils to talking 'posh' but it is still the case that 'non-standard dialects are discriminated against' (Halliday, 1978, p. 104). In many walks of life, what all this can often add up to is non-Standard-English-speaking students being deprived of the linguistic competence they need to travel educationally, socially and economically 'without let or hindrance'.

In twenty-first-century Britain, diverse non-standard dialects are appreciated more, in many circles, than they have ever been before and are often a source of pride. Yet *The Language Trap* unambiguously argued that we should 'face the sad but true fact that in a plural society the handicaps of disadvantaged groups can be increased by promoting linguistic diversity, as they can be reduced by fostering greater linguistic conformity' (Honey, 1988, p. 181). The implications will not be lost on those educating disadvantaged groups of children who do not routinely speak Standard English. Difference to the standard has consequences that can curtail freedom and limit the potential a young person has to make progress in a society where Standard English is valued and associated with a good education. Whether we like it or not, linguistic difference can be social deficit (Edwards, 1988). An inability to communicate in Standard English constrains rather than liberates and can deny young people important opportunities. There are strong social advantages attached to the ability to speak in the standard dialect, not least if one wishes to communicate with speakers of English who are not native speakers where clarity in Standard English is all the more important.

It has been put, rather simplistically, that 'If children are suffering because of their dialect, why do they not learn another one?' (Halliday, 1978, p. 104). Certainly, many children who are non-Standard English speakers in England are able to imitate Standard English and even RP (Received Pronounciation) for comic purposes, if mimicking royalty, for instance. Yet many children are unlikely to realize they are 'suffering' or that only speaking a non-Standard dialect may be a disadvantage until after they have left school and travelled more widely. It has been suggested that 'the whole of our educational system, as at present constituted, presupposes the ability to handle Standard English. This is the variety of English used by teachers themselves' (Honey, 1988, p. 175), but in twenty-first century classrooms in England many teachers of English can be heard giving instructions or responding to questions in non-Standard English, especially in schools where many of the students regularly use non-Standard English.

The teacher of English must be a good model as a language user and should have an excellent command of Standard English as a speaker in the classroom. When young people are aware of the value of the gift that English is, there is all the more reason for them to make the most of it and to enunciate, speaking clearly without mumbling or slurring words. To teach children and young people to speak well is one of the most potent and strategic of ways in which to overcome social disadvantage and yet this is so 'politically incorrect' among some educators that this opportunity is sadly missed. While teachers of English and their classes often enjoy discussing the richness of linguistic diversity it is important, if English is to liberate learners, that they possess a linguistic repertoire that includes the most powerful dialect of the most powerful language in the world.

Freedom of interpretation

English teachers have a moral obligation to help children to acquire the vital skills they need to live well in a free society. In this way, English has the capacity to contribute to human flourishing (*eudaimonia*) in a free, vibrant and fair society. The curriculum and students' choices within it can constrain or liberate and we need to think carefully about how 'liberal' the education is which schools provide for students in the United Kingdom and elsewhere. When I led English in a large sixth form in the South of England one young man came to see me soon after starting his Science and Maths A levels (which he needed to take for the career he wanted to pursue) to complain that there was no room for personal interpretation and individuality in the subjects he had chosen. He wanted the freedom to express himself. We negotiated a place for him on an Arvon creative writing course at Totleigh Barton in Devon and he became a regular contributor to the school magazine. Having the liberty (being free from economic constraint) to seek knowledge for its own sake rather than for its utilitarian value is what a liberal education is all about. The distinction is often made between English and literacy because only the former is 'liberal' in the sense that studying literature can be for its own sake. The paradox is that by studying English (and reading poetry rather than writing business letters, for instance) one is being prepared rather well for *life* in a liberal society. We do not spend all our waking hours at work and an ethical English education is a good preparation for life, not just work.

We need to be sufficiently discriminating though with regard to 'freedom' and 'democracy'. Andrew Stables emphasizes that 'freedom is not co-terminous with democracy', acknowledging that the rule of the majority can 'restrict or remove the freedoms of minorities' (Stables, 2005, p. 237). Consequently, Stables directs attention away from the hard sciences, as a model for understanding such a plural society, towards hermeneutics, and the importance of interpretation. Stables's semiotics calls for an education that respects diversity and difference (rather than promoting democracy necessarily). For Stables, 'to live morally is to respect interpretation' because those 'who respect and welcome other interpretations will be slow to condemn them' (Stables, 2005, p. 46).

While the liberal state acknowledges that restricting the freedom of some people to engage in certain cultural practices is necessary because these limit others' freedom, we need to acknowledge that Western liberal interpretations are not the only ones that are worthy of respect. Where non-liberal interpretations do not result in harm, these may not be the threat to community cohesion that many suppose (Pike, 2009c, 2011e). Stables advocates a 'non-judgmental exploration of individuals' life experiences'

(Stables, 2005, p. 41) and seeks to 'valorize the unpredictable, the individual and *the sense of freedom* that accompanies the play of individual difference, as well as the held-in-common concerns of any group at any time' (Stables, 2005, p. 163, my italic). He argues that a 'truly moral concern for others' must entail a genuine search to 'appreciate otherness' (Stables, 2005, p. 43), an issue to which we return in relation to literature from different cultures and traditions in Part Three.

Democratizing interpretation, within responsible boundaries, rather than enforcing a state-sponsored reading of the state's values in state schools (a stance that hardly recommends itself as neutral), would seem to be a valuable way of enhancing engagement in English. Yet equality (ensured by rights) needs to be considered in the light of the experience and ethos of liberty we enjoy in a liberal society. We need to ensure that being different to the majority does not necessarily entail discrimination. We need to protect the freedom of some citizens to hold different views to the majority of their compatriots and to resist unjustified attempts to mould everyone to be just like everyone else (even though homogeneity may make us easier to manage).

This is important because, paradoxically, increasing regulation through rights legislation can reduce the freedom people experience in a democracy. We need to be reminded of 'the power of majorities over minorities' and of 'a government over the people' (Lewis, 1996/1958, p. 420). It is even asserted that 'rulers have become owners' (Lewis, 1996/1958, p. 178) under the guise of protecting our 'rights' and 'equality'. This is a controversial notion but is timely. Security threats after 9/11 and 7/7 have reduced our liberty. Ensuring that people have certain minimum 'entitlements' means submitting to a certain 'paternalism' but this cannot be achieved without losing 'personal privacy and independence' (Lewis, 1996/1958, p. 182). In order to be 'protected' we need to be identified, visible and measured. We saw in Chapter 3, with reference to the work of Foucault, measuring and assessing citizens has serious consequences for the freedom young people experience. Yet, in order to ensure 'equality' citizens have to be measured. When the 'ethic of contract becomes more and more the pervasive ethic of society' (Wolterstorff, 2004, p. 91) we should consider the implications for the choice citizens exercise and the freedom they enjoy.

With reference to agents of the State we might well conclude that the 'more completely we are planned the more powerful they will be' (Lewis, 1996/1958, p. 182). If English is to prepare students for life in a free society, it must help to protect fundamental freedoms. It should help us to reappraise rarely challenged assumptions concerning 'equality' that are rapidly forming a new orthodoxy which it is almost deemed heretical, in a democracy and in many schools, to challenge. Although 'Legal equality' is seen as 'protection against cruelty' (Lewis, 1996/1943, p. 29) we should be sufficiently discriminating;

calls for 'equality' should not extend to higher planes for 'Ethical, intellectual, or aesthetic democracy is death' (Lewis, 1996/1944, p. 41). We return to these issues and explore the outworking of core liberal values in a society characterized by cultural and religious diversity in Part Three.

Critical literacy and Education for Democratic Citizenship (EDC)

Ethics and politics are at stake in English. Reading is an inescapably socio-political activity (Harrison, 2004; Pike, 2006b) and English in schools should undoubtedly foster 'active readers and writers who can be expected to exercise some degree of agency in deciding what textual positions they will assume or resist as they interact in complex social and cultural contexts' (Hall, 2003, p. 187). Critical literacy necessarily assumes that the teaching of literacy itself is 'never neutral but always embraces a particular ideology or perspective' (Powell et al., 2005, p. 13). Indeed, critical literacy is an important element of English because it 'acknowledges the differentials of power in society and seeks to realize a more equitable, just, and compassionate community' (Powell et al., 2005, p. 13). As *Literacy: Reading the Word and World* (Friere and Macedo, 1987) suggests, understanding words and world go together. The similarities between the aims of critical (rather than functional) literacy within English and Education for Democratic Citizenship (EDC) in England have been noted (Pike, 2011b). English in schools has a major contribution to make in the teaching of such reading not least because critical literacy 'promotes social justice and a strong participatory democracy, the kind of democracy where power is with, not just some people (like special interest groups or the wealthy) but all people' (Hall, 2003, p. 175).

The democratic values underpinning Citizenship education in schools in England are not, however, uncontested. Unlike France and the United States, England is not a republic but a constitutional monarchy with no written constitution. Further, it has been argued that 'there are no shared values' in Britain which is home to 'a series of sub-cultures each of which has its own priorities, its own agenda' (Sachs, 2005). Citizenship education 'provokes heated debate and controversy in schools' with 'certain critics even questioning whether schools should be engaged in this area of learning' (Osler and Starkey, 2005, p. 4). It has plausibly been claimed that a democracy, whether or not it admits it, 'wants and needs to produce men and women who have the tastes, knowledge, and character supportive of a democratic regime' (Bloom, 1987, p. 26) and the 'idea of citizenship-as-outcome reveals a strong instrumental orientation in the idea of citizenship education' (Biesta and Lawy, 2006, p. 72). The 'transformative' aims of the citizenship curriculum might be regarded, in McLaughlin's (2000) terms, as 'maximal' not 'minimal'. Transformation is also, as we have seen, overtly the aim of critical literacy. Citizenship education (QCA, 1999) in England does not simply entail learning *about* citizenship; it is *for* active citizenship as it aims to produce citizens who have specific beliefs and commitments (Pike, 2008b). Twin emphases within EDC are democratization and human rights.

If Citizenship is the 'new RE' there is one important difference between the two subjects beyond their content that should be noted. Since the 1960s, RE (Religious Education) in most schools in England has made the transition from a 'confessional' approach, (which was designed to nurture children in the Christian faith), to a 'phenomenological' approach (whereby religion is studied as a phenomenon). Citizenship is not *about* democracy it is *for* democracy as it seeks to nurture children in the democratic faith. Citizenship education might therefore be regarded as 'confessional' rather than 'phenomenological' as it teaches children and young people to 'believe in' its doctrines (Pike, 2008b). We have to be careful about encouraging a 'blind faith' in our current system.

Many from conservative faith communities will not share the civic republican emphasis on *political* activity preferring to direct their energies to areas of social, community and religious service for instance where high levels of critical literacy might not be appreciated. The assertion that freedom can be experienced by a society 'only when a nation state is unified around a set of democratic values' (Banks et al., 2005, p. 7) may well be seen as legitimating a single, democratic reading which teachers and students of English may feel is exclusive rather than inclusive. In democratic, capitalist societies the voice of minority groups and the poor may be hard to hear. The democratization of schools may not be welcomed by all. A minority ethnic family who have first-hand experience of injustices and inequalities experienced within a liberal democratic society may not see democratization as a panacea for all perceived injustice. If they privilege hierarchy and respect for authority above democratization, they may view the prospect of their children's schools becoming *more* democratic with dismay. There is certainly 'a tension between cultural and religious tradition on the one hand and universal notions of rights' (Gearon and Brown, 2003, p. 205) on the other. We should not forget that 'dignity does not depend solely on individual *rights*' (Burtonwood, 2000, p. 281, my italic).

The opportunity for children and young people to become autonomous adults has a high priority in evaluating education policy in a liberal country. While liberal theorist Will Kymlicka (2003) argues that acquiring a range of dispositions, virtues and loyalties is inseparable from the practice of democratic citizenship, ethical English places a premium upon allowing young people to come to their own decisions on a range of political and social issues. Indeed, ethical English in schools should help young people to 'read' the plural society they live in with all its contradictions and inconsistencies. Questions certainly need to be asked about the freedom allowed to divergent readings in English; any attempt to impose one reading of democratic values on all will restrict the freedom of some readers. It has been argued that 'in a multicultural society, realizing the goal of equity would mean that everyone had a voice' (Powell et al., 2005, p. 13) but we need to consider what this means given the influence of competing value systems. We might list as examples, postmodernism (Wheen, 2004) or radical feminism (cf. Graham, 1994) as well as religious worldviews such as the Islamic and the Christian (cf. Halstead, 2004, 2007; Pike, 2005c, 2010a). As there are 'different visions of society, using different discourses' (Bottery, 2003, p. 101) ethical English will help young people to understand different 'interpretive communities' (Fish, 1980).

Good readers and good citizens

English teaching should foster critical analysis of the particular 'mode of associated living' (Dewey, 2002/1966, p. 101), which is Western liberal democracy. Professor Sir Bernard Crick, the architect of the citizenship curriculum in England, has claimed that 'a liberal education' should 'change our collective mentality from being subjects of the Crown to being both good and active citizens' (Crick, 2000, p. 160). Crick is quite explicit about the values underpinning the Citizenship curriculum and states that the 'philosophy behind the Report' is 'what scholars call civic republicanism, and also pluralism' (Crick, 2000, p. 120). The aim of citizenship education in England is for young people to become 'active citizens' (QCA, 1998, pp. 7–8) because civic republicanism regards participation in public affairs as the duty of citizens (as it was in the republic of ancient Rome) and the way in which liberty is best preserved. Yet only thinking of oneself as an 'active citizen' has significant moral limitations.

If one is to be a good citizen rather than simply active one needs to be a sufficiently ethical reader of the world one inhabits. Consequently, 'reading' comes to mean the decoding of bias in society. This does not mean that if we can read critically we will necessarily act well but ethical reading of people and situations (as well as books) is a prerequisite for good behaviour and good citizenship. The similarities and differences between character education and citizenship education have been discussed elsewhere (Davies et al., 2005). Put simply, the emphasis in citizenship is upon *political* knowledge and activity (the 'informed' and 'active' citizen) rather than *moral* knowledge and activity or the development of good character. Importantly, Ian Davies (2012) observes that being 'virtuous' is important in the fulfilment of both the civic republican and liberal aims of citizenship (Heater, 1999, p. 177) and Eamonn Callan (1997, p. 3) has promoted a 'politics of virtue' aimed at 'creating virtuous citizens'. If the 'most successful societies and elements in society are those that combine liberalism with a belief that humanity's purpose lies beyond material gratification' (Koch and Smith, 2006, p. 130) the same is also true of ethical English.

Citizens of good character

In the West it is often assumed that democratic values and civic republicanism provide the best foundation for moral and citizenship education. However, there are significant limitations to such a project. As we have seen previously, the *Tao*, the Chinese term for 'the Way' or 'the Road' of harmony, derives its force from the need for 'harmonising the things inside each individual' as well as the need for 'fair play and harmony between individuals' (Lewis, 1981/1952, p. 67). Although citizenship and character education are sometimes considered to be quite different, citizenship education, rightly conceived, should seek to work with young people on the development of personal, moral as well as political virtues (Pike, 2014). In the Athens of the fifth-century BC the separation of character and citizenship would not have made much sense. It also makes no educational sense whatsoever for 'citizenship' to be seen as a lesson or a subject that has little or no relevance to classroom discipline or the 'behaviour management' in a classroom or school. Issues of behaviour provide the opportunity to work with young people on the development of virtues that underpin good character.

It is sometimes misguidedly assumed that if a teacher makes his or her lessons sufficiently interesting, then children or young people will not misbehave or engage in chatter and small-scale disruptive activity. Indeed sometimes the teacher is even blamed for the behaviour of pupils and it is suggested that had the teacher's lesson been more interesting the children would not have misbehaved (as if there is a simplistic cause–effect relation). Of course, teachers do have a responsibility to design lessons to ensure student progress and to engage learners but it is morally wrong to assume that children have the 'right' to misbehave if they do not happen to find lessons adequately entertaining. Teachers are called to educate, not entertain. Students need to respect teachers, behave courteously and develop patience; teachers need to plan lessons that are stimulating, challenging and inspiring rather than boring, tedious and monotonous. Both teachers and students have moral obligations and responsibilities: teachers need to plan well in order to meet the needs of learners and ensure progress and students need to behave well even in lessons that they do not happen to find the most entertaining. High standards are expected of both teachers and students; school leaders have a moral obligation to monitor learning in lessons and to ensure excellence in behaviour and teaching. However, respect for a teacher must not be contingent upon how interesting the learner finds his or her lessons.

Students who have been brought up in what we might call a 'fast food' culture of almost instant gratification where they multitask using social media make channel hopping with a remote control in front of a television look decidedly 'twentieth century'. Those used to the speed and rapid action of digital interactions, not least gaming, need to learn the importance of delayed gratification (Lickona, 2004). They need to appreciate that much learning is investing today in order to receive dividends tomorrow. For instance, learning to play a musical instrument, or memorizing the vocabulary and grammar of a foreign language and doing exercises, does not bring immediate satisfaction. It is only after consistent application over a sustained period of time that they might enjoy playing the instrument or speaking a new language. Schools have a vital role to play in building intellectual stamina and helping students to develop longer concentration spans by enabling them to devote serious and sustained thought to one task rather than giving superficial attention to too many.

In English, learning spellings by using a 'look, cover, say, write' strategy may not bring instant success or gratification but accurate spelling is still required. Reading Shakespeare or classic literature is also often an acquired pleasure. If students only read in school the sort of texts they might read outside school, their reading experience will not be broadened and augmented by being in school. We also need to think ethically about the reasons or motives for a teacher's action in the classroom. If lessons really are to be in the students best interests and are to help them to learn and make progress, teachers have to be very careful to do things for the right reasons. They need to consider if a task or activity is planned simply to entertain, to control behaviour or whether it provides a cognitive challenge and fosters real learning and student progress. Students (and teachers) should not mistake education for entertainment. Being a student is about sowing today in order to reap tomorrow and schools have a responsibility to help students appreciate the importance of this if their English as well as their character is to develop.

Behaviour Management and the Literatures of Dignity and Freedom

Many schools today operate a behaviour policy whereby students must be consistently rewarded for good behaviour and sanctioned for misbehaviour. In many schools 'stamps' or 'merits' or other rewards are given. Hook and Vass argue that 'in addressing in appropriate behaviour you should always make it clear that it is the behaviour and not the person you are critical of' (2011, p. 44). It is generally assumed that this depersonalizes a member of staff who is seen as punishing the behaviour rather than the student. He or she is simply following the policy or strategy, which is consistently applied. Yet, distancing the person from the behaviour can militate against an accurate and honest appraisal of character and an acknowledgement of the young person's personal responsibility. There are a number of problems with this sort of approach, which is rooted in the psychological theories of behaviourism of B. F. Skinner. This is not to say that there should not be sanctions and rewards and a consistent approach but there is far more to a school of character than behaviour modification and training for compliance.

Behaviour strategies, like those espoused by Canter (2010), are influenced by the behaviourism of B. F. Skinner. As we saw in Chapter 5, Skinner placed rats in what has become known as a Skinner Box, where food pellets were released if they pushed a lever; in other words the right behaviour was rewarded as the rats came to associate an action with a particular result. This is similar to Pavlov's dogs that salivated when his laboratory assistant appeared as they associated the appearance of this person with food. On this basis, many believe that the theory of behaviourism 'explains the interaction between human behaviour and environmental factors' (Maag, 2004, p. 15). The behaviour policy in many schools is firmly based on Skinner's principle of Operant Conditioning or 'the establishment of functional relations between behaviour and consequences' (Maag, 2004, p. 48). Skinner's behaviourism underpins systems that operate on the principle that students will modify their behaviour, as a result of consequences, as they will have formed a 'functional relation' between the two through repeated patterns being reinforced. There are, however, serious problems with the theory of Operant Conditioning forming the basis for a behaviour policy in schools. Unlike the rats in Skinner's experiments young people are endowed with the capacity to respond to more than negative or positive associations. A child or young person is responsible for their actions (rather than a product of environmental factors) and has the ability to work together with trusted adults on their character development. Human beings can choose to behave ethically and Rogers admits 'no plan or policy . . . can hope to address all the issues raised by human fallibility and disobedience' (Rogers, 2000, p. 214).

Clearly, it would be inconsistent to believe in the power of literature in the cultivation of good character and good behaviour and to pay insufficient heed to the importance of the 'literatures of dignity and freedom'. In Chapter 9, 'What is Man?', of his influential book *Beyond Freedom and Dignity* B. F. Skinner directly attacks the view of C. S. Lewis in *The Abolition of Man* that by failing to educate the character of students and to develop humane virtues, we were dangerously close to abolishing 'man' or what makes us really human. According to Skinner:

> C. S. Lewis put it quite bluntly: Man is being abolished. . . .What is being abolished is autonomous man—the inner man . . . the man defended by the literatures of freedom and dignity. His abolition has long been overdue. (1971, p. 200)

While C. S. Lewis defends human freedom and dignity, B. F. Skinner asserts the importance of going beyond such 'unscientific' anachronisms in order to make 'progress':

> To man *qua* man we readily say good riddance. Only by dispossessing him can we turn to the real causes of human behaviour. Only then can we turn from the inferred to the observed, from the miraculous to the natural, from the inaccessible to the manipulable. Science has probably never demanded a more sweeping change in a traditional way of thinking about a subject; nor has there ever been a more important subject. In the traditional picture a person perceives the world around him, selects features to be perceived, discriminates among them, judges them good or bad, changes them to make them better (or, if he is careless, worse), and may be held responsible for his action and justly rewarded or punished for its consequences. In the scientific picture a person is a member of a species shaped by evolutionary contingencies of survival, displaying behavioral processes which bring him under the control of the environment in which he lives, and largely under the control of a social environment which he and millions of others like him have constructed and maintained during the evolution of a culture. The direction of the controlling relation is reversed: a person does not act upon the world, the world acts upon him. (1971, p. 200)

There could not be a clearer illustration of the forces that C. S. Lewis is fighting in *The Abolition of Man*. These forces are powerfully at work in many schools in the twenty-first century and will be fought by English that is truly ethical and has a high view of learners. A serious problem with seeing children and young people as 'products' of their environment (which is not to say that environmental factors do not exert an influence) is that their power to 'act upon the world' is undermined and their human capacity to choose well, act with integrity and develop good character is undermined. The sobering truth is that 'if man chooses to treat himself as raw material, raw material he will be' (Lewis, 1978/1943, p. 44).

Study questions

1 Are good readers good citizens?

2 How can English promote virtuous citizenship?

3 What is the unique contribution of English to citizenship in school?

4 What are the similarities between critical literacy and education for democratic citizenship?

5 How might English contribute to the cultivation of good character?

6 What are the limitations of approaches influenced too strongly by behaviourism?

8

The character of professional learning

This chapter illustrates the importance of English teachers as ethical professionals. In doing so it focuses attention on the significance of personal qualities in professional learning and the importance of the *character* of the teacher. It suggests that acknowledging the importance of personal and 'poetic' qualities liberates teachers of English to develop as ethical professionals who teach for social justice and are committed to fostering the good character of their students. This chapter explores the development of teachers' personal virtues and values and those that may be developed through engaging in teacher research (Pike, 2002b).

Developing as an ethical English teacher

Ethical English concerns *who* a teacher is not just *what* he or she does. In order to be a good teacher one needs to be a certain *kind* of person. There are essential qualities of character one needs to develop in order to continue learning and make progress as a teacher. Of course, we have to be careful to distinguish between *personality* and *character* but may concur that:

> On the one hand, then, teaching may seem more professionally commendable when it is carried out by those who are trustworthy, respectful of others, fair, patient, loyal, principled, discrete, responsible, conscientious, good humoured, witty, optimistic, self-restrained, persistent or lively; on the other hand, it may seem less so where those who teach are untrustworthy, disrespectful, unfair, spiteful, indiscreet, lazy, bullying,

humourless, charmless, poorly motivated and self-obsessed. (Carr, 2007, p. 370)

In Part Two of the *Teachers' Standards* (DfE, 2012, see Appendix 2, p. 205) makes it similarly clear that the personal as well as the professional matter in teaching and that 'high standards' of 'personal' as well as 'professional conduct' are required. When we speak of the character of the teacher we are referring to something more important than personal style for, 'the qualities commonly associated with character have the moral stamp of virtues, those associated with personality have more the aesthetic flavour of personal predilection or taste' (Carr, 2007, p. 370). We may appreciate a colleague's ability to perform, tell jokes and recount anecdotes in the classroom (and the staffroom) but these will not compensate for lack of diligence or self-control in these respective areas. We are more likely to censure a colleague for laziness (and failing to prepare lessons or mark work) than for being dour. We tend to be more tolerant of occasional disorganization than deliberate dishonesty. In professional learning, we should therefore consider the character, as well as the charisma, a teacher of English needs in the classroom.

The virtues and values of a teacher are integral to his or her capacity to improve as a professional. If I do not have the humility and patience to be teachable, and if I am not committed and determined to learn, this will impede my development as an ethical teacher (and I will be hard to live with as a colleague too). If my work ethic is poor and I am unreliable I will not possess the moral authority to inculcate a good work ethic in my students. Previously we have explored the notion of the teacher as a 'parent' (to recall the emphasis upon English as a 'home' and the relational quality of 'being' with children in Chapter 2); on this view, it should not surprise us if children 'inherited' certain qualities from their educational 'parents'. The focus on the *values* of teachers is important because it helps us to distinguish between personality and character. A short definition of 'values' is that these are *'principles and fundamental convictions which act as justifications for activity'* and the fuller definition below indicates that our values enable us to judge what is good and worthwhile:

> Values are principles and fundamental convictions which act as justifications for activity in the public domain and as general guides to private behaviour; they are enduring beliefs about what is worthwhile, ideals for which people strive and broad standards by which particular practices are judged to be good, right, desirable or worthy of respect. (Halstead and Pike, 2006, p. 24)

Not only do teachers of English need to possess ethical attitudes and values but these qualities will underpin their ability to make good judgements in the classroom. 'Values' cannot be limited to one strand of any *Teachers' Standards* (DfE, 2012) because they underpin everything teachers of English do.

The character of the English teacher

From an ethical perspective, an English teacher cannot be considered to be a *'excellent* teacher' on technical grounds alone. Being an excellent teacher of English requires more than technical craft of the classroom skills or effective and efficient behaviour management techniques; it rests upon particular values and the development of certain virtues (Pike, 2004a). The reason we cannot judge English teaching by technical norms alone is that, as a profession, it is profoundly implicated in ethical concerns.

Aristotle's virtue ethics (1987) is important to teachers of English because it attends to the personal, emotional, moral and critical dimensions of their work. Unlike Plato (for whom affect may impede moral agency) and Kant (for whom emotion was irrelevant to moral reasoning), Aristotle's virtue ethics concern the rational ordering of virtues and commitments and will appeal to teachers and student teachers of English because the importance of motivation is acknowledged. For Aristotle, one cannot be an ethical person simply by doing the right thing if your heart is not in it; one's feelings and motives have to be congruent with good judgement. Virtue ethics will also appeal because they are an ethics of judgement and are therefore flexible enough to be applied to different situations.

Certainly Aristotle's *doctrine of the mean* might inform English teachers' rational ordering of, and reflection upon, their emotions, values and actions in the classroom. English teachers will appreciate that following the *doctrine of the mean* enables a course to be charted between excess and deficiency in different contexts. Steering a middle course between too little or too much rational detachment and between too little or too much emotion is only possible with the exercise of *phronesis* or good judgement. Indeed, ethical teachers of English will already be charting such a course having had their judgement, as well as their values, honed in the ethical gymnasium of the English classroom. Being a teacher in school (and especially being on teaching practice) is often a character-building experience. After all, one is thrust into a position of responsibility for leading young people into doctrines such as that of the *mean* so that they live balanced lives.

Much that has been written about professional learning, teacher development, teacher research or teachers as action researchers emphasizes the importance of *reflection*. Yet we have to ask how much of this reflection is upon *the teacher's own values and character*. Professional learning concerns one's development as a *reflective practitioner* and it is generally agreed that 'powerful learning takes place for participants through combining research with reflection on practice' (Wilson, 2009, p. 198). Yet those engaged in action research 'tend to be working intentionally towards the implementation of ideas that are from deep seated values that motivate them to intervene' (McNiff et al., 1996, pp. 9–10). Developing as a professional educator (as a 'phronemos') who cultivates 'phronesis' (practical wisdom or wisdom in action) is a fuller and more holistic vision of teacher development than one that sees a teacher simply as the possessor of certain skills or being adept at particular techniques. Action research is also of value when one wishes to explore learners' 'attitudes and values' (Cohen, Mannion and Morrison, 2000, p. 226). There are important similarities between the focus on the experience of the learner in much action research, where the 'long term aspiration' is necessarily 'always a collaborative one' (Altrichter et al., 1993, p. 6) and character education where the learner collaborates with the teacher on the development of his or her character.

Ethical English favours responsible reading and personal moral response over 'second-hand' comprehension and criticism when it comes to both literature and life. The congruence between character education, rightly conceived, and the aims of emancipatory action-research are significant in that both seek to perform a transformative social and moral function. Other forms of research only tell us what a situation is, whereas action-research tells us how it should be which 'is a totally different matter and belongs to ethics' (Gaulthier, 1992, p. 192). Much action research 'located at the social justice end of the political continuum' (Day, 1998, p. 273) is fundamentally ethical in character because it is not only concerned with achieving change so that a practitioner may be more efficient or effective, but more fundamentally with 'how to act rightly' (Bryant, 1996, p. 116).

The dialectical relationship between theory and practice in teacher research is the hallmark of 'praxis' in the Aristotelian sense carried out by one who is a 'phronimos' who exhibits a combination of good judgement and action. Although many English teachers already demonstrate the attributes of Aristotle's 'phronimos', the value of working within the recognized framework of action research and attending to the importance of character development and moral education in both teachers and learners, is that it can enable teachers to reflect more systematically, and ethically, on their practice (Carr, 1993). As such, English teachers are invariably engaged in 'phronesis', or moral and ethical deliberation. In a similar way, action researchers, for whom the 'exchange between research and practice is immediate' (Schön, 1983, p. 309), address the ethical issue of justice as theorizing leads immediately to the question of what should be done which is an issue of the transformation of reality and not simply the description of it.

Action is important but so too is reflection; to teach ethically requires both. For Aristotle (1987), the ethical person cultivates virtue in two ways: first, through serious moral reflection upon the human condition and the purpose of human life and secondly through practice. In other words, I tend to get better at something the more I do it (according to Aristotle I am therefore likely to become more just or courageous by committing just and courageous acts). Professionals deliberate ethical matters and develop as professionals by getting better at such deliberation. Teaching is therefore de-professionalized when it only focuses on the way we do things at the moment. If it is reduced to the following of routine technical procedures in a localized context, without attention to the 'big picture', professional judgement is undermined. Thinking about the way things should be is an integral aspect of being an ethical professional. One of my student teachers recently wrote an email to me in which she explained she had become more aware of her own values when she noticed behaviours such as bullying. As a teacher of English I become more aware of my own values and the ways in which my own character and behaviour need to develop through both real and vicarious experiences (those provided by both life and literature).

In *Character Matters*, Thomas Lickona relates the experience of a high school English teacher who saw one young man as a 'problem' because he was a poor student and had failed to pass English with her the previous year. Seeing this young man back in her class resitting English did not fill her with enthusiasm and consequently she did not view him positively. However, when her car had a flat tyre and this young man helped her to change the wheel at the garage where he had a part-time job after school, their relationship changed (not least because she reflected on her attitude towards him). Through their conversation she realized she felt the same way about her inability to change a tyre as he felt about his English assignments (both experienced feelings of frustration and failure). Their teacher–student relationship improved dramatically after that as both teacher and student changed their attitudes and perceptions. They began to see each other as people.

Although bonding does not always have to be around vehicles my beloved 750cc Honda motorbike did help me relate to Darren, a 14-year-old boy, who was always in trouble at school, forgetting his books and equipment, sometimes sleeping outdoors in summer and coming to school without having breakfast. As an exceptional (and temporary) measure we had a system whereby Darren would be permitted to excuse himself from a lesson if he thought he was about to 'explode' in the face of a teacher and report to me. I found out that he was badly bullied by his brother at home and that his largely absentee father was a member of a motorbike gang. He knew all about motorbikes and it was a point of common interest. Darren needed someone to talk to who would take an interest in him and be a real 'person' rather than just a 'teacher' who focused only on academic work (at which he generally failed).

This is one reason why extracurricular activities are so important to a school community. Taking groups of children away to the Lake District and the Isle of Wight on residential activity holidays enabled me to relate to children in a more practical environment than the English classroom. School connectedness, where a student feels close to people at school, boosts resilience and acts as a protective factor; young people, who have overcome considerable challenges, often cite a special teacher who was important to them personally (Lickona, 2004, Chapter 5). There are many 'English-related' opportunities for extracurricular activities too. Many teachers of English get involved in the school play although I preferred taking students on creative writing courses, editing the school magazine and organizing media events.

The teacher as role model

It is difficult to overestimate the importance of the teacher as a role model. Consequently, as teachers we need to practise and exhibit the qualities of character we want to see in our students. According to Comenius, one of the great educators, the teacher offers moral and character education by providing: (1) example, (2) explanation and (3) practice for children and young people. Teachers need to be a 'good and living example to children, for imitation is one of the key elements of human learning' (Hábl, 2011, p. 11). We need to give 'an adequate explanation of every rule or principle that is to be obeyed' and should also provide 'opportunity for everyday practice' (Hábl, 2011, p. 11). Teachers are under scrutiny in every lesson, every day, and are closely observed by students who need positive role models.

A brief examination of some of the virtues or character traits of an excellent teacher of English (bearing in mind that excellence in teaching involves moral legitimacy and not just technical skill) follows. Reflection upon teacher development could profitably employ a framework such as Lickona's 'essential virtues' but it is fitting in a book devoted to the spiritual, moral and religious significance of English that the theological and cardinal virtues are used here (unsurprisingly all of Lickona's 'essential virtues' as well as the *Tao* can be found in them). The ancient Greeks are renowned for reason but in Christianity it is faith, hope and love that are the greatest virtues; the New Testament teaches that 'the greatest of these is love' (1 Cor 13:13). To seek to teach is a considerable responsibility and teachers make mistakes; as none of us is perfect it is worth noting that 'love covers a multitude of sins' (1 Peter 4:8).

A very important virtue related to love is humility. The most serious vice (the opposite of humility), is regarded as pride. C. S. Lewis was an exceptional teacher of English at Oxford University where he gave individual tutorials as well as immensely popular lectures to halls packed with students. In a letter to his good friend, Arthur Greeves, he wrote that he had found out 'terrible things' about his own 'character' confessing 'I catch myself posturing before the mirror, so to speak, all day long. I pretend I am carefully thinking out what to say to the next pupil (for *his* good, of course) and then suddenly realize I am really thinking how frightfully clever I am going to be and how he will admire me' (Green and Hooper, 1979/1974, p. 105). Teachers who know they can 'perform' in front of a student or class need to guard against pride.

Virtues in the classroom:
The character of the teacher

1   **Faith:** The original meaning of 'faith' as a theological virtue is to trust in Christ for one's salvation but it also signals believing the right thing. Arguably, it would not be possible to 'believe in' behaviourism and treat one's students with proper respect and dignity. Teachers who 'believe in' their students believe they can succeed and overcome obstacles. They acknowledge that children will not always do what is right but believe they can achieve their potential when they make the right choices that develop the sort of character that will support them. They trust students with responsibility while ensuring accountability. Teachers who have 'faith' in their students' potential help them to achieve it. This is closely allied to the virtue of hope.

2   **Hope:** Hope is traditionally interpreted as hope of the world to come. It has a spiritual dimension. It involves looking ahead with optimism and appreciating that there is far more to life than the material here and now. If a teacher of English has hope he or she is not pessimistic but optimistic about life. Being around hopeful teachers cheers children up and supplies them with energy and creativity rather than draining it from them. A teacher with hope is a positive rather than negative person. Teachers who have hope inspire and engage students and communicate well. They are aspirational and see excellence before it is achieved. They are also grateful for their students and do not take them for granted.

3 **Love:** Teachers are *in loco parentis* and good parents love their children and want what is best for them. Sometimes this will require 'tough love' whereby one disciplines students and has the courage to act with justice and integrity so they do not get away with what is wrong and have bad habits reinforced. Love is kind and patient and puts the student first. Teachers who show love to those they teach will not lose their temper or show irritation but will show self-restraint. The teacher who loves students does not have to try to impress them and is not proud. Teachers who put others first are not on an ego-trip. They are humble enough to care more about their students' learning than their own 'performance'. A teacher who shows love will appreciate the dignity and worth of each student as a human being and will smile and display warmth and generosity to them.

4 **Prudence (Wisdom, Phronesis):** A wise teacher is willing to learn. A prudent teacher considers the consequences of a course of action. It is unwise not to reflect and improve. It is prudent to become a reflective practitioner. This necessitates hearing, accepting and acting upon good advice from those who are wiser than oneself and have greater expertise in a particular area. Sometimes others see things that we cannot; we tend to have 'blind spots' about ourselves. Knowing where to get help and mentoring is prudent, but it takes humility to seek wisdom.

5 **Temperance (doing things to the right degree, getting the balance right):** Many teachers leave within their first few years in the classroom. Teacher stress and burnout is an issue. Teachers work hard (planning, marking, attending parents evenings, engaging in extracurriculum activities and doing further study) and need time off if their efforts are to be sustainable and they are to remain engaging and lively in the classroom. To be temperate is to exercise self-control. A teacher needs to 'push' students to just the right degree. This requires knowledge of individuals and is built upon good relationships. Teachers will explain *and* demonstrate (not do one or the other) so their teaching is balanced. The teacher of English will set enough work but not too much, will ensure a balance between the modes of language use and a balanced reading diet.

6 **Justice (fairness, honesty, truth):** Just teachers act with integrity even at personal cost. They are truthful, honest and keep their promises. They do the right thing and are fair. This does not mean that they will not spend more time with some students than others (some may need or want more help than others) but they will not show 'favouritism' and act unfairly. They will attend to what *merits* their

attention. Just teachers will help the most able to excel, support the least able and not forget those in the middle, they will treat students as individuals and meet individual needs justly.

7 **Fortitude ('guts', courage):** It takes courage to teach and to put any of the other virtues into practice. The courageous teacher establishes their authority and requires courtesy and good behaviour from students while not being threatened by the intellectual curiosity of those students who want to know 'why' as they study. It takes courage to strive for excellence rather than becoming complacent. The courageous teacher does not back down in the face of pressure when the right thing is to stand one's ground (with peers, pupils and parents). A teacher with fortitude will be courageous but will also persevere when it would be easier not to. Teaching is hard work and good teachers are hard workers. They are also resilient.

Developing good character through literature and life

While teaching practice (and teaching too) can be daunting, we should remember that our task is to 'irrigate deserts' (Lewis, 1978/1943). As it has been suggested that 'teaching placement itself clearly provides much scope for the further character development of teacher trainees' (Carr, 2007, p. 384) a recent study was undertaken where student teachers of English, who had just completed their first teaching placement, were asked if they felt they had developed *personally* as a result of the experience (Pike, 2011f). Their reflections lend credence to Carr's view that teaching practice may contribute to *personal* as well as *professional* development. One student teacher, who was candid about her lack of patience, remarked:

Teaching has taught me . . . that when one has a responsibility for another human being's learning, patience is more essential than anything else. It doesn't matter how many times their/there/they're needs to be explained, or how many times the plot of *Of Mice and Men* needs to be repeated, or how many times the right spelling of 'necessary' has to be written on the board – it has to be done. As that pupil's teacher, I can't walk away from them with an exasperated shake of the head, much as I might want to do so. I can keep practising on classes – if I make a mistake, I'll just try to make sure it doesn't happen again – but that pupil doesn't get to be a teenager going through education again. (Pike, 2011f)

There appear to be no shortage of opportunities for engaging in ethical reflection and activity in the English classroom. While personal virtue is sometimes acknowledged to be a major factor in professional development, insufficient attention is often devoted to it in models of professional learning. The character of the teacher of English and his or her values need to be taken into account in explaining educational processes. Another of my student teachers, Emily, reflecting upon her professional and personal development after her first teaching practice, recently explained:

> The greatest change that the English PGCE course has realized in me is my ability to be endlessly resilient: in the face of both disaffected students and difficult staff members! I have learnt that relentless positivity and kindness towards both these groups is the key to building successful working relationships. These relationships are crucial for effective teaching and I now realize that to be a successful teacher – especially in English – it is just as much about building trusting relationships with students, as it is about having extensive subject knowledge; because English teachers must teach to the heart as well as to the head. I think that 'love' sums up the kind of teacher I hope I can be: one who teaches for the students, not for themselves or the prestige of 'being a teacher'; one who cares deeply about the success of all their students, both academically and socially; and one who takes the time to smile and talk to their students, listens, and remembers what they have been told. (Emily, PGCE student)

Another student, Ceri, explained that prudence and fortitude were the most important for her and reflected that she needed to be wise as well as courageous to teach literacy skills in an area where non-Standard English was the norm. English teachers are also aware that literary texts function as 'suggestive templates for assessing and directing our lives' (Stibbs, 2001, p. 42). We often see virtues displayed by characters in high quality literature. For instance, the 'Knightly Virtues' project based at the Jubilee Centre for Character and Values at Birmingham University in the United Kingdom has provided 9- to 11-year olds with the opportunity to explore the virtues of knights in the King Arthur legends (and heroes and heroines from different traditions and faiths) while helping them to reflect upon their own virtues of character.

Good literature offers us an especially rich source of characters that display virtues and vices that enable students and teachers to engage in character and moral education in a way that captures the imagination. A novel popular with teenage boys as well as girls, such as *The Lord of the Rings*, offers us a leader who evinces the cardinal virtues (Wood, 2003). Aragorn exercises prudence when Frodo and Sam make towards Mordor by deciding to seek the rescue of Merry and Pippin who have been captured by orcs. While it might have been more strategic or congruent with mission objectives to follow the Ring-bearer, Aragorn is wise enough not to micro-manage, to trust Frodo and to seek to protect and rescue the most vulnerable who are in the greatest danger. Aragorn follows his heart not just his head as is fitting for a king of Gondor. He seeks the good of others and demonstrates wisdom in relationships. He is loyal to Arwen (despite Eowyn's affections) to whom he is betrothed. Aragorn does not only seek justice for himself but just recompense for others and at his marriage to Arwen he invites all to Gondor. Tolkien has Aragorn fighting a just war and *The Lord of the Rings* provides countless examples of courage. Aragorn's own courage is displayed as he climbs the wall of Helm's Deep and defies the orcs alone. Yet he is temperate as well as courageous and exercises self-discipline. The role of literature in helping teachers and students to reflect on ethical behaviour should not be underestimated.

Response to works of art such as Hogarth's *The Harlot's Progress* (1732) and Raymond Briggs's *When the Wind Blows* (1982) may be especially powerful in developing moral understanding (Pike, 2004d). It has been noted that 'Hogarth's titles deliberately echo Bunyan's *The Pilgrim's Progress*, and their themes are primarily about the moral and spiritual journeys of a symbolic protagonist set against the values of a corrupt society: Moll Hackabout and Tom Rakewell are the ignoble, seedy descendants of Bunyan's Christian' (Benton, 1995, p. 34) where 'it is the utter waste of a young life and the despoiling of innocence by the corruptions of a sick society that have provoked Hogarth's indignation' (Benton, 1995, p. 36). The moral relevance for children and adolescents is apparent when one recognizes 'the present day parallel of the friendless, vulnerable, provincial teenager arriving in London' (Benton, 1995, p. 36).

Moll is a country girl who becomes a fashionable courtesan and then, falling on hard times, a street prostitute who is eventually committed to prison. After some years she has a little son but is in a desperate state as venereal diseases are ravaging her body. As Moll, diseased and dying, crouches in agony by the fire the nurse steals her remaining possessions. Finally, Hogarth depicts the funeral of Moll, aged 23, where the pitiful figure of her little boy is the chief mourner. The reality that this desperate situation is being enacted even now in cities across the world, indicates that the present generation in schools need to experience spiritual and moral lessons such as the one Hogarth teaches. The capacity of social satire such as this, that is intended to expose human vice and folly, can provide valuable moral education. This is an important area for research, which should not just focus on how to be more 'effective' or 'efficient' or concentrate on how to help students get better grades. Moral education matters and given the prevalence of Internet pornography and teenagers' exposure to this, it is all the more important for them to understand the reality of life for those working in the sex industry who have sexually transmitted diseases and infections. Moral education in such realities may come more from literature than the PSHE (Personal, Social and Health Education) lesson.

Another work that can offer valuable and moving moral education (although there are many from which to choose) is Raymond Briggs's classic satire, *When the Wind Blows* that is firmly in the tradition of Hogarth. The cosiness and warmth of Jim and Hilda's domestic life in the countryside, with cups of tea and dialogue that highlights their complete naivety serve to render the scenes that follow even bleaker and darker as they depict the slow deaths of Jim and Hilda from radiation poisoning following a nuclear blast, the glare of which is depicted by the white light of its centre pages. Here the 'Biblical fragments ("Lay me down in Green Pastures . . .") that Jim and Hilda recite in the steadily darkening frames of the last page as they enter "the Valley of the Shadow of Death" recall the bright sunlit fields with which the story had begun' (Benton, 1995, p. 38). Those teachers who have watched the animated video of this journey with an English class can attest to the moral education many children experience when they have followed Jim and Hilda's journey to the Valley of the Shadow of Death.

What is at stake is more than physical death; it is the death of our humanity. According to Hunter it is already too late, just as it was for Jim and Hilda. In *The Death of Character* the claim is made that 'Character is dead. Attempts to revive it will yield little. Its time has passed' (Hunter, 2000, p. xiii). For Hunter, 'While we desperately want the flower of morality to bloom and multiply, we have at the same time, pulled the plant up out from the soil that sustains it' and he argues that: 'We so urgently desire the cultivation of moral qualities, but under conditions (we insist upon) that finally render those qualities unattainable' (Hunter, 2000, p. 226). Our society has changed irrevocably in the post-war era. Most children are no longer provided with a comprehensive moral culture; 'where earlier generations of children were socialized primarily within the boundaries of family, school, religious organization and community, consumer and popular culture is now the principal mode of early childhood socialization' (Luke et al., 2003, p. 254). The educational situation is riven with contradiction and some of the most memorable lines from *The Abolition of Man* are those in which Lewis similarly concludes that we 'castrate and bid the geldings be fruitful, we laugh at honour and find traitors in our midst' (Lewis, 1978/1943, p. 20).

However, the difference between Lewis and Hunter with regard to the sources of values is striking. For Hunter 'what we think of as "innate" in our moral sensibilities – derive from cultural resources that are dwindling' (Hunter,

2000, p. 227), whereas for Lewis there really are innate and objective values. For both, however, character is eschewed:

> In the older systems both the kind of man the teachers wished to produce and their motives for producing him were prescribed by the *Tao* – a norm to which the teachers themselves were subject and from which they claimed no liberty to depart . . . It was but old birds teaching young birds to fly. This will be changed. Values are now mere natural phenomena. Judgments of value are to be produced in the pupil as part of the conditioning. Whatever *Tao* there is will be the product, not the motive, of education. (Lewis, 1978/1943, pp. 37–8)

The authors criticized by C. S. Lewis in *The Abolition of Man* are sceptical about certain values and yet do not offer their students any that are better. Being critical is all well and good but we also need to have appropriate educational virtues that underpin our criticism. In Chapter 6 the view was advanced that moral values stand outside of us; they must be independent of our subjectivities for: 'unless the measuring rod is independent of the things measured, we can do no measuring' (Lewis, 1967b, p. 73). Moral relativism and subjectivism make it impossible to evaluate different moral codes and provide meaningful moral education:

> Supposing we can enter the vacuum and view all Ethical Systems from the outside, what sort of motives can we expect to find for entering any one of them? One thing is immediately clear. We can have no *ethical* motives for adopting any of these systems. . . . How then does it come about that men [*sic*] talk as if we could stand outside all moralities and choose among them . . . nevertheless exhort us (and often in passionate tones) to make some one particular choice? (Lewis, 1967a, p. 48)

Put another way, I can only privilege, recognize or value one morality over another if I have already accepted and privileged particular moral claims:

> This thing that judges . . . that decides which of them should be encouraged, cannot itself be [one of those instincts]. You might as well say that the sheet of music which tells you, at a given moment, to play one note on the piano and not another, is itself one of the notes on the keyboard. (Lewis, 1981/1952, p. 20)

Whether moral values and morality stand outside of and apart from the human imagination, and are already established outside the 'whole interlocked system', is of fundamental importance. We are faced with a choice: 'Either the maxims of traditional morality must be accepted as axioms of practical reason which neither admit nor require argument to support them and not to "see" which is to have lost human status; or else there are no values at all' (Lewis, 1967b, p. 75).

Study questions

1 How important is character in teaching English?

2 How has your character developed while you have been teaching English?

3 Why is moral relativism and subjectivism so dangerous to one's character development?

4 What virtues or character traits does a teacher of English need to demonstrate?

5 How has reading literature supported your professional learning and character development?

6 What would you like your students to read that might foster their moral and character development?

7 What tasks or activities would you set to encourage personal moral response to these works?

PART THREE

Ethical English as religious education

In Part Three of this book, the word 'religious' signifies the focus on people's beliefs about ultimate reality and the human condition. It takes into account our worldviews, what we 'worship' or hold to be of greatest value. It concerns the role of English in mediating answers to ultimate questions such as: Who am I? What is the nature and meaning of my life? What is my purpose? Ethical English is concerned with 'something more' than communication or even aesthetic and literary response, to recall Portia's speech in *The Merchant of Venice*.

The focus on religion as human beliefs about ultimate reality and the 'religious' as different interpretations of how this reality relates to us is congruent with that of Plato and Aristotle (Jaeger, 1960), William James in *The Varieties of Religious Experience* (1929) and Paul Tillich (1951), who defined religion in terms of our 'ultimate concern'. Hermann Dooyeweerd (1955), C. S. Lewis (1960) and Hans Küng (1986) also adopt broadly similar definitions of 'religion'. Contrary to popular notions of 'religion' that tend to focus on the most observable phenomenon (such as rites, rituals, holy days, dress codes behaviours, and buildings) these thinkers focus on what is considered fundamental in life: beliefs about what is true or axiomatic and upon which all other things depend. Such beliefs are very much the concern of ethics because, as we shall see, 'a belief about what has independent existence' also 'delimits a distinctive range of acceptable conceptions of human nature, of destiny and of what can or can't be done to improve the human condition' (Clouser, 1999, p. 26). The thesis of Part Three is that it is impossible to consider the ethics of teaching English (or of any other subject) without acknowledging the importance of 'religious' belief in this sense.

Here we address the 'religious' quality of English itself, the 'faith' put in it and the ways in which it deals with issues of 'religious' significance. If the values underpinning English are broadly 'liberal–humanist' (Newby, 1997, pp. 284–5) we need to bear in mind that, according to the definition of 'religious' adopted here, even the Humanist Manifesto is religious. Education in general, and English teaching in particular, are inherently 'religious' as they engage with ultimate questions and concern meaning and purpose. Teaching (even if it does not recognize it) proceeds on the basis of assumed answers to foundational epistemological, ontological and theological questions. English is not regarded here as a technical exercise that has nothing to do with beliefs and values. English is of religious (as well as spiritual and moral) significance.

The aesthetic and existential experiences offered in English can be regarded as 'religious' phenomena (although not in the sense of being linked to any particular religion) and are the subject of Chapter 9. Equally, many of the societies where English is important are increasingly plural and cosmopolitan and many students and teachers of English are Hindus, Sikhs, Buddhists, Muslims, Jews, Christians or followers of other faiths and traditions. The value of multicultural literature in helping us to understand the beliefs and values of different groups is explored in Chapter 10. In addition, many teachers and students are secular. Yet even secularism and materialist atheism are not neutral; they are what some people 'believe in'. The rationale for Part Three of this book is that these 'faiths' often inform linguistic and literary response and cannot realistically be left outside the classroom like a coat hung on the peg. To a greater or lesser degree 'religious' garb is always worn even if invisible. In England and many other Western nations which are increasingly secular, there is still the influence of historic Christianity upon values and vision, customs and culture, language and literature. Indeed, about a third of the teaching and learning that goes on in English in England does so in schools that have a Christian ethos or foundation as they were originally established by the churches. Before the Forster Act of 1870 the churches provided much of the schooling on offer and they still have a considerable investment in schooling in the United Kingdom and elsewhere in the world. Even in more secular educational contexts such as public schools in the United States, it has been asserted that the legacy of Christianity has a pervasive influence (Burke and

Segall, 2011). Such a context is likely to inform the culture of the English classroom and this is examined in Chapter 11. The impact of secularism upon English and the way an increasingly secularist society often fails to appreciate religious perspectives is explored in Chapter 11. Finally, in Chapter 12 we look at the importance of beliefs and values in English teachers' professional learning.

9

English as a pseudo-religion

It is perhaps unsurprising given the importance of English that it has acquired a quasi or pseudo-religious status. Recently, the way English is often seen as 'more than a subject' and considered to be a 'pale substitute for religious faith', being concerned as it is with the meaning of life, has been described:

> The subject English has indeed always been something more than a subject, at least for many of its practitioners: at pains to counter a sense that the subject English, especially in its Romantic conception, had arisen as a somewhat pale substitute for religious faith, David Holbrook pointed out that 'It is not a "religion": but it is a discipline in which we use language, to grope beyond language, at the possible meaning that life may have.' (Stevens, 2011, p. 46).

This chapter explores the 'religious' nature of the 'something more' in the identity of English. Part Three as a whole analyses what this means for English in the plural societies of the twenty-first century.

The gods of the house

In Chapter 2 we considered 'English' as a spiritual 'home' or 'house'. My contention here is that every 'house' has its 'gods'. Aristotelian thinking has been drawn upon throughout this book and is helpful once again in this respect. In the Book 11 *Metaphysics*, Aristotle sets out upon a quest to find what is of utterly independent existence. He writes 'if there is such a kind of thing in the world, here surely must be *the divine*' (2013, 1064.a.33–8, my italic). Aristotle refers to what is non-dependent and changeless as 'divine'.

English is regarded here as a 'pseudo-religion' or at least as 'religious' as it concerns what is 'non-dependently real' (Barnes, 2014, p. 121). Every English classroom has its own 'gods'. Answers to questions concerning ultimate reality are personally important because what we consider to be 'divine' influences our destiny, at least in the sense that: 'our idea of the divine strongly influences the view we take of human nature and that, in turn, influences what we believe about values and many other issues ranging over the entirety of our experience' (Clouser, 1999, p. 25). Many of the issues discussed in English lessons are of religious significance. Studying advertising and the ways in which people are persuaded to 'buy' certain 'truths' (not just products) is a particularly good example of how religiously significant the content of non-literary texts can be in English. Looking at ethical advertising (aimed at persuading people to stop smoking, to eat more healthily or to stop domestic violence for instance) is theologically as well as ethically important. The debates within English classrooms on moral issues such as cloning, euthanasia, abortion, the death penalty, the environment or in response to the motives and behaviour of characters in literary texts (such as *An Inspector Calls* by J. B. Priestley or *Heroes* by Robert Cormier) mean that English is one of the most 'religious' subjects on the curriculum.

Different religions give different answers to the question of what is divine but so do all worldviews. Indeed, 'implicit in all claims to knowledge of the divine is some account of human nature, of salvation and how salvation is achieved: basically some account of how and on what basis human beings find their fulfilment (or release) in the divine' (Barnes, 2014, p. 122). What one believes about the purpose or *telos* of English is 'religious' as it concerns our proper relation to the 'divine' or what is 'self-evident'. Arguably, 'If nothing is self-evident, nothing can be proved. Similarly if nothing is obligatory for its own sake, nothing is obligatory at all' (Lewis, 1978/1943, p. 28). Blaise Pascal referred to 'self-evidency' as knowledge of the 'heart' and this may appeal to teachers of English who are not persuaded that exclusively rational explanations should guide their subject or their lives. According to Pascal, 'We know truth not only by reason, but also by the heart, and it is in this last way that we know first principles' (Pascal, 1966, p. 58). English teachers are likely to be particularly aware of knowing by the heart.

In Chapter 5 we saw that behaviourism (which still exerts an influence in many schools) was found wanting as it failed to recognize or appreciate some of the most fundamental aspects of what it is to be a human being. The 'divinity beliefs' underpinning this theory warrant analysis as does a consideration of how these apply to the teaching of English. J. B. Watson who coined the term 'behaviorism' asserted that 'consciousness' was as fictional as the notion of the 'soul' (Watson, 1930, p. 6). This is especially relevant to English where 'inner experiences' would be regarded by many as of central importance.

Following Watson, Skinner asserted that such inner experiences do not cause behaviour, but are always caused by behaviour (Skinner, 1965/1953, p. 33). He even declared that 'when a man writes books' this is only the 'effect of past history upon him' and therefore 'He didn't initiate anything' (Time magazine, 20 September 1971, p. 52). According to Skinner we do not have free will. The perspective that even an author does not 'initiate anything' will be especially problematic for teachers of English. Indeed, one might wonder what Wordsworth might have thought of this perspective on 'inner states'.

Materialism (the view that physical matter is the ultimate reality) fails to offer a credible explanation that does justice to the richness, variety, depth, creativity, beauty or originality of the texts, teachers and learners in English, that most humane of subjects. Clearly, 'a materialist theory of reality lies behind behaviorism' (Clouser, 2005, p. 167) because 'the physical aspect is given the status of self-existence' in that it 'explains and causes everything because everything depends on it'; in other words, 'the materialist perspective presupposes the religious belief in the divinity of the physical' (Clouser, 2005, p. 168). In *The Merchant of Venice*, Portia was right, we need to 'tarry a little'. There is more to explaining human behaviour than 'stick and carrot' or stimulus and response. The aesthetic responses and creativity of young people are not adequately explained by behaviourism or the materialism upon which it is founded.

That 'literacy policy in England is hugely influenced by the cognitive-psychological perspective' (Hall, 2003, p. 109), rather than a socio-political one, is significant ideologically. In its most undiluted form 'the cognitive-psychological take on reading considers it to be value-free and more about skills than cultural knowledge' (Hall, 2003, p. 189) and it should not therefore surprise us that a behaviourist approach to literacy instruction will be especially difficult for teachers of English who privilege the 'personal growth' model of their subject. Consequently, many teachers of English may see the appeal of social constructivism, which is often contrasted with behaviourism. Constructivism acknowledges that learners actually make meaning, they construct their own knowledge; they ascribe meanings rather than passively receiving them. According to this theory we construct our own understandings of the world by engaging in reflection upon our experiences and attributing meaning to them. Social constructivism is normally associated with Vygotsky for whom the construction of knowledge and understanding was a profoundly social activity. Indeed, even infants are comprehensively social and cognitive development is brought about through interaction with others: 'Human learning presupposes a specific social nature and a process by which children grow into the intellectual life of those around them' (Vygotsky, 1978, p. 88). Vygotsky's is an apprenticeship model whereby cultural tools become part of the child's own mental resources. The movement is from *inter*mental to *intra*mental reasoning, from social to individual. What we can do with help from others, we are subsequently enabled to do on our own. On this view, research into classroom learning will require an investigation of interactions and their meanings (Pike, 2003b, 2008a).

In a sense, while in behaviourism the human subject is manipulated and acted upon, in constructivist thinking the learner acts upon and manipulates the world. The inadequacies of the former have been discussed but there are also problems, from a moral and ethical perspective, with the latter. In short, we should not respect every meaning that is constructed. We will roundly condemn some interpretations. As we saw in Chapter 5, the way some people interpret the world results in them harming others. We do not condone female genital mutilation because some people interpret the world in a way that leads them to believe that this is culturally necessary. Some interpretations in life and literature are more valid and worthy of respect than others. If an English literature graduate did not consider Shakespeare to offer a more profound depiction of the human condition than J. K. Rowling we would have good cause to doubt their discernment when it came to literary texts. If a teacher of English refused to consider one student's work to be better than another's we would question their professional ability to discriminate accurately. However, to claim that human beings are the final arbiters of truth and that there is no objective standard of ultimate truth (that we make our own meanings) will be found wanting by teachers who believe that children and young people need to learn objective standards of right and wrong rather than simply making their own meanings. If truth is regarded as a social construction there is danger of subjectivism.

If English is so interpretivist that 'man is the measure of all things' as Protagoras (the teacher and philosopher of the fifth-century BC, who is usually regarded as the first humanist) put it, there will be legitimate moral and ethical concerns. It has been suggested that English as a subject is liberal–humanist in orientation (and much depends on definitions of terms such as 'liberal' and 'humanist') but if the Protagorean sense of 'humanist' is taken, it will be found lacking by many teachers of English dissatisfied with the status accorded to human reason as the arbiter of truth. This is not to advocate the irrational but reason may not be regarded as providing a sufficiently secure foundation to support them in nurturing the human spirit, stimulating creativity and teaching the 'literatures of dignity and freedom'.

In a world where much faith is put in science and the technical model teachers need moral support not just technical skills to help them when they are *in loco parentis* (in the place of the parent). The importance of beliefs, in the professional learning and development of teachers of English is explored further in Chapter 12. For now, it will suffice to note that to be a truly liberal subject, and a liberal art, English will not seek to indoctrinate young people in comprehensively liberal or secular materialist values (although it may recommend politically liberal ones); rather, it will be generous towards non-secular perspectives (providing they are ethical) and will foster criticality. To treat young people as citizens rather than 'subjects' we need to be transparent about the philosophical foundations (the 'gods' of the house) underpinning their learning so that they can judge for themselves the ways in which English is a liberal art worth 'believing in' (Pike, 2012a).

That scholars from Holbrook (1979) to Stevens (2011) prefer to distance themselves from 'religious' conceptions of English is not insignificant and may be indicative of the dominance of secularism in our discipline (an issue taken up in Chapter 10). There is, however, a rich heritage of seeing the religious significance of English as evinced by titles such as *The Preachers of Culture* by Margaret Mathieson (1975) or *The Education of the Poetic Spirit* by Marjorie Hourd (1949) that implicitly assert the 'religious' importance of English. The use of terms such as 'spirit' to signify that English reaches the central core of the person and to describe English teachers as 'preachers' has much to commend it.

The English teacher as pastor, prophet and priest

The claims made for the status, influence and power attributed to these 'preachers' of culture, the teachers of English, are elevated indeed. Similar claims tend not to be made even for teachers of that highest status of subjects, science. This is curious for the latter often 'preach' logical positivism with regard to how the world can be known. Teaching English is often regarded as a 'vocation' or a 'calling', a term that has religious connotations. It has even been suggested that there is far more similarity between 'religious ministry' (Carr, 2007, p. 177) and teaching than between the professions of teacher and lawyer. Certainly, many English teachers (especially the majority that subscribe to the 'personal growth' model of English) engage in the pastoral care of their students as their needs become apparent in personal responses to texts and topics that deal with the human situation. Recently our attention has been drawn to the ways in which English teachers have been seen as 'a lay priesthood, called to the cure of young souls' (Chubb, 1902, p. 393) and the relation between Sunday schools and the development of English as a subject is significant (Brass, 2011).

The teacher of English seeks to enable children to have new experiences and to discover their moral and spiritual significance (Pike, 2002a). It is a role closely related to that of the prophet or priest. Just as the artist and poet 'could both be said to function as priest' (Long, 2000, p. 149), the same is true of the teacher. It is no coincidence that the Romantic poets cast themselves in religious or prophetic terms and that Romanticism is so influential upon English today (Stevens, 2010b). The Old Testament prophets, to whom the Romantics looked, challenged unjust and inhumane practices and advocated social justice. The child labour of chimney sweeps condemned by Blake is perhaps the best-known example studied in English. Clearly this is congruent with the social justice commitments of many teachers of English who see empowering young people, so that they have a voice, as a vital aspect of their role.

English teachers also 'forth-tell' or 'foretell' as their expectations of their students and their hopes for them are expressed and often become 'self-fulfilling prophecies' (see Chapter 12 on the virtue of 'hope'). The notion of teachers of English as prophets and priests deserves serious consideration as English, and her teachers are more 'religious' than they often care to admit. The importance of the teacher as mediator between art and life, curriculum and learner, text and reader, is redolent of the priest because the teacher often brings *significance* as well as coherence to learning encounters and has an obligation to turn any given curriculum 'into a dynamic series of learning experiences with a sense of cumulative purpose' (Stables et al., 1999, p. 450). The teacher of English as 'priest' can be seen as mediating the 'aesthetic distance' between the reader and the work of literature across a developmental area not dissimilar to Vygotsky's ZPD (zone of proximal development) where spiritual rather than necessarily cognitive development occurs. Learning of this sort is often a 'significant event' (Stables, 1999, p. 450) and might be compared to Maslow's 'peak experience' which is defined as 'a transient moment of self actualization' (Chiang and Maslow, 1977, p. 259).

It is the teacher who mediates such significance for the 'formal curriculum is rarely, if ever, framed in these terms' because it is 'atomistic, with related elements linked thematically but not in terms of building towards significance' (Stables et al., 1999, p. 450). Those who see the teaching of English as an art or a discipline belonging to the humanities will appreciate the importance of the role of English teachers as 'priests' as they mediate meaning-making. We interpret the world for learners and in doing so teach them how to interpret that world for themselves. The 'religious' nature of English, can also be appreciated by looking at its 'sacred' texts and its most metaphysical of activities: reading.

Reading sacred texts: Shavuot

If we are to understand English as a pseudo-religion, reading is a good place to begin. An example from one religious tradition will help. In medieval Jewish society, being able to read was celebrated at a religious festival (Manguel,

1997). The young boy who had learned to read would be wrapped in a prayer shawl (yarmulke) and taken by his father to the teacher (Rabbi) at the Feast of Shavuot. The young reader would sit on his teacher's lap and read the Hebrew alphabet, a passage of Scripture and the words 'May the Torah be your occupation' which were written on a slate. After reading the words aloud, the slate was covered in honey and he licked it clean. Biblical verses were also written on honey cakes and on hard-boiled eggs that the child would eat after reading them aloud to his teacher. The words disappeared and were assimilated bodily. The scene is proleptic of Christ's statement in the Gospel of Luke that 'man shall not live by bread alone, but by every word of God' (Luke 4.4). Conceiving of these 'words' as fundamental to living, more so even than 'bread', shows how important they can be to teachers and learners of English. Teachers and students of English cannot 'live by bread alone'.

Such a perspective directly challenges theories such as that of Maslow whose paper 'A Theory of Human Motivation' (1943), developed in *Motivation and Personality* (1987/1954), is still influential today. According to Maslow, human needs can be seen as a pyramid, or hierarchy, with the most basic, physiological needs (for 'bread', for instance) at the base, and higher order needs (such as the need to be creative) at the top. The model is not just problematized but turned upside down if one considers words and creativity to be basic to human beings and not simply a higher order need that emerges once the need for food has been satisfied. When the literary, aesthetic, spiritual and moral needs of human beings are recognized Maslow's model begins to look distinctly secular and materialist.

The young reader physically eating words followed by feasting to celebrate becoming a reader is striking. We celebrate other accomplishments more now, such as passing a driving test. Reading and learning to read tend not to be celebrated in secular Western culture; a community celebrating 'reading' might prompt us to consider whether we should re-learn how to celebrate it. The closest we get might be seen in the images in local newspapers of teenagers jumping and waving their exam results on slips of paper showing their success (where English is particularly prized due to its economic value). This may be a faint echo in our secularized society of celebrations such as those of Shavuot. The partying surrounding the occasions also differ. At Shavuot, there was all-night reading of the Torah, recital of poetry, reading of the biblical book of Ruth and the eating of dairy products in homes and synagogues decorated with greenery. It was a celebration of joining a community of interpretation and having access to its most prized literary works.

Celebrating reading at a religious festival might surprise us but even outside of religious traditions, reading literature is a 'religious' activity in the sense that our reading and responses relate to our vision of the good life. Reading is an inherently 'religious' activity, not only in the sense that it is important within established religious traditions, but because it cannot be understood apart from the beliefs and values of readers and writers. Reading is central to both English in education and to many religious traditions. Moreover, religious beliefs are generally based upon an interpretation of sacred books that are considered authoritative for living (Pike, 2010a). In a sense *a book* is at the centre of each of the great monotheistic religions. The adherents of Judaism, Christianity and Islam are 'people of the book'. Scriptures are important too in Hinduism, Buddhism and Sikhism.

We should certainly consider what the 'sacred' texts of English are and what this tells us about the beliefs, values and priorities of those choosing them. The 'canon' is a term derived from Biblical Studies to denote a standard or measuring rod and English as a subject in schools has its own canon. Sometimes a government will prescribe a list of authors (see Appendix 1), but English departments and teachers also make choices about which texts children should read in English. Shakespeare (through the work of Rex Gibson and others) and works from the English literary heritage have secured positions in the 'school canon'. Among many English teachers there is also the belief that young people have something important to learn about the nature of life and relationships from contemporary works such as *Of Mice and Men* by John Steinbeck or *Holes* by Louis Sachar. English department stock cupboards contain more than 'old favourites': they contain texts that give us clues about what a particular teacher or English department 'believe in'. Reading is one of the daily spiritual disciplines practised by many religious communities which generally subscribe to the view that students are 'formed by the reading they do' and by the 'views of self and world such reading presents' (Palmer, 1993, p. 19).

Texts often contain 'clues about our view of ultimate reality' and hold 'the images of self and world in which our students are formed' for reading 'is one of the "disciplines" to which our children are required to "disciple" themselves' (Palmer, 1993, p. 19). The rationale for choosing a particular book to read reveals a great deal about what one 'worships' and views as most 'worth-while' in life. The ways in which religion and faith are represented and explored in texts is also significant and students need to be able to detect and critically engage with bias and authorial intentions. *Abomination* by Robert Swindells, where the extreme religious beliefs of parents result in child abuse might be regarded as perpetuating aggressively secular attitudes and promoting the view that we are all much better off without religious constraints. Novels such as the *Harry Potter* series by J. K. Rowling beg questions about the sources of the powers that the characters use. The nature of the supernatural is explored in works such as *The Hobbit* and *The Lord of the Rings*, by J. R. R. Tolkien, the *Narnia* novels by C. S. Lewis, *His*

Dark Materials by Philip Pullman and *Shadowmancer* by G. P. Taylor. The latter two authors are certainly on different sides theologically and Taylor writes that *Shadowmancer* was intended to counter the depiction he perceived in Pullman's *The Amber Spyglass* that 'God is a liar, God is senile. God is the enemy of humanity.' (Taylor, 2006, p. 196). Yet while Taylor disagrees with Pullman about God, he states 'I don't want to live in a country where books are burned, where authors are not free to write what matters most to them' (Taylor, 2006, p. 197). We consider book burning in England further in Chapter 11 as freedom in reading is a key issue for ethical English.

Free readers

We have seen that the festival of Shavuot in the Middle Ages marked the freedom to read. It commemorated the day on which practising Jews believe God gave the Torah, including the Ten Commandments, to Moses on Mount Sinai and thereby to the people of Israel. The date of Shavuot is calculated in relation to the Passover; seven weeks after Passover comes Shavuot and the linkage is important. At Passover, Jewish believers remember their rescue, when they were freed from being slaves of Pharoah in Egypt (we will recall the dramatic plagues, the Exodus and the parting of the Red Sea). At Shavuot what is remembered is becoming a nation, whose identity was based around a shared reading of sacred texts. Reading was celebrated at a festival which commemorated the reception of a code for living, an explanation of origins and the purpose of a community.

Becoming a 'free reader' is something worth celebrating because it really can bring freedom. It marks the transition from a state of dependence (of needing to be 'read to') to independence where the world is at one's fingertips. Reading is central to education because once you can read you can teach yourself rather a lot, especially in our information age, if you have sufficient motivation. I can remember being surprised when our eldest son was just five or six years old and seemed to know far more about the planets of our solar system than I did. I discovered that this small boy had acquired a large, colourful children's encyclopaedia presenting all sorts of information about the planets in which he had been immersed, lying with the book open on the floor of his bedroom. It reminded me that once you can read you can find out just about anything.

Finding out 'anything' can be for good or ill and encouraging responsible reading is an important element of ethical English. What children and young people should read is a moral issue. W. H. Auden suggests that instead of asking 'What can I know?' we should ask 'What, at this moment, am I meant to know?' (Auden, 1962, p. 272) and from an ethical perspective, we need to help young readers ask such questions as, 'What is it good for me to read?'

Clearly, 'the adolescent needs to encounter literature for which he possesses the intellectual, emotional and experiential equipment' (Rosenblatt, 1968, p. 26). Yet:

> The concept of having to be a certain sort of person, morally or theologically, in order to read a book aright – with the implication that perhaps, if one is not that sort of person, then the book should be withheld from one – is alien to the assumption of liberal modernity that every rational adult should be free and is able to read every book. (MacIntyre, 1990, p. 133)

The 'alien' perspective may be the ethical one. It would appear naïve and insufficiently aware of the diversity and nature of young readers to argue that the 'reader is the final arbiter of a text's morality' (Gallagher and Lundin, 1989, p. 140) or that 'it is the reader's will that determines the moral form the reading takes' (Jacobs, 2001, p. 31). Especially with regard to children and adolescents, to suggest that the reader 'determines' the morality of the text seems foolhardy. Some adults, like St Augustine, may be willing 'to reconfigure a reading experience in order to profit, spiritually and morally, from it' (Jacobs, 2001, p. 23) but we need to take into account the ways in which readers who have 'not yet arrived at a consistent view of life' (Rosenblatt, 1968, p. 31) respond to different texts.

Reading is at the very heart of English and it is the love of reading literature that motivates most English teachers. Speaking, listening and writing are all important but reading is the most elusive, the hardest to pin down and the most 'metaphysical' of all the modes of language use. I am referring here to reading in the sense of understanding and interpretation rather than phonic decoding and reading aloud. We have no direct, unmediated, access to 'reading' as we can never really see what is going on in another person's head. We are always at one remove when it comes to assessing reading as teachers. When we do encounter 'reading' we often get a privileged glimpse of the reader's personal response to a range of important issues.

Reading is certainly the 'odd-one-out' among the modes of language use. We have direct access to what someone is *saying* and we can see what someone has *written* but *reading* is different. What we know about someone's 'reading' always comes to us via another mode of language use; we only know about someone's reading by what comes out of their mouth or their pen (or keyboard). We only know about someone's 'reading' by what they *say* about it or what they *write* about it. That is why it is sometimes so difficult to assess reading; if a reader has difficulty writing or speaking it is harder to get access to their reading. Real reading is locked away, deeper down, in the reader's head and heart, soul and spirit (we may use different terms depending on our beliefs).

If reading in general is somewhat metaphysical, reading literature is especially so. Fictional characters are ontologically bizarre. We will recall Rosenblatt's view that a reader is needed to bring a text to life, for it to become a 'poem'. Receiving life through appropriation, by reception, when words come to be experienced and offer a vibrant spiritual experience, is the parallel here. It is strangely apt that the Divine Author is known as the 'Word' ('In the beginning was the Word and the Word was with God and the Word was God' John 1.1). English classrooms, which are not dominated by literacy but foster literary and aesthetic reading and response, can be seen as 'sacred' and spiritual spaces.

Personal growth and individual autonomy

Rather than regarding English as a utilitarian subject, and a vehicle for delivering economic success and productivity, English teachers, as we have seen, have traditionally favoured the personal growth model of their subject (Marshall, 2000; Goodwyn, 2011). At Shavuot, reading meant that one could be initiated into a shared understanding and interpretation of key texts. In English, the purpose of reading, if it is underpinned by a vision of 'personal growth', is to nurture the individuality, independence and autonomy of the child. We need to appreciate though that learning to express one's individuality is a very Western or liberal way of seeing the world.

The influential legal theorist Joseph Raz has noted that the 'autonomous person is a part author of his own life' (Raz, 1988, p. 369) which sums up the mission of many English teachers who want their students to exercise their freedom and creativity to make their own decisions and choices concerning the stories of their lives. We shall return to Joseph Raz, but for the present it is important to appreciate that what many take for granted as a desirable goal, may well be far from universally endorsed. We need to understand different religious and cultural perspectives on autonomy and personal growth if English in education is to serve children and young people from minority ethnic and religious groups that are counter-cultural to the secular mainstream. The notion of 'personal' growth is often unquestioningly accepted as a desirable goal by English educators but the emphasis upon the 'personal' or 'individual' is not unproblematic. Autonomy or 'personal growth' might be regarded by some committed religious believers as too secularist and too individualistic by far. There is certainly the potential for conflict. In general, those subscribing to the 'personal growth' view of English may feel a greater loyalty to the individual child than his or her family or religious community. Put simply, 'liberals stress that educational authority should not be rested exclusively with parents' because 'the autonomy of the family sits uneasily with liberal values' (Halstead, 1999, p. 276).

It is important to recognize that the 'liberal state *based on propositions about the desirability of individual autonomy* is bound to be committed to educational programmes which are incompatible with the beliefs and values of parents from non-liberal religious and cultural minorities' (Burtonwood, 2000, p. 269, my italic). Consequently, there is the distinct possibility that some will see the liberal views of English teachers and the emphasis upon the individual as the 'neo-colonial imposition of majority liberal values on minority non-liberal religious communities' (Wright, 2003, p. 142). Fostering autonomy or 'personal growth' will not be considered to provide an adequate or overarching educational aim for many religious believers or communities for: 'Egalitarian liberalism has its origins in the Enlightenment commitment to individual autonomy: it is suspicious of 'community', preferring to use education to free the individual from the constraints associated with the membership of groups' (Burtonwood, 2000, p. 241).

In the next chapter we look at how multicultural literature can help us learn about different cultures and traditions: it can also help students to consider the respective rights of the group and the individual in different contexts. We saw in Chapter 5 how the group or family is often privileged above the individual in the short story 'Anil' by Ridjal Noor. In this story the right to life of Marimuthu's wife and the right of seven-year-old Anil to be brought up by his parents are treated with scant regard. Protecting the village's hierarchy from shame is of primary concern and 'trump' the rights of the child or parents in this story. In another story, 'Something Borrowed, Something New' by Leila Aboulela, the priorities of the lovers are subservient to the Muslim family and community in the Sudan. Personal desires, wishes and priorities cannot be acted upon without Islamic sanction. The young couple cannot be together, marry or have sexual relations (all of which might be considered 'personal rights' by secular Westerners) unless the religious authorities sanction it. The young couple cannot simply retire to their hotel room; religious and communal obligations have to be fulfilled first. The story shows how in this culture personal relationships and sexual desires are subject to religious law.

English, for many teachers, is fundamentally about liberation and freedom but we need to be aware that autonomy or 'personal growth' will not be seen by everyone in a diverse plural society as synonymous with freedom. Indeed, even in Western cultures autonomy as an educational aim has been challenged because it is not always the case that 'actions one has determined for oneself are more effective, appropriate or worthwhile than actions performed under the direction of others' (Hand, 2006, p. 539). Such a view leaves scope for acknowledging the importance of parents and elders within a faith community in determining what is felt to be an appropriate course of action. Hand contends that autonomy is not a justifiable educational aim because 'there will often be people in a better position than me' who are 'willing and able to direct me' and consequently it is 'foolish not to submit to their direction' (Hand, 2006, p. 538). On this view, it might even be considered negligent for young people to be 'abandoned to make crucial life decisions from a position of dangerous inexperience' (Stables, 2005, p. 236). The logical conclusion of this line of reasoning will make liberals decidedly uncomfortable. If it is better to listen to those with greater authority or expertise than to make one's own choices, in some communities this would be a justification for an arranged marriage. I should make it clear that I am not advocating such practices but seeking to show how the aims of English (that are taken for granted by many English educators) will be viewed by those who 'believe in' different goals and have a different set of priorities. Arguably, the belief in autonomy and commitment to personal growth, while appearing to be secular, are actually very 'religious' because they represent the secular liberalism that many English teachers 'believe in'.

Cultural analysis and criticality

The 'cultural analysis' and critical literacy models of English are closely related to the 'personal growth' model because criticality is foundational for autonomy. Even when the rationale for reading is 'cultural analysis', the purpose in English is to be critical rather than to conform. In the West, criticality, like autonomy and 'personal growth', is generally unquestioned as a desirable good in education. This will not, however, be a view shared by some communities and even if we 'believe in' criticality, we have to be critical enough to admit that if critical thinking itself is seen in terms of promoting pluralistic democracy it may be 'a strongly didactic, polemical educational offer' which allows 'little space for truly non judgemental exploration of individuals' life experiences' (Stables, 2005, pp. 40–1).

Although the English teaching community might claim to be *allowing* children to exercise choice and autonomy, the reality is that in our sort of society (Raz, 1988) we do not have any option. We cannot choose whether to choose. Our whole system is based on exercising choice. A liberal democratic system has choice (rather than direction) at its core. Promoting choice and autonomy (or even liberal democracy) is not a neutral stance. Although the conventional wisdom is that 'no one conception of the good life is favoured in liberalism, and a vast range of lifestyles, commitments, priorities, occupational roles and life-plans form a marketplace of ideas within the liberal society' (Halstead and Pike, 2006, p. x) it is also the case that liberalism tends to be much less accommodating to those who do not fully subscribe to liberal values.

Approving of a 'vast range of lifestyles' rather than advocating a particular way of life as many religious groups do, is a specific vision, not a neutral one. Indeed 'the claim to be culturally neutral or to be a meeting ground for all cultures, which is sometimes made on behalf of liberalism, is itself a cultural stance' (Halstead, 1995, p. 268). This means there is the danger that English education in the common, state school in a liberal democracy may view the beliefs of those who do not share its values 'through the lens of an illicitly comprehensive liberalism' (McLaughlin, 1995, p. 251).

The mandatory English curriculum in England not only aims to teach skills and convey an appreciation of literature but seeks to influence learners' values and actions. If the aims of English are not communicated to learners and they do not have the opportunity to consider 'personal growth' or 'cultural analysis' or 'critical literacy' as goals, these can be seen as beliefs or ideological positions that readers are to submit themselves to rather than critically evaluate. We must declare our 'bias' as English teachers if we are to show respect for the autonomy and freedom of learners. By disclosing the 'lens' through which we see the world we enable learners to take this into account when 'reading' us and what we say. When there is to be the inculcation of beliefs concerning democracy, rights and autonomy, the degree of freedom that young citizens experience to read their world should be appreciated by those exercising their critical faculties.

As it is 'in dialogue with others we learn to read the world' (Stables, 2005, p. 1), education should enable young people to explore the readings and interpretations of differing groups in their society including religious perspectives rather than legitimating a single, secular 'reading' or fostering their uncritical allegiance to secular liberal values. It has recently been suggested that 'to understand living as interpretation is to re-conceptualize freedom and democracy' (Stables, 2005, p. 1). It is certainly important to us to attend to differing perspectives and 'readings' in a diverse, plural society. We need to consider how accommodating English is to religious, social and cultural diversity (and how accommodating it should be). We may assume that English is welcoming to a wide range of students in our plural democracy but how accommodating it is to religious perspectives warrants careful evaluation. In the next chapter I argue that English should help everyone in a plural society to 'read' religious cultures and traditions that differ from the secular mainstream.

Study questions

1 Why is English a 'pseudo-religion'?

2 What faith is put in English?

3   How 'religious' is English?

4   What are the implications of the beliefs and values underpinning English for learning and teaching in a multicultural, plural society?

5   How do you respond to students from conservative religious homes and communities?

6   How does English address students' needs?

7   What is your view of behaviourism and social constructivism?

8   Why is liberalism not a neutral stance?

9   Why might secularism or humanism be considered 'religious'?

10 What do you 'believe in'?

11 What do you believe to be 'divine'?

10

Multicultural English

Young people growing up in a plural society need to appreciate the differences (as well as the similarities) between the beliefs and values of the majority and significant minorities. The argument of this chapter is that a key issue for ethical English teaching is how such 'difference' is viewed:

> Political multiculturalism begins with a concept of negative *difference* and seeks the goal of positive *difference* and the means to achieve it. (Modood, 2007, p. 61, my italic)

English and multiculturalism

From a liberal perspective, it is unity in diversity that is to be cultivated in a plural society. Such a stance is supportive of participation in a diverse, liberal culture and is congruent with the multicultural project:

> Multiculturalism as a policy or ideology, in other words, is oriented towards not just the recognition and celebration of cultural difference, but the active overturning of negative perceptions of such difference. (Johnstone, 2011, p. 126)

There is an umbilical link between approaches to literature from different cultures and traditions and political and ideological views of multiculturalism. Arguably, 'English teachers have a vital role to play in the survival and flourishing of multicultural British society' (Johnstone, 2011, p. 125). If we see a diminution in the aspect of the English curriculum concerned with appreciating such difference we should not, however, be surprised as it reflects a wider, political, trend. English teachers committed to multiculturalism may be placed in an invidious position if one believes the headlines that followed David Cameron's speech at the Munich Security conference in 2011: 'State multiculturalism has failed, says David Cameron' (*BBC*); 'Cameron: My war on multiculturalism' (*The Independent*) and 'David Cameron's attack on multiculturalism divides the coalition' (*The Guardian*).

This sort of rhetoric did not begin with the Conservative-led coalition. Gordon Brown before David Cameron was making speeches that asserted 'Britishness' and 'British' values and explicit reference is made to these in the new *Teachers' Standards* (DfE, 2012). This was also the line taken by Tony Blair in speeches made after 7/7, the suicide terrorist attacks in London. David Cameron is following the 'party line' established by the Blair–Brown government of New Labour. Johnstone (2011) quotes Gordon Brown as Prime Minister to the effect that overemphasizing *difference* was perceived as a problem:

> What was wrong about multiculturalism was not the recognition of diversity but that it over-emphasised separateness at the cost of unity. Continually failing to emphasise what bound us together as a country, multiculturalism became an excuse for justifying separateness, and then separateness became a tolerance of – and all too often a defence of – even greater exclusivity. (*Daily Telegraph*, 2007)

David Cameron's speech made in 2011 at the Munich security conference takes this further and advocates a more 'muscular liberalism' which it is important to see in context:

> Under the doctrine of state multiculturalism, we have encouraged different cultures to live separate lives, apart from each other and apart from the mainstream . . . We've even tolerated these segregated communities behaving in ways that run completely counter to our values . . . The failure, for instance, of some to confront the horrors of forced marriage, the practice where some young girls are bullied and sometimes taken abroad to marry someone when they don't want to, is a case in point. This hands-off tolerance has only served to reinforce the sense that not enough is shared . . . Frankly, we need a lot less of the passive tolerance of recent years and a much more active, muscular liberalism. A passively tolerant society says to its citizens, as long as you obey the law we will just leave you alone. It stands neutral between different values. But I believe a genuinely liberal country does much more; it believes in certain values and actively promotes them. Freedom of speech, freedom of worship, democracy, the rule of law, equal rights regardless of race, sex or sexuality.

It says to its citizens, this is what defines us as a society: to belong here is to believe in these things. (Cameron, 2011)

These issues are addressed, both here and in the following chapter, as they are of central importance in ethical English. The question raised is whether teachers of English who support multiculturalism have been manoeuvred to reflect Cameron's policy through the re-framing of the curriculum that excises 'different' and replaces it with a focus on appreciating 'contemporary' literature? It would appear that similarity and common values are now more fashionable, politically, than cultivating an appreciation of difference. The semantic (and ideological) trajectory of this element of English, especially for 14–16-year-olds in England, needs to be sketched briefly for it to be appreciated.

'Other', 'Different' or 'Contemporary' cultures and traditions?

Several writers on multicultural English (Yandell, 2008; Doug, 2011; Johnstone, 2011) have recently engaged with the changing way in which students of English literature at GCSE (in particular, those studying the anthology produced by the largest examination board in England, the AQA) have been presented with literature from various cultures and traditions. How this aspect of the curriculum is framed is likely to be influential upon how multiculturalism is perceived. This issue concerns far more than semantics in relation to one anthology produced by one exam board; what is at stake is how certain authors or works are construed and presented within English in general when teachers talk about them or design sequences of lessons or schemes of work based on them. This is because what young people are encouraged to focus on and how they are encouraged to read in this area of the curriculum is likely to be influential upon their reading of the world as well as words.

In *Moon on the Tides*, the AQA's GCSE anthology for study from 2010–15, poetry from 'different' cultures and traditions is included within each of the themes: *Character and Voice, Place, Conflict and Relationships* (while not being labelled as 'different'). The eclectic selection of poems for each theme that appear in the 'contemporary' section includes some from 'different cultures and traditions' in contrast to the 'literary heritage' (although not named as such). Students might, for instance, compare and contrast Tennyson's 'The Charge of the Light Brigade' with 'The Right Word' by Imtiaz Dharker. Within the theme *Character and Voice*, there are 15 poems including 'Singh Song!' by Daljit Nagra alongside 'Give' and 'The Clown Punk' by Simon Armitage and 'The River God' by Stevie Smith within the 'Contemporary' selection.

Also within the theme *Character and Voice* are poems from the English 'literary heritage' such as 'Ozymandias' by Percy Bysshe Shelley and 'My Last Duchess' by Robert Browning.

It has not always been this way. Experienced teachers will recall a poetry anthology for GCSE that included a distinct section labelled 'Poetry from *Other* Cultures and Traditions'. The change from 'Other' to 'Different' came in 1995 and was considered more acceptable by some teachers given that many of the 15- and 16-year-olds they taught would themselves be positioned as 'Other' if they were members of a minority ethnic group. More recently, however, a similar argument has been made against the use of 'Different'. Roshan Doug certainly asks important questions:

> Why are Black and Asian poets living in the UK like Grace Nichols, Benjamin Zephaniah, Daljit Nagra and John Agard viewed as poets from 'different' cultures? Different from whom? White British, white Europeans? White working class? What about poets of mixed race; should the AQA continue classifying them as 'different'? If so, does not 'different' in this context imply one's race and convey rather racial connotation/assumptions? Does it just extend to colour of skin? Clearly it does. (Doug, 2011, p. 452)

While these questions are important, Doug's conclusion is much less convincing because far more is 'different' here than ethnicity. These poets are able to offer perspectives on life from a different cultural and religious milieu to that of the secular, 'white British, white European' majority in the United Kingdom. This is important because recognizing and appreciating 'difference' in a plural society, especially as a learner aged 15 or 16, is rather important. To replace 'different cultures and traditions' with 'contemporary' would seem to be exactly what politicians such as Cameron would want. Here the English curriculum seems to mirror the current policy shift.

Alongside contemporary poets in the anthology such as the 'white' Armitage (who was born, grew up and went to school in West Yorkshire) are 'non-white' poets (to keep Doug's terminology) such as Dharker, Khalvati and Nagra. But there is much more to this than skin colour. The cultural and religious background of writers as well as their ethnicity is significant. Daljit Nagra's father came to Bradford, West Yorkshire in the late 1950s from the Indian side of Punjab, before moving to London and then Sheffield. Being a Sikh boy, in a predominantly white working-class area of Sheffield is significant; being a member of a minority ethnic community, visually different by virtue of wearing a turban and Sikh dress and attending a Gurdwara, should not be ignored. There are important religious and cultural differences that it is entirely legitimate to focus upon and about which it is beneficial for all children to learn in a multicultural society.

It is a mark of difference *to the majority* that Imtiaz Dharker was born in Lahore to Pakistani parents, was brought up in Glasgow and lives in London, Wales and Mumbai. Most people belonging to the ethnically white majority in the United Kingdom do not divide their time between Mumbai and London and it is important that they learn from British citizens such as those of Pakistani origin who do live in two cultures. That Dharkar describes herself as a 'Scottish, Muslim, Calvinist' immediately distinguishes her from the secular majority in England. That Choman Hardi was born in Kurdistan and raised in Iraq and Iran distinguishes her *from the majority* in the United Kingdom. To have been raised in countries steeped in Islam rather than a largely secular environment with a legacy of historic Christianity differentiates Hardi, in important respects, *from the majority* of her British compatriots who are 'white'. It also distinguishes her from those with Sikh or Hindu backgrounds or those of Afro-Carribean origin who have a different type of Christian heritage to traditional Anglicanism or Catholicism. Writers of high quality that have a wealth of experience to share on the basis of being members of a minority ethnic group, who know about the religious beliefs and practices of members of that group, may offer us all a great deal.

The ways in which faiths and cultures different to one's own are studied is critically important. John Yandell points out that the stance of the young reader is likely to be influenced by the categorization of the literature studied and approaches informed by this:

> When exploring texts 'from different cultures and traditions', the student is placed in the role of cultural anthropologist; when encountering the 'English literary heritage', it would seem that awe and wonder are more appropriate responses. The assumption is that the student will encounter difference in reading texts from different cultures, but will be inducted into her or his own 'heritage' in worshipping at more canonical shrines. (Yandell, 2008, p. 31)

It is important to challenge assumptions regarding one's 'heritage'. There are, after all, significant differences between contemporary readers and canonical texts (Pike, 2003a, 2005a). Indeed, the difference between a reader saturated in twenty-first-century culture and a text written several hundred years ago can be a valuable resource. In our final chapter the problems created for learners by adopting the role of anthropologist or that of phenomenologist (where religion is studied dispassionately as a 'phenomenon') are discussed in more detail. The importance of learning 'from' (not just 'about') different cultures and traditions is affirmed. The majority of young readers will experience difference in relation to both 'heritage' literature and 'multicultural' literature. In both cases religion is a key aspect of the difference. When studying the works of dead 'white' Christian authors, many young, secular twenty-first-century readers will be culturally different to the world about which they read.

For now it is sufficient to note that difference (whether cultural or chronological) between the world of the reader and that of the author can provide the sort of 'aesthetic distance' (Jauss, 1982) that motivates learners and fosters personal growth (Pike, 2002a). We need to be aware that there are losses as well as gains associated with substituting 'Contemporary' for 'Different' as in the 2010–15 AQA anthology, where these poets do not stand out in their own category as 'Different' as they once did under the previous incarnations of the anthology. Referring to the singling out of poetry from different cultures and traditions in a distinct category, Roshan Doug sees the 'crux of the problem' (in the old anthology) as:

> the segregation of poets in the Poetry Anthology whose very format, that departmentalizes Black and Asian poets, acts as a tokenistic gesture of political correctness, a form of political appeasement. (Doug, 2011, p. 453)

Arguably though it is political 'correctness' that has now led to the inclusion of Black and Asian poets under the term 'contemporary' which fails to foreground and celebrate 'difference'. It is entirely legitimate for students to learn about differences between majority views and practices and those of significant minority groups. Doug, however, sees the removal of 'difference' as a sign of progress and greater inclusion:

> It is, therefore, reassuring to learn that these criticisms of the Poetry Anthology – in which Black and Asian poets are marginalized and segregated – were addressed by the AQA (2010) when the board finally abandoned 'different cultures and tradition' in favour of a new format for their 2010 edition. The current Poetry Anthology [2010–2015] presents the poets/poetry in a far more inclusive way by grouping poems in terms of themes and not in terms of cultures defined on rather questionable racial grounds. (Doug, 2011, p. 453)

To see only 'racial' grounds for black and Asian poets being 'segregated' appears decidedly secular and does not sufficiently attend to *cultural* and *religious* difference. Such an approach, despite good intentions, may exacerbate the marginalization of minority perspectives as attention is now focused on the difference between 'contemporary' and 'heritage' literature rather than between different groups in contemporary society. The label 'contemporary' can lead to less (not more) attention being paid to the nature of the differences between groups in our diverse contemporary society and less (not more) attention being devoted to the heterogenous nature of plural, cosmopolitan societies. We need to think carefully about where our attention is being directed by such curricular framing.

As a result of a 'contemporary' section in an anthology including poets of different ethnicities and cultural backgrounds, but not signalling difference, students may not be encouraged to explore cultural differences between groups in contemporary society. Ceasing to appreciate such difference may be precisely what is advocated by the current political emphasis on shared 'Britishness' and 'British values'. Rather than talking about differences, English is being encouraged to focus on common values and what binds us together. This is important but the result of such assimilation or 'inclusion' may not encourage an appreciation of difference. Including 'ethnic' voices and perspectives as 'part and parcel of the main-stream poetry, like local accents and regional identity' (Doug, 2011, p. 453) is likely to entail less of an emphasis upon cultural difference. This takes us right to the heart of the debate about multiculturalism.

If less attention is paid to cultural difference, less attention may be given to understanding the perspectives of minorities. This can all too easily lead to a failure on the part of members of the secular majority to understand the views of their religious compatriots who do not belong to the secular mainstream. Arguably, ethical English should help us understand the subtleties and nuances of our differences rather than pretending we all agree with each other all the time; this is vital because there will need to be a principled and respectful disagreement some of the time (see Chapter 11). Such a situation is hardly a recipe for social cohesion. Indeed the new AQA anthology contains *less* poetry from 'other' cultures and traditions than it did before. Clearly, including these poems under the heading 'contemporary' may fail to foreground their importance and distinctiveness. As majorities can so easily pay scant regard to the wishes of minorities in a democracy, it is vital to educate members of the majority about the perspectives of minorities. Arguably, what is needed is not an abolition of the term 'different' or its replacement with 'contemporary' but a more nuanced and discriminating appreciation of contemporary difference and diversity.

English and the 'Otherness' of all

Crude stereotyping fails to do justice to the complexity of people's lives and the influences upon them. Yet failing to understand 'other' cultures (those different to one's own) and traditions is only likely to exacerbate unwarranted generalizations and misunderstanding. For Yandell, multicultural literature should be studied in English for reasons of 'solidarity' defined as 'the recognition of common interest: 'your struggle is our struggle' . . . the movement from the binary opposition of 'I'/'not I' to the collective point of view' (Yandell, 2008).

The tension between 'yours' and 'ours' goes to the very heart of the debate about multiculturalism and the English curriculum. A focus on understanding and appreciating the differences between the cultural background of minority ethnic groups and the majority should not be eschewed. It is important that young readers, as much as curriculum planners, do not adopt a view of culture as 'stable, single and essentialist' (Yandell, 2008, p. 32). There are undoubtedly problems with a multiculturalism which 'maintains a distinction between "us" and "them", rather than recognizing the fluidity and inter-mingling of cultures and identities in contemporary multicultural societies' (Johnstone, 2011, p. 128). If we are genuinely committed to teaching young people growing up in a plural society in ethical ways we should not shy away from 'difference' and we must be wary of 'either dissolving or clarifying *differences* between "us" and "them" and must engage in a genuine quest to understand the Otherness of all' (Stables, 2005, p. 43, my italic). While affirming solidarity and our common humanity, we must also guard against a 'lowest common denominator' approach where legitimate differences are insufficiently acknowledged. The designers of the AQA poetry anthology were caught between Scylla and Charybdis: either include poems from minority ethnic groups in a section such as 'contemporary' and risk less attention being paid to them as 'different' or single them out in a separate category and be accused of segregation rather than 'inclusion'.

Johnstone draws an important distinction and points to the richness and importance of literature *about* multicultural Britain. What is meant by the term 'multicultural literature' (which would be a good title for a section in an anthology for schools), and why it should be read, is worth reflecting upon. The term denotes:

> not so much literature in English that is written in or about other countries and cultures, but literature that engages with the experience of multiculturalism itself . . . such writing 'produces', as well as 'reflects', multicultural Britain, because it helps to create our sense that this is the way our country, culture and society are, and helps us to know what that feels like – even to ourselves. (Johnstone, 2011, p. 127)

Certainly what we might call 'multicultural experience' (both the sense of affiliation to more than one culture and of living in a multicultural society) needs to be explored. Johnstone, drawing attention to the claims that multiculturalism has failed and noting that Modood (2007) has called for its reinvigoration, makes the following claim:

English teaching . . . needs to be part of that continued effort [the reinvigoration of multiculturalism] – in practice, at least, if not in policy. The teaching of the 'Different Cultures' poems, and 'texts from different cultures and traditions' more generally, must be at the heart of this project. What is at stake is less the understanding of different cultures, than the ongoing forging of our own multicultural society and the very survival of multiculturalism itself in this country. (Johnstone, 2011, p. 132)

Arguably, developing an understanding of different cultures is a vital aspect of ethical English that prepares young people for participation in a plural society.

Eschewing religious differences?

Understanding different cultures cannot be based on the illusion or pretence that they are all secular; we need to acknowledge religious differences even if this is an area from which some English teachers might be tempted to shy away. Certainly the teaching of multicultural literature to each cohort of students is part of an ideological project. Understanding different cultures is a prerequisite for building a tolerant multicultural society but, all too often, 'religious' differences are simply brushed under the carpet. Whether the particular poems by multicultural authors, chosen to be read in schools, are the most appropriate to enable children and young people to learn about cultural and religious difference is another matter. According to Mohammed Shafiq, chief executive of Muslim youth group The Ramadhan Foundation, multiculturalism is about 'understanding each other's faiths and cultures whilst being proud of our British citizenship' (2011).

Exploring our differences is vital in education. I was privileged as an undergraduate at the University of Leeds to visit Sikh gurwaras, Muslim mosques and Hindu temples as well as black Pentecostal churches. Reading what was then called 'Commonwealth literature' in the School of English while also attending a course on the Religions of Ethnic Minorities in Britain (of enormous benefit to those who become teachers) was a highlight. Everyone I met on my visits was respectful and courteous; it would, however, be patently absurd to suggest that they agreed with each other any more than with secular worldviews. Disagreement exists between religious groups upon their most cherished beliefs. A Muslim will not agree with the Christian truth claim that Jesus is God any more than the Christian will agree with the truth claim of Islam that Mohammed is God's prophet. Both will disagree with the secularist or atheist. This is not just a theological argument; committed religious believers are also likely to disagree with comprehensively liberal and secular attitudes to sexuality. English classrooms might well be considered the best places for cultivating an understanding that such faith-based positions are derived from an interpretation of 'sacred' texts, and are based on reading. Given the increasing marginalization of Religious Education in schools in England, the teaching of literature from different religious cultures and traditions may become the primary vehicle on the English school curriculum for exploring religious perspectives on key societal issues, a significant responsibility for teachers of English.

In ethical English, children and young people will be taught how to express themselves so that there is an honest acknowledgement of difference; learners will need to agree to disagree but not to be disagreeable about it. Avoiding a discussion of difference fails to tackle the issue and it is in English of all subjects where difference should be discussed and young people should learn how to express their differences respectfully. All too often, we are afraid to discuss our differences in England because of inadequate and insufficiently robust notions of tolerance (an issue taken up in the next chapter). We often fail to appreciate that an important aspect of multiculturalism entails the development of an appreciation of the *religious* beliefs and values of different groups.

Secular readings seem to be encouraged by the AQA resources and in the notes that accompany the short story 'Something Borrowed, Something New' by Leila Aboulela (from the AQA GCSE Anthology *Moon on the Tides*) where there is little or no mention of Islam. This seems to be missing out on something rather important considering that the story portrays a young man from Edinburgh who converts to Islam as a result of talking to his school Chemistry teacher. He subsequently meets a young Sudanese Muslim woman (who had divorced after six months of an arranged marriage) and eventually goes to the Sudan to marry her in an Islamic ceremony. There is certainly a contrast between his life in Scotland, with privacy and personal possessions, and the more communal way of life his fiancée is accustomed to in the Sudan. But there is more to be learned from this story than an awareness of such *cultural* differences:

> To understand the religious believer's world one needs to understand the beliefs and values that give purpose and meaning to his or her actions and behavior. One becomes aware of the role of doctrines and beliefs in facilitating experience and the way in which religious rituals and practices give expression to beliefs and values. (Barnes, 2014, p. 122)

This is particularly important in this case as the central male character has converted to Islam and participates in an Islamic wedding, reciting the *Fatiha* with the bride's brothers and abiding by Sudanese Islamic custom. If one has had a secular upbringing it can be difficult to appreciate the significance of religion in believers' lives. Comprehensive liberals may also find it difficult to appreciate religious teachings that are in opposition to comprehensively liberal attitudes towards sexuality. Yet a liberal commitment to multiculturalism should not only entail the understanding and appreciation of *cultural* diversity, it should also entail respect for *religious* diversity. To expect children from religious homes to read in a secular way betrays an inequality of respect and is illiberal.

Ethical English must acknowledge the different backgrounds and stances of students and liberate each to read holistically and with integrity rather than in a way that expects those with religious beliefs to become secularized in English lessons at school. According to T. S. Eliot:

> If we, as readers, keep our religious and moral convictions in one compartment, and take our reading merely for entertainment, or on a higher plane, for aesthetic pleasure, I would point out that the author, whatever his conscious intentions in writing, in practice recognizes no such distinctions. (Eliot, 1935, p. 394)

Yet even when reading and discussing multicultural literature in English, it seems more common to discuss *cultural* rather than *religious* difference. At best this is a missed opportunity and at worst it deprives young people of the ethical education that English should offer with attendant consequences for life in a fair, vibrant and plural society. All too often important religious perspectives go unnoticed within the English lessons of a society where the majority is increasingly secular, an issue to which we return in the next chapter.

Study questions

1 How do you believe that multicultural literature should be framed on the English curriculum? How should it be taught?

2 In your experience, in what ways is 'religion' left out when reading literature from different cultures and traditions?

3 What strategies might work for a more intellectually honest inclusion of religion in English lessons?

4 What cultural and religious knowledge do you need to teach certain texts well?

11

English as secularist subject

The question posed in this chapter concerns how accommodating English is to religious perspectives. The allied ethical question of how accommodating it should be is perhaps even more important. While the image we have of 'English' is of an inclusive subject, this chapter examines whether it has a secularist 'blind spot' when it comes to religion. This has important implications not only for the study of multicultural literature and the learning of children from minority religious and cultural groups, but for how we read texts that are of religious significance in English.

Secular attitudes in English

Many English educators may consider that children generally have their freedom curtailed and rights infringed by parents and faith communities who provide them with religious nurture. This is unsurprising in an increasingly secular society where religious perspectives are often misunderstood. The beliefs of teachers are, however, critically important with regard to the inclusion of many children with religious commitments who may feel that secular perspectives are privileged and that their faith-based perspectives are marginalized.

The influence of English teachers who may be somewhat suspicious, or at least cautious, of religion and religious influences upon their students needs to be evaluated. It is important to consider the implications for the English classroom of secularist assumptions as it has been plausibly suggested that:

children's responses and judgements can be limited as much by their encountering *teachers with anti-religious views* and school policies which assume a secularist view of religion or are insensitive to families from religious backgrounds as by encounters with teachers holding religious views. (Jackson, 2003, p. 96, my italic)

While we would need to consider the particular home and religious context to be sufficiently discriminating (rather than reaching unwarranted generalizations about the benefits or dangers of 'religion' in general) we still need to give serious consideration to the implications of Jackson's view for English.

The importance of families and faith groups as 'interpretive communities' (Fish, 1980) must be acknowledged and appreciated in English lessons because there are 'different visions of society, using different discourses' (Bottery, 2003, p. 101). The difference between what is assumed to be quite normal and acceptable in different groups within a plural society is striking. We have to concede that liberalism is often much less accommodating to those who do not fully subscribe to liberal values. Comprehensive liberals approve of a wide range of lifestyles rather than advocating a particular way of life (as many religious groups do) but, as we have seen, this is a specific vision and not a 'neutral' one. In a plural society it is important to appreciate the non-neutrality of secularism as well as of liberalism. There is the danger that English education in the common, state school of a liberal democracy will be hostile to the beliefs of those who do not share its own values or assumptions. An exclusively or aggressively secular approach in English lessons is unlikely to protect the freedoms, or respect the rights, of those students who do not share the views of the secular majority.

English and other subjects often 'promote the adoption of secular core values on the basis that they constitute a common denominator, to which religious and secular people alike can subscribe' but fail to grasp that if values are limited to the secular 'they are in practice anti-religious since they leave religion out' (Copley, 2005, p. 109–10). This necessarily results in intolerance of religious perspectives but tolerance of secular perspectives (Pike, 2010e, 2011e, 2013). Tolerance of religious perspectives is a key issue for a liberal subject such as English. Clearly, 'social cohesion and democratic values are primary concerns for liberals' (Wright, 2003, p. 149) but if these are imposed through a 'neo-colonial educational regime' such an approach may 'threaten the sense of security of minority religious communities, put them on the defensive and consequently exacerbate the breakdown of social cohesion' (Wright, 2003, p. 152). Evidently there is 'a tension between cultural and religious tradition on the one hand and universal notions of rights' (Gearon and Brown, 2003, p. 205) on the other. In a context where democratic values are valorized it should not surprise us that a fundamental aim for many state schools is to foster autonomy and the freedom of young citizens to pursue their own interests and desires. Raz argues that in a non-directed, non-traditional society it is the only way to flourish for 'there is no other way to prosper in such a society' (Raz, 1988, p. 391). We should consider, though, just how 'non-directed' or 'non-traditional' a secular, liberal society is. While liberals may see themselves as 'non-traditional', many quite rightly perceive a democratic society to be steeped in 'a form of thought and experience – itself a tradition' (Wilson, 1991, p. 50).

It has been argued that in a liberal, democratic society 'there is no choice but to be autonomous' (Raz, 1988, p. 391). According to John Stuart Mill in *On Liberty*, 'He who does anything because it is the custom makes no choice' (1914/1859, p. 116). We ought therefore to consider just how much choice people in a liberal democratic society really exercise. Autonomy entails 'choosing between goods' (Mulhall and Swift, 1996, p. 325) and is of value to people living in the kinds of society 'whose social forms are such that they are based on individual choice' (Mulhall and Swift, 1996, p. 326).

According to Raz (1988), in our culture the majority of institutions are premised on the ideal of individual autonomy and White acknowledges that 'the institutions to do with marriage, work, residence, consumer choice' and so on 'embody conventions', suggesting that 'it would be quite easy for people in our kind of society to make choices within these areas, yet never to reflect on the conventional structure itself' (White, 1991, p. 88). For instance, 'young people in many Western cultures will be little aware of the "freedom to marry" because there is no longer any question of marriages being arranged for them' (Stables, 2005, p. 236). This is a good example of the way in which 'institutions that are insufficiently known cannot reach discursive status' (Stables, 2005, p. 130) because 'distance' from them has not been achieved. If 'an autonomous agent must also have distanced himself in some measure from the conventions of his social environment' (Gray, 1983, p. 74) exchanging 'readings' at different distances from these conventions and institutions could prove liberating.

Reading and engaging with new and different texts and interpretations (other worldviews) can result in a 'change of horizons' but texts that force no 'horizonal' change merely fulfil expectations because 'no turn to the horizon of yet unknown experience' is stimulated (Jauss, 1982, p. 25). In literary response theory the term 'horizontal distance' refers to 'the disparity between the given horizon of expectations and the appearance of a new work whose reception can result in a change of horizons through negation of familiar experiences or through raising newly articulated experiences to the level of consciousness' (Jauss, 1982, p. 25). Engagement with alternative readings may promote participation rather than subservience to the most popular reading at a given time in a particular group. It is especially important that 'discursive status' (Stables, 2005, p. 130) is attained in English classrooms.

Learners should engage with the worldviews of others within an interpretative *community*. Rosenblatt recommended 'spontaneous interchange among students' (1985, p. 49) and participation in the dialogue of the interpretative community often results in readers choosing to revise their readings in the light of other interpretations. If readers are not encouraged to invest anything of themselves in their reading (Pike, 2007c), they can all too easily become passive recipients rather than active and engaged 'readers' who author their own lives (Raz, 1988, p. 369). If 'free institutions depend on a high level of popular participation' (Crick, 2007, p. 244) institutional discursiveness should be stimulated, not suppressed. A free society requires discursiveness by institutions, about institutions and for the people who make up those institutions. Supporting and stimulating such discursiveness is the task of the ethical English teacher.

If English promotes democracy and democratic practices it must be acknowledged that democratic values are unlikely to be subscribed to by all students of English. In English, children persuade and negotiate and make up their own minds about issues such as the death penalty or euthanasia and yet if there is a class debate and a vote (good democratic practices) some young readers will still feel that morality cannot be determined by majority vote. What their parents, community and sacred texts say about such issues may 'trump' the views of the majority of their classmates or compatriots. If the religious freedom of young citizens is to be respected, a secularist view of religion, where the view is taken that 'the truth claims of religion are purely private matters', must not be privileged. Logically, 'Nothing at all is ever entirely private or entirely public, since no act by a human being can have no external effect at all, and no public act can be undertaken other than by a human being' (Stables, 2005, p. 120). If English is to be genuinely ethical it must 'take the religious beliefs of children and parents seriously' (Jackson, 2003, p. 97).

Militant and aggressive secularism which is 'incompatible with deeply-held beliefs about personal and family life that are based on religious teaching' could end up creating 'a gulf between the family and the state by insisting that, as a matter of formal educational policy, schools should impose on children a view of how toleration is to be interpreted and applied' which is determined by the state rather than parents and families (Almond, 2010, p. 132). Secular and comprehensively liberal perspectives on sexual freedom or other issues often override and take precedence over religious perspectives and we should be wary of approaches to morality that marginalize the perspectives of religious groups. Almond's view is that:

> tolerance is good, discrimination is bad and children should be brought up by their parents and teachers to respect others, especially those

who differ from them in religion, race or culture and, also, perhaps more controversially, those whose way of life at a more personal level differs from that of the majority, for example, in terms of their sexual relationships and their approach to marriage and family life or in their moral views and conduct. (Almond, 2010, p. 131)

According to Almond, 'legislators and educators who deliberately or thoughtlessly ignore these considerations, create an inevitable conflict for religious believers, forcing them to choose between compliance and conscience, especially where matters of family and sexual relationships are concerned' (p. 141). Equally we would not expect a secular citizen with comprehensively liberal views about sexuality to agree with the statements in the Qu'ran or the Bible to the effect that *any* sexual relations outside of heterosexual marriage are sinful. Reconciling 'freedom of speech, freedom of worship' and 'equal rights regardless of . . . sexuality' (Cameron, 2011) in a tolerant liberal society will be a major challenge to which English will have to rise in the twenty-first century. English, of all subjects, must defend freedom of speech. But that does not mean that it will tolerate homophobia any more than bullying on the basis of someone's religious views. Nor does it mean that it will condone religious practices such as forced arranged marriages or 'honour' killings. But equally it cannot claim to be liberal or respectful of diversity if it privileges exclusively secular or comprehensively liberal perspectives. Arguably, among communities living in Western liberal democracies that do not subscribe to 'democratic values' there is the 'danger of liberalism contradicting itself by imposing a liberal regime through distinctly illiberal methods' (Wright, 2003, p. 147).

English teachers will know all about the Thought Police in Orwell's *1984* and will be acutely aware of the problems associated with telling people (especially in law) what they should or should not think or believe. According to Orwell, liberty is being able to say what other people don't want to hear. If English in schools is to contribute to a harmonious, plural, cosmopolitan society it cannot seek to indoctrinate children and young people from different communities in comprehensively liberal attitudes towards different forms of sexual conduct as this issue is one on which different communities will necessarily differ (Pike, 2011b, 2011c). Seeking to foster faith in *comprehensively* liberal views and values (rather than simply *politically* liberal views and values) in English is to demonstrate an inequality of respect. We might even ask 'if it is unreasonable to expect one's fellow citizens to accept the imposition of comprehensive doctrines with which they might reasonably disagree, why is it not equally unreasonable to impose political liberalism upon those who disagree with it?' (Mulhall and Swift, 1996, p. 234). Rawls's argument that political goods trump other goods 'will carry little conviction with those who reject his general vision of the political realm altogether, for reasons grounded in their acceptance of a fundamentally non-liberal comprehensive conception of the good' (Mulhall and Swift, 1996, pp. 224, 231). For Almond (2010) tolerance does not mean agreement but forbearance or courteous and respectful agreement to differ. In reviewing the way in which the State increasingly expects religious minorities in a predominantly secular society to celebrate and approve of lifestyles and practices that are in opposition to their own, Almond asks:

> Must we approve as well as permit? Must we refrain from judgment? Can we not condemn what we ourselves think is bad? *Or is it wrong even to think in terms of bad and good?* Is moral neutrality the new virtue? (Almond, 2009, p. 132, my italic)

It is of the utmost importance that we define 'tolerance' in genuinely liberal rather than in aggressively secular terms if a firm foundation is to be laid for the discussion of difference in English classrooms. To be positive about diversity one needs to know that one will not be persecuted for being different. Tyranny on either religious or secular grounds has no place in a plural, liberal, democratic society.

Free speech, freedom of religion and the Bible

Beliefs about the respective place of rights, liberty, equality, inclusion, freedom of expression and interpretation are all informed by the doctrines, beliefs and practices of the religion that has had a pervasive influence on the liberalism of England and the subject of English. We should not forget that 'Liberalism was an offshoot of Jewish and Christian belief' (Koch and Smith, 2006, p. 130). Belief in the 'priesthood of all believers', asserted at Reformation emphasized that ordinary people mattered. This is not to suggest that Luther and Calvin were early liberals but the emphasis on being able to read and decide on matters of faith for oneself, rather than being dictated to by religious authority, was one of the results of the Reformation. The battles fought (against the government and ecclesiastical authorities) for the Bible to be available in English in England for anyone who wanted to read it, not just the wealthy or powerful, has had a profound influence upon the development of a 'free country'. It is worth sketching the story briefly in order to appreciate how freedom of interpretation has been hard won.

Popular pressure for a Bible in English (rather than Latin) to be freely available in England began in the fourteenth century with Wycliffe and his followers, who came to be known as the Lollards. Wycliffe's translation of the Bible into Middle English was the first in a European language for over a thousand years. Wycliffe asserted that English people should be allowed to read for themselves what the Bible had to say rather than listening only to what the clergy chose to read to them or tell them about it in church. His translation of the Bible was banned in England in 1408; it is perhaps strange to think of a book being illegal that is now so influential upon the English language and literature. The Council of Constance in 1415 pronounced Wycliffe a heretic posthumously, decreed that his remains were to be exhumed and burned like his books.

By the end of the century Gutenberg's invention of printing made it much more difficult to prevent the distribution of the Bible in English as so many were produced so much more quickly and cheaply than previously. The spread of printing technology (like the Internet today) made it increasingly difficult to control what people read. Even though hauls of imported Bibles in English (printed on the Continent and smuggled across the North Sea or English Channel) were seized and burned by the authorities, still more were printed. It was, however, still illegal to buy a Bible in English and there were severe penalties for being found with one. This was a subversive, banned book that could cost one's life. Astonishingly, the Bible was still unavailable to ordinary English people in their own language.

In 1526, a New Testament in the English language was produced on the Continent by William Tyndale who was committed to 'make a boy who driveth the plough know more of Scripture than the priest himself'. Tyndale had fled England on account of taking up one of the most dangerous professions of the time and had settled in Antwerp, the centre of the publishing trade on the Continent. In 1535, he was betrayed. One Henry Philips lured Tyndale to leave the safety of the house in which he was staying to go to dinner. Tyndale was arrested and burned at the stake the following year.

To put this in context, shortly after the first Bible in German was printed in 1483 there were no fewer than nine German translations in print. Bibles in French were available in France from 1500. Although many of the English nobility could read the Bible in French, in England the Bible was unavailable in English for peasants to read. Monarchs and bishops feared a peasants' revolt if the Bible in England was freely available because the difference between the power and wealth of the Church and the simplicity of the early church and Christ's teaching would be obvious. This illustrates how repressive the church in England was and how different it was to the community of believers advocated by the life and teaching of Christ.

The first whole Bible, rather than just the New Testament, to be published in English in 1535, was the work of Miles Coverdale and borrows heavily from Tyndale. In 1537 what is known as Matthew's Bible, influenced by Coverdale and Tyndale, gained royal approval and was authorized for sale. However, the marginal notes to Matthew's Bible, which could lead to it being read in a radical Protestant manner, led to serious objections on the part of the Establishment to this version. The next translation, which appeared in 1539, came to be known as the 'Great Bible' and drew upon Tyndale and Coverdale but did not have the notes of Matthew's Bible that caused offence.

The easing of restrictions in the late 1530s did not spell an end to the burning of Bibles though as is made clear from an entry made by the London diarist, Wriothesley, in 1546:

> The seventh daie of Julie was proclamation made in the cittie of London with a trompett and an Harold-at-arms, with the serjeant-at-arms of the cittie . . . for certaine Englishe books which contain pernitious and detestable errors and heresies to be brought in by the last daie of Aufust next coming, the names of theise: the text of the New Testament of Tindales or Coverdales translation: the books of . . . Tindalle, Wyckliffe . . . Coverdale . . . which books after the bringing unto the mayor or bishop shal be brent [burned]. (Dickens, 1982/1959, p. 12)

To give an idea of how such books influenced personal beliefs outside of centres of power such as London, we might take the case of Robert Plumpton as one example of the many young men who brought the influence of Tyndale's New Testament in English to the regions. Around Christmas of 1546, the same year that Wriothesley reported in his diary that the work of Tyndale and others was to be burned, Robert Plumpton was buried at Luddington in the Isle of Axholme nearly two hundred miles north of London (between present day Hull and Leeds). He was aged only 31 when he died, but letters survive from his student days in London ten years previously. On 12 January 1536, he had written home to his mother, Isabel Plumpton, explaining that he was sending her a 'godly New Testament' and suggesting 'Yf it will please you to read the introducement, ye shall see marvellous things hyd in it. And as for the understanding of it, dout not; for God wil give knowledge to whom he will give knowledge of the scriptures, as soon to a sheppard as to a priest' (Dickens, 1982/1959, p. 132). He went on to tell her, 'I write not this to bringe you into anie heresies, but to teach you the cleare light of Goddes doctrine' (Dickens, 1982/1959, p. 134). This 'introducement' would have been the preface 'W.T. unto the Reader' which Tyndale had included in editions of his New Testament from 1534 onwards. His mother knew of the dangers of heresy and the need for caution but by the time Isabel died in 1552 (a much safer time) she had written her will, not according to the formula used by her husband but in her own words: 'I comende my sowle into the most mercyfull hands of my Saveior and Redeemer, Jhesus Christe . . . ' (Dickens, 1982/1959, p. 136).

After Isabel Plumpton's death, the Geneva Bible (produced by English Protestant exiles living in Geneva in 1560) became popular during Elizabethan times. This is the version of the Bible that Shakespeare used and which he quotes in his plays. By 1600 the Geneva Bible was the most popular with English-speaking Protestants and John Knox promoted it in Scotland. However, James VI of Scotland, who became James I of England, took 'an intense personal dislike to this Bible' (McGrath, 2001, p. 141) on account of the marginal notes that did not support his view of the 'divine right of kings' and was too republican in emphasis. Consequently, James I decided to produce a better one to beat the competition. As the King James Bible (the Authorized Version) was to be read aloud in churches, it had to sound good not just read well and it drew upon the best of all previous versions.

In the seventeenth century refugees from England, fleeing religious persecution, took copies with them. The global influence of Britain in the nineteenth century and dominance of America in the twentieth century, guaranteed English its status as a world language and also the place of the Authorized Version as its foremost literary text. In the more secular twenty-first century the story of the political as well as linguistic importance of the Bible in English is often untold. Yet the battles for the Bible chart the quest for religious liberty and freedom of interpretation. Freedom to read the Bible in English in England and to interpret it for oneself was a key factor in gaining the freedoms now enjoyed in England and other liberal democracies. Often the King James Bible is described as a landmark or a monument but it would be more accurate to depict it as the result of a seismic shift socially and politically.

Liberal attitudes and the Bible as literature

It has been plausibly claimed that 'the main legacy of modern liberalism' is that, 'many if not most citizens of contemporary liberal democracies cannot take *religious stories and narratives* seriously' (Carr, 2004, p. 391, my italic). This has led to the marginalization of the Bible as a seminal literary text, partly because it is at the centre of the historically dominant faith where English has been spoken. According to the Newbolt committee report *The Teaching of English in England* the 'special difficulty' of the Bible is that it faces 'on the one hand, feeling and belief, on the other hand, disbelief and indifference' (HMSO, 1921, p. 34).

T. S. Eliot is at least partly right when claiming that 'the Bible has had a literary influence upon English literature not because it has been considered as literature, but because it has been considered as the report of the Word of

God' (Eliot, 1935, p. 390). C. S. Lewis once quipped that 'those who read the Bible as literature do not read the Bible' (Lewis, 1950, p. 23):

> It is, if you like to put it that way, not merely a sacred book but a book so remorselessly and continuously sacred that it does not invite, it excludes or repels, the merely aesthetic approach. You can read it as literature only by a tour de force. You are cutting the wood against the grain, using the tool for a purpose it was not intended to serve. It demands incessantly to be taken on its own terms: it will not continue to give literary delight very long except to those who go to it for something quite different. I predict that it will in the future be read, as it always has been read, almost exclusively by Christians. (Lewis, 1950, p. 25)

There are, however, very real dangers associated with religious or sacred texts only being read by adherents of the religions to which they belong. If people outside the religion in question have not taken the time to read its main texts, this leaves those living in a liberal society in a position of ignorance. A liberal education is to liberate one from ignorance, and to prepare one to live in a plural society (which is religiously diverse). There are particular dangers with the Bible only being read by Christians because it puts such a text in a category (such as the canon or poetry) that only a certain group reads. An aspect of the process of democratization applied to English entails making such high status texts accessible to all and not, to all intents and purposes, keeping them out of reach of the secular majority.

Even in the United States where public (state) schools are secular 'religious and educational organizations support a literary study of the Bible in public schools because it is great literature and because it is foundational for understanding Western culture' (Wachlin, 1997, p. 7). Yet it is more 'unusual' than 'universal' (Wachlin, 1997, p. 8) in the classrooms of public (state) schools there. In the United States, although the Bible 'may not be used either to disparage or to encourage a religious belief', it is entirely legitimate for the Bible to be 'taught as literature' (Wachlin, 1997, p. 11) which is what one would expect in a liberal society. Despite being of seminal literary and cultural importance, and of particular value to students of English, the Bible appears to suffer acute neglect in most English classrooms in state schools in the United Kingdom. Research has shown that the Bible is *never* read by two-thirds of 13- to 15-year-olds in secondary school in the United Kingdom (Francis, 2000, p. 165). The Biblos project at Exeter University reached similar conclusions. That English in England tends to have a 'blind spot' when it comes to religion might be illustrated by the dearth of articles during 2011 (the King James Version's 400th birthday) in the journals of the English in Education community.

Given that Shakespeare and the Bible are the two greatest influences upon the English language the omission is significant.

Although the Bible is often read for its meaning and influence on other texts there is no reason why the sorts of personal response approaches with poetry, informed by reader response theory, cannot be employed with selected biblical passages (Pike, 2000b, 2003a). Many of the active approaches used to make Shakespeare accessible could also be used with the King James Bible. Legitimating personal interpretation and fostering active rather than passive reading may be one of the most valuable approaches, for this can facilitate personal response (Pike, 2003e, 2003f, 2005b). In this way, English teachers who believe in the importance of enhancing and stimulating the imaginative and aesthetic development of their students (the 'personal growth' model) can be liberated to make creative use of the Bible. It is certainly important in an increasingly secular twentieth-century society that the Bible is not rendered 'out of reach' in a way that is, to all intents and purposes, analogous to the way the State sought to keep it out of the reach of ordinary people in the sixteenth century (Pike 2002c).

The King James or 'Authorised' Version of the Bible (1611) and Shakespeare's plays, are normally cited as the two most important and influential works in the English language. They were written at about the same time (the Authorized Version was published in the year Shakespeare began work on his last play *The Tempest*) and are influential for different reasons. Whereas Shakespeare 'ransacked the lexicon' the King James Bible employs a vocabulary of barely eight thousand words as it was written to be accessible in 1611:

> From that day to this, the Shakespearean cornucopia and the biblical iron rations represent, as it were, the North and South Poles of the language, reference points for writers and speakers throughout the world. (McCrum et al., 1986, p. 113)

Much has been written about Shakespeare in English but much less has been written about the Bible (Pike, 2002c). Shakespeare's poems and plays and the range of texts by different authors anthologized in the Bible are the highest status of texts. For instance, although Charles Dickens contributes as many as *two hundred* quotations to my edition of the *Oxford Dictionary of Quotations*, around *two thousand* quotations are included from each of the Bible and Shakespeare. The 'Top 10' most-quoted authors in English literature are Tennyson, Milton, Browning, Kipling, Dickens, Byron, Wordsworth, Shelley, Keats and Shakespeare. What is striking is the difference between the prevalence of quotation of Shakespeare and the Bible on the one hand and 'the rest' of the most quoted canonical authors on the other.

It is certainly remarkable that Shakespeare, as a single author, is quoted ten times as much as the next most quoted leading literary author. Nevertheless, as a whole, the Bible has inspired more poetry, music and works of art than any other text:

> Without the King James Bible, there would have been no *Paradise Lost*, no *Pilgrim's Progress*, no Handel's *Messiah*, no Negro spirituals, and no Gettysburg address. (McGrath, 2001, p. 2)

Students are unable to understand and appreciate works by John Donne and many other canonical and non-canonical authors without biblical knowledge of key Christian doctrines and narratives (Crossref-it.info is a helpful resource in this regard). In fact, the Bible is 'probably the most important single source for all our literature' (Alter and Kermode, 1987, p. 2) and as 'the most formative influence on Western literature' it provides us with potent cultural symbols, many of which enable us 'to interpret our experience of the world even while the intellectual current apparently flows strongly against the belief systems in which those images were born' (Jasper, 1999, pp. 12–13).

For David Crystal, who is well-known to English teachers, the 'most interesting cases of the Bible shaping our language are when we find expressions in daily use, where people take a piece of biblical language and use it in a totally non-biblical context' (Crystal, 2010, p. 6). For instance, when an Arsenal football club website used 'the race is not to the swift' they did so not because they wanted to promote the spiritual dimension of the 'race' of life but to make the point that in a bid for league success endurance rather than speed mattered. The extent of such biblical idioms in the English language is startling. David Crystal is our best guide here and *Begat – The King James Bible & the English Language* (Crystal, 2010), published to mark the 400th anniversary of the King James Bible, offers nuanced findings with regard to the linguistic significance of the King James Bible. In *Begat* the items discussed 'are not quotations: they are everyday expressions used by speakers and writers of modern English, most of whom will have no religious motivation for their use' (Crystal, 2010, p. 257). In all, Crystal found 257 modern English expressions in the King James Bible and while he acknowledges that a different analyst 'could arrive at a different total' because not everyone will share his intuitions 'about what counts as an idiom (and thus to be included) as opposed to a quotation (and thus to be excluded)' he concludes that 'the totals will not differ greatly' (Crystal, 2010, p. 258). To put this in context, Shakespeare is the next most prolific contributor 'but the number of idioms we can confidently attribute to him (such as *to the manner born*) is under a hundred' (Crystal, 2010, p. 258).

Idiomatic expressions unique to the King James Version include: 'east of Eden' (Gen. 4.16), 'how are the mighty fallen' (2 Sam. 1.19), 'a still small voice' (1 Kings 19.12), 'to everything there is a season' (Eccles. 3.1), 'beat their swords into ploughshares' (Isa. 2.4), 'be horribly afraid' (Jer. 2.12), 'lay up for yourselves treasures in heaven' (Matt. 6.20), 'turned the world upside down' (Acts 17.6) and 'a thorn in the flesh' (2 Cor. 12.7). From expressions that the King James Version shares with only one other version we have, among many, 'be fruitful and multiply' (Gen. 1.22,28), 'there were giants in the earth in those days' (Gen. 6.4), 'love thy neighbour as thyself' (Lev. 19.18), 'white as snow' (Num. 12.10), 'shibboleth' (Judg. 12.6), 'out of the mouth of babes and sucklings' (Ps. 8.2 and Matt. 21.16), 'from strength to strength' (Ps. 84.7), 'render unto Caesar the things which are Caesar's' (Matt. 22.21) and 'the way, the truth and the life' (John 14.6). When it comes to the Bible, Crystal concludes:

> No other single source has provided the language with so many idiomatic expressions . . . when it comes to idioms the Bible reigns definitely supreme. (Crystal, 2010, p. 258)

Commenting on the abilities of learners of English to understand and use idiomatic expressions such as 'fly in the ointment' (which is biblical), Crystal quite rightly declares, 'their religious beliefs are neither here nor there . . . they may have no religious belief of any kind' but 'the biblical expression will be part of their English language ability' (Crystal, 2010, p. 5). For Crystal, these instances are 'the clearest cases where we could assert with confidence that the King James Bible has helped to shape the modern English language' (Crystal, 2010, p. 5). According to Nicolson (2011) 'the King James Bible has sewn itself into the fabric of the language':

> If a child is ever the apple of her parents' eye or an idea seems as old as the hills, if we are at death's door or at our wits' end, if we have gone through a baptism of fire or are about to bite the dust, if it seems at times that the blind are leading the blind or we are casting pearls before swine, if you are either buttering someone up or casting the first stone, the King James Bible, whether we know it or not, is speaking through us. (Nicolson, 2011, p. 43)

Powerful and memorable biblical phrases have entered the linguistic repertoire of global speakers of English and 'People who use these are often well aware of their biblical origin' (Crystal, 2010, p. 5). When writers use an idiom from the Bible in an inventive way such as 'Frequent fly in Qantas ointment' or 'Unto us a blog is born' (Crystal, 2010, pp. 114–15):

> The writers aren't expecting us to know which bit of the Bible the allusion refers to, only that they've done something clever with the English

language. *And we enjoy the joke – as long as we recognize it.* (Crystal, 2010, p. 6, my italic)

But what if we don't recognize it? Appreciating the inventive and imaginative use of language depends upon 'knowing that the allusion will be recognised' (Crystal, 2010, p. 6). If the Bible comes more and more to be read only by Christians, there will be less and less recognition of the biblical sources of allusions, idioms and quotations. English teachers have a vital role to play in introducing learners to key passages such as the Creation, Ten Commandments, the Twenty-Third Psalm and The Lord's Prayer. Reading The Lord's Prayer, in several versions (especially Wycliffe, Tyndale and the Authorized Version) enable us to see how the English language has changed over time. Yet, as we have seen, the history of the Bible in English concerns more than linguistics, it gives an important insight into the history of freedom. It is worth reflecting that the Lord's Prayer in English was once banned in England. In 1513 John Colet, Dean of St Paul's was suspended from his position for translating The Lord's Prayer (Luke 11. 2–4) into English:

The Lord's Prayer
Old English (Anglo-Saxon, 995)

Fæder ūre, þū þe eart on heofonum;
Sīe þīn nama gehālgod,tō becume þīn rīce,
gewurþe þīn willa,on eorðan swā swā on heofonum.
Urne gedæghwamlican hlāf sele ūs tōdæg,
and forgif ūs ūre gyltas,swā swā wē forgifaþ ūrum gyltendum,
and ne geld þū ūs on costnunge,
ac ālȳs ūs of yfele,
sōþlīce.

Wycliffe's translation (Middle English, 1382)

Oure fadir that art in heuenes,
halewid be thi name; thi kyngdoom come to;
be thi wille don `in erthe as in heuene;
yyue to vs this dai oure `breed ouer othir substaunce;
and foryyue to vs oure dettis, as we foryyuen to oure
dettouris; and lede vs not in to temptacioun,
but delyuere vs fro yuel.
Amen.

Tyndale's translation
(Late Middle English, 1534)

O oure father which arte in heven,
hallowed be they name. Let they kyngdome come.
Thy wyll be fulfilled, as well in erth, as it ys in heven.
Geve us this daye oure dayly breede. And
forgeve vs oure treaspases, even as we forgeve oure
trespacers. And leade vs not into temptacion: but
delyver vs from evell. For thyne is the kyngedome
and the power, and the glorye for ever.
Amen.

King James or Authorized Version
(Early Modern English, 1611)

Our father which art in heauen,
hallowed be thy name. Thy kingdom come.
Thy will be done in earth as it is in heauen.
Giue us this day our daily bread.
And forgiue us our debts as we forgiue our debters.
And lead us not into temptation,
but deliuer us from euill. Amen.

Douai Rheims (American edition, 1899)

Our Father who art in heaven, hallowed be thy name.
Thy kingdom come. Thy will be done on earth as it is in heaven.
Give us this day our supersubstantial bread.
And forgive us our debts, as we also forgive our debtors.
And lead us not into temptation. But deliver us from evil. Amen.

American Standard Version (1900)

Our Father who art in heaven, Hallowed be thy name.
Thy kingdom come. Thy will be done, as in heaven, so on earth.
Give us this day our daily bread.
And forgive us our debts, as we also have forgiven our debtors.
And bring us not into temptation, but deliver us from the evil one.

New International Version (1984)

Our father in heaven,
hallowed be your name,
your kingdom come,
your will be done,
on earth as it is in heaven.
Give us each day our daily bread.
Forgive us our debts, as we also have forgiven our debtors.
And lead us not into temptation,
but deliver us from the evil one.

Performances of Old English and Middle English versions of *The Lord's Prayer* can be found on YouTube and similar websites. We can enjoy watching and hearing *The Lord's Prayer* dramatically read by hooded students of English (specializing in Old or Middle English), dressed like monks who appear to be roaming windswept Northumberland moors or the coast around Lindisfarne (Holy Island). In the English classroom it can be a stimulating task to identify the words that have changed over time such as 'gyltas' (Old English, we would now say 'guilt'), 'dettis' (Middle English) and 'debts' (Early Modern English) especially when students hear the words read while seeing the subtitles. A comparison of *The Lord's Prayer* in several versions (Old English c. 995, Middle English 1200, Wycliff 1388, Tyndale 1526, Authorized Version 1611 and contemporary English translations) enables us to see how words have changed and is especially good for language study on the associations and connotations or words and their semantic fields (such as 'debt' and 'guilt').

It is important that students appreciate the influence of the King James Version. David Crystal (2010) estimates that around 60 expressions from Matthew's gospel alone in the King James Version have found their way into our present-day English language. To give just a few that are immediately recognizable we might take: 'salt of the earth', (Matt. 5.13), 'an eye for an eye' (Matt. 5.38), 'pearls before swine' (Matt. 7.6), 'the lost sheep' (Matt. 10.6), 'the blind lead the blind' (Matt. 15.14), 'the signs of the times' (Matt. 16.3), 'den of thieves' (Matt. 21.13) and 'thirty pieces of silver' (Matt. 26.15). The problem, when it comes to assessing the influence of the King James Version (KJV) in particular, is that *all* the sayings just quoted are also found in *all* the other major sixteenth-century translations of the Bible. Arguably, though, it is not simply the linguistic (or literary) influence of the Bible that has had an impact upon 'English'.

The emphasis on social justice and liberty in a liberal arts subject such as English should not be divorced from its intellectual, moral and theological roots. Although social justice is emphasized in many religions, 'of all faiths primitive Christianity was the most radical, egalitarian and inclusive, smashing down all barriers between people, and even the barrier between individual's and God' and it is 'no accident that the West was the only civilization to abolish the slave trade and slavery voluntarily' (Koch and Smith, 2006, p. 39).

The influence of the Judeo-Christian belief in the inherent equality of all people is foundational in our society and in many schools (Pike, 2009a). It has been plausibly suggested that the emphasis on the individual self originated in the Christian belief in a unique and immortal soul (Koch and Smith, 2006, p. 47) and that the commitment to respecting every individual is rooted in the Christian teaching that each person is made 'in the image of God' (Gen. 1.27). We take it for granted that the professor of politics does not cast ten votes in an election while the cleaner of her office casts only one but such equality owes a considerable debt to Christianity:

> The early Christians came up with the most subversive political idea yet to hit the world – that of the equality in Christ of all nations and races, of slaves and masters, and of men and women. The idea that ordinary people mattered and the individual soul had infinite value was peculiarly European; this emphasis was absent in other great religions and cultures, in Islam, in Confucian China, and in Hindu India. (Koch and Smith, 2006, p. 118)

Radically, for the time, the importance of making religious choices for oneself rather than following other people was emphasized in the Gospels where Jesus was critical of those who followed the 'tradition of men' rather than making their own decisions about whether or not to follow him. When such an emphasis was rediscovered, 'the Reformation had an incalculable effect in stimulating religious pluralism, freedom of thought and political liberty' (Koch and Smith, 2006, p. 120).

Yet views of freedom and autonomy and 'personal growth' differ quite markedly in a plural society. It has been claimed, for instance, that from an Islamic perspective 'personal and moral autonomy . . . is a kind of nonsense' (Halstead, 2007, p. 289) because in Islam personal and moral autonomy is not the goal of development. Indeed, the word 'Islam' means 'submission' and no 'body of work exists that is comparable to that of Bentham, Mill, Kant or Rawls in the West in the sense of seeking to provide a framework for moral decision-making without any necessary link to religion' (Halstead, 2007, p. 284). Significantly, a liberal society's political institutions are largely separate from its religious institutions. Theocratic states are very different to those nations where religious and secular powers are separate. Whereas Christ preached 'Render unto Caesar the things that are Caesar's and to God the things that are God's' (Pike, 2009c), in Islam 'the legal order is founded in divine commandment' (Scruton, 2002, p. 4) and many mullahs exercise temporal, political power. Of course, we should not forget that it was bishops who ordered the burning of Bibles and bodies in sixteenth-century England in a desperate attempt to shore up their temporal power.

Ethical English teaching will support the student's freedom of choice in matters of religion. The ability to act autonomously or to make up one's own mind and come to one's own decisions and choices in life, is one of the main aims of a liberal education and it has a high priority in English. Yet we have to consider on what basis choices and decisions are made. In a sense, when we consider if certain behaviour is appropriate in the English classroom, in school or in society, we are always asking the question of whether it is reasonable or not. There are, however, issues with rationality as the core liberal value that mediates between equality and liberty. Challenging authority and learning to question accepted assumptions is part and parcel of learning English but we also need to be discriminating when we think about what we mean by rational thinking. We must not fall into the trap of assuming that all religious positions are irrational. Arguably, it would be wrong to assume 'there is no place for rationality in Islamic ethics' for the 'superstructure is very rational' and can be seen in the judgements and application of Islamic (Shariah) law that is based on religious texts' (Halstead, 2007, p. 285). In the Christian tradition the apostle Paul gave a rational explanation of his faith in Athens (Acts 17.17) and a 'reasonable' defence before Festus, the Roman governor (Acts 26.25). The 'religious' basis of a learner's reasoning needs to be appreciated.

Although as liberals we tend to think decisions are generally made on the basis of rational justification, we should be sufficiently attuned to debates concerning diversity to appreciate that not all citizens will read and respond to 'reason' or to 'autonomy' in the same way. For liberals, the core liberal value of rationality is employed to mediate between freedom and equality but some 'believers' would not endorse the view that important choices are always to be based on logically consistent rational justification. Many will no doubt take the view that 'an open mind, in questions that are not ultimate, is useful' but having such a mind, 'about ultimate foundations' is 'idiocy' when such questions are rightly 'matters of faith' (Lewis, 1978/1943, p. 10). That liberalism itself (and English as a discipline) is founded upon certain premises, presuppositions or ways of seeing the world demonstrates both are 'faith-based'.

Study questions

1 How secular is English? How secular are you? What ways can you think of to ensure secular assumptions in lessons do not marginalize and exclude students from religious backgrounds?

2   How important is the Bible as a text in English?

3   Why should students of English language and literature read the Bible?

4   What activities can you devise based on reading different versions of 'The Lord's Prayer'?

5   How important has the fight for a Bible in the vernacular been to English society?

6   How important has the Bible been to the values of English?

7   Why is the most important literary text in the English language read so little in English lessons?

8   How can strategies be adopted for active approaches to the literary text?

12

Believing in professional learning

As a teacher-researcher, insight is gained not only into the researcher's environment, but into the researcher's perception of that environment. Arguably, to develop as an English teacher one has to know about one's worldview because this influences behaviour and development; it informs the course of action taken and the rationale for it. The problem is that one's worldview is rather like the windscreen of the car we drive or the glasses we wear: we tend to look through the glass rather than at it. Identifying our taken-for-granted views is not always easy. Identifying where we got them from can be harder still. The challenge is for teachers to begin to identify their presuppositions and assumptions. The task is to raise to the level of awareness what is unconscious and to become aware of the spiritual, moral and religious aspects of practice. Here, at the end of Part Three, we look at the significance of the beliefs and values of teachers of English and the parallels between professional learning and learning from 'religious' perspectives.

Seeing the 'Movie' not the 'Snapshot': Validity and generalizability

The teacher of English is in a privileged position when it comes to understanding the classroom context and the total situation in which the transactions between learners and texts are embedded. A teacher-researcher working within the qualitative paradigm, has numerous advantages over a visiting outside researcher because understanding of educational processes develops over time and in a context. Indeed, Barnes and Todd (1977) showed that classroom discourse could not be adequately understood by reference only to a 'content' frame in ignorance of the 'interaction' frame. More recently, Schofield (1993) has argued that quantitative research is liable to produce a 'snapshot' of a situation and has suggested that qualitative research can give access to the 'movie'. We must remember, though, that even qualitative researchers run the risk of viewing a 'snapshot' and the closer we can get to taking into account the whole 'movie' the better.

The knowledge gained by the English teacher-researcher who is carrying out a study while based in an institution is of a special sort. Such a researcher is more likely to have been involved in, or to have witnessed, the start of the 'movie' or a particularly salient episode. The visitor, on the other hand, may well be oblivious to such events and is therefore unable to draw upon such knowledge to inform any judgement made. The advantages of being an insider with privileged access to insider knowledge are often insufficiently acknowledged by teachers of English and also more conventional researchers. In ethical teacher-research, the focus is not just on observed behaviour (as in behaviourism). Teacher research does often record classroom behaviour and will document changes and improvements, but if it is to be holistic and to respect the dignity of teachers and students, the purposes and beliefs behind the observed behaviours need to be appreciated.

The aims of ethical English teachers can be mediated through action research, as it is 'the study of a social situation with a view to improving the quality of action within it' (Elliott, 1991, p. 69). Moreover, in action research any theories generated are 'validated through practice' (Elliott, 1991, p. 69). In other words, the researcher's role is not to be an objective, dispassionate and impartial spectator, but to be an integral part of the action that improves the situation. It is not about being a fly on the wall: the sort of transformation that action research aims to achieve is necessarily an essential part of the English teacher's professional role, which is to improve situations and not to observe them only:

> Action research is primarily concerned with change, being grounded in the idea that development and innovation are an essential part of professional practice. At the heart of teaching lies the complexity of social interactions (usually involving large groups) in which there is always opportunity for improvement. (Altrichter et al., 1993, p. 201)

Yet teachers of English who are reflective practitioners sometimes lack the confidence to share their action research in a wider context because of doubts about its status as 'research'. At the heart of the debate about whether small-scale practitioner research is, in fact, 'research' are issues of validity and generalizability: whether the conclusions drawn by one teacher are valid and whether these conclusions can inform the work of other teachers or learning in other classrooms.

Case studies such as those produced by much action research, are generalizable to 'theoretical propositions' and not necessarily 'statistical populations' (Yin, 1994, p. 10). This is because action research case studies, in common with all case studies, set out to illuminate how and why decisions were taken, and therefore seek to expand and generalize to theories and not frequencies. Although it has been acknowledged that 'neat generalisations' are not yielded in the traditional sense in action research as each classroom is unique 'that does not mean it can have no effect beyond its particular context' because:

> it is the understandings of the complexities of the particular situation and the recognition of the different ways in which the familiar can be interpreted that is the aspect that is so readily transferable to other situations. (Green, 1999, p. 107)

The views of Cohen and Mannion, (1994) that the small-scale, restricted, qualitative action research case study prohibits generalizations can be questioned on the basis that knowledge of finite cases, however large or statistically representative, never allows researchers to infer with total certainty about a more universal claim. Clearly, a basis for 'induction' through logic has never been achieved (Popper, 1959). We are necessarily, therefore, forced to relinquish the notion that a claim has to be proved beyond all conceivable doubt before it is considered to be valid. Simons and Humble (1978, p. 189) have observed that teachers in general assume that case studies are low in generalizability.

Teachers tend to assume that the research a teacher does with one class may tell us about that class and the pupils in it, but not about the teaching of any other teacher or the learning of any other pupils. This is a particularly invidious notion because it devalues and marginalizes the knowledge a teacher generates by asserting that it is only locally applicable. If 'teachers generalise from past to present experience' then there is a good case for assuming that other professionals' case studies can provide vicarious experiences which are 'generalisable to their own situations, and vice versa' (Elliott, 1991, p. 65). In most cases, once teachers read a fellow teacher's case study, albeit from a different context, they are able to transfer elements of it to their own situation (Pike, 2002b).

Seeing the 'Selfie': Values and worldviews in teacher research

The notion of the 'selfie', a photograph we take of ourselves, often on a mobile or cellphone, is helpful here. But seeing what is inside our head (our worldview (made up of our assumptions and presuppositions) is much more difficult than taking a photo of the outside of it. Identifying the aims and beliefs of English teachers, and thereby enabling them to reflect on their ideological position is valuable because it facilitates a clear description of the research lens through which reality is viewed when research is conducted. However, English teachers' beliefs (about personal growth) and their talents (for reading readers as well as texts) may not be enough on their own to underpin the ethical English described in this book. Sobering advice has been given about our idealistic aspirations:

> If one is not forced into working out the practical implication of one's aims – which involves thinking about how they might be translated into desirable outcomes for all students – then there is every chance that the feel-good satisfaction of boasting about the humanising effect of one's work are not likely to lead to much actual good in the classroom. (Davies, 1996, p. 29)

When evaluating and analysing educational phenomena, a teacher-researcher might well focus on the *effects* of an action or intervention, strategy or policy. But we need to evaluate *purpose*, not just *effects* if we are to better understand what is going on. This applies not only to pedagogy for a particular aspect of a subject such as English but also to whole school processes and policies and even to entire educational systems in whole countries. The reason we need to focus on *purpose* not just *effects* is because we cannot adequately or intelligently analyse the latter without the former. It is 'difficult to criticize the way things *are* without some sense of how they *ought to be*' which makes 'the normative/philosophical at some point unavoidable' (Standish, 2010, p. 7).

This book concerns ethics and seeks to provide a bigger picture than is gained by looking only at the way things are now in English teaching. This is critically important because we need to 'say what the purposes of education should be, regardless of what is in fact going on now' (Standish, 2010, p. 7). A person's view of the purpose of education and of English in education will be derived from their worldview. What their priorities are, what they 'worship' or deem to be most important and of greatest value in life will influence their view of purposes in education. Of course, this is not always admitted and in the sociology of education it is sometimes claimed that the researcher is merely describing the way things are now. However, it is hard to see how critical reflection is possible at all without thinking about the way things should be. Put simply, ethics concerns the way things should be and teachers engage in such ethical reflection every day. When teachers look at a child's progress the question is not just where the learner is now but the progress he or she can make with further help. When an innovation or intervention is planned and evaluated we need to look at purpose and effects (Standish, 2010, p. 7). This is where action research comes in. It is of ethical value because it provides English teachers with the research perspective needed to transform practice and to set an agenda for change. Indeed, action research itself has been defined, not by reference to specific methods and techniques, but by:

> a continuing effort to closely interlink, relate and confront action
> and reflection, to reflect upon one's conscious and unconscious
> doings in order to develop one's actions, and to act reflectively in
> order to develop one's knowledge. (Altrichter et al., 1993, p. 6)

What we believe is 'self-evident', and of 'ultimate reality' or greatest worth, does not only influence teaching and learning but also the researching of teaching and learning. It influences how we interpret what we see and hear. We will recall from the Introduction to Part Three that any theory about education and schooling in general, or teaching and learning in the English classroom in particular, 'can't avoid presupposing something as having divine status, even if they never mention what it is' because 'whatever is presented as the explanation of all else is tacitly being given divine status' (Clouser, 1999, pp. 28–9). What is 'regarded as unconditional and non-dependent is appropriately designated "divine"' (Barnes, 2014, p. 121) and, 'In every religious tradition the divine is whatever is unconditionally, nondependently real. It is whatever is believed to be "just there"' (Clouser, 1999, p. 21). The answer of Christianity to what is 'just there' is 'Christ' or 'God' as 'all things have been created through Him and for Him. He is before all things, and in Him all things consist' (Col. 1.16–17). The word 'consist' here is also translated to convey the meaning that Christ 'sustains' or 'holds together' all things. Of course, many people in increasingly secular societies now give a different answer to the question of what they believe to be 'divine' or 'just there'.

Implicit in claims about the 'divine' are beliefs about happiness and fulfilment, not just salvation. The difference between a materialistic or naturalistic worldview and one that accepts that there is more to life than can be explained by scientific explanation is of central importance: 'Materialist atheism says we are just a collection of chemicals. It has no answer whatsoever to the question of how we should be capable of love or heroism or poetry if we are simply animated pieces of meat' (Wilson, 2009). Darwin himself was candid enough to concede 'with me the horrid doubt always arises whether the convictions of man's mind, which has been developed from the mind of lower animals, are of any value or at all trustworthy' (Darwin in Clouser, 1999, p. 87–8). Clearly, human beings are concerned with their origins: 'not just in the sense of how they originated (the processes that produced them) but in the sense of what it is they ultimately depend on' (Clouser, 1999, p. 40).

One school with a Christian ethos in which research has been recently carried out attributes its high view of human beings to the belief that children are 'made in God's image', a powerful theological resource that underpins the view that everyone has dignity and potential that 'trumps' socio-economic background or family histories of educational underachievement (Pike, 2010d). On this view, students cannot be regarded as 'grade raw material' or, worse still, as 'exam fodder' and schooling cannot be seen as a qualification production line that aids and abets the commodification of children and young people. Students are seen as ends in themselves rather than as means to ends. This is not to say that schools without a Christian ethos and teachers working in them cannot have faith in human potential but the source of their 'divinity' belief may be more humanistic.

'Ontology' (the nature of 'being' or 'existence') is rather important as one's 'doctrine of man' or view of humanity derives from it. If one believes a child can 'create' something original from their heart, soul or spirit and that this is not simply a function of their background, training or conditioning, then a materialist vision (at least of the exclusivist type) is untenable. Arguably, what a great many teachers of English believe about children and young people cannot be supported by a materialist explanation of ultimate reality. Humanity is indeed defended by the 'literatures of dignity and freedom'. In the light of their experience of humane relationships in the classroom and their reading of literature exploring the human condition English teachers do not tend to see human beings as simply products that are governed, conditioned and regulated by their environments. Attending to beliefs and values including the notions of meaning and purpose at the heart of English need to be acknowledged in any research about it. For instance, if one wishes to increase the level of motivation of adolescents and help to develop their insight as readers of literature, this cannot be approached rightly in a behaviourist way (see Chapter 8).

As a teacher, if an adequate foundation is to be laid for authentic and sustainable professional learning, one's beliefs and answers to ultimate questions need to be examined. One's worldview is particularly influential as it has a profound influence upon one's views of English and the pedagogy appropriate for different aspects of it. The worldview of the teacher will determine the strategies, approaches and initiatives that can be accommodated into his or her authentic professional practice with ethical integrity; it will influence both what is researched and how it is researched. Reflecting upon what one believes to be *most important* is often a considerable challenge but answers are of determining significance for both teaching and research. Recognizing what we 'believe in' is not always easy but we still have to go through the challenging process of interrogating what we believe to be most worthwhile if we are to understand the lens, through which observations are seen, that colours our interpretations and underpins our research. Looking at religious perspectives may help us to identify what we really 'believe in' as teachers and to consider existential matters.

Imaginatively learning about religion

Ways of knowing other than the rational, such as an aesthetic or spiritual sort of knowing, are rarely drawn upon in researching teacher development. We saw in Part Two that teachers' responses to literature can inform their professional learning but we also need to consider what teachers of English might learn from religion that would inform research into their practice. Throughout Part Three we have seen the need to be religiously literate in order to evaluate and respond to the truth claims of our students and the society in which we live. The 'religious education as ontology' thesis of Hella and Wright (2009) is helpful:

> Different religious and secular traditions offer contested accounts of reality. Hence the basic unity of learning about and learning from religion is ontological: the personal and spiritual development of pupils is dependent on their understanding of the good life, and hence their understanding of ultimate reality. Since in a plural context, such understandings are contested, the unity of the twin dimensions of religious education lies specifically in the pursuit of truth and truthfulness (Hella and Wright, 2009, p. 58)

What might be added is that this applies not only to the learning of students but also of teachers. In order to function in a fully human or humane way we will need to have considered other ways of living, in other places and at other times. An important part of this will entail being imaginatively and spiritually literate, in order to 'learn from religion' a term familiar within RE (Religious Education) in the United Kingdom.

It has been suggested that 'learning from religion' is less problematic in confessional religious education than in its liberal forms:

> In confessional forms of religious education, the contrast between learning about and learning from religion does not normally present itself as a problem. This is because students are attempting to live their lives within the worldview presented to them by the curriculum. Thus for a Christian student to learn about Christianity is simultaneously to learn from Christianity: the knowledge and insights gained from their learning about their faith tradition will have a direct connection to their own beliefs and values. In liberal forms of religious education, however, the contrast between learning about and learning from religion becomes problematic. . . . A secular humanist studying Islam, or a Christian studying Buddhism, may not immediately perceive the value of such study for their personal development. (Hella and Wright, 2009, p. 56)

While distinguishing between 'confessional' and 'liberal' religious education is helpful, it should be added that 'learning from religion' is not entirely unproblematic in 'confessional' religious education. Hermeneutics has taught us that it is not always a straightforward and simple process for readers saturated in twenty-first-century culture to find personal relevance in, respond to, and apply sacred texts of their own tradition to their present personal concerns. The theory of the 'reading event' as a transaction between reader and text (Rosenblatt, 1978), that is central to ethical English, is particularly valuable when seeking to facilitate 'learning from religion' because the relevance of the text is made apparent to the reader and is applied by the reader to his or her own life. When we, as readers, engage with key religious themes, we need to consider these issues at a personal level and see their relevance to our own lives and not simply to be dealt with as themes to be 'objectively' explored (Pike, 2011e).

Pedagogy informed by the transactional theory of the literary work (Rosenblatt, 1985) has much to offer and is philosophically congruent with Variation Theory. A short literary work such as 'The Right Word' by Imtiaz Dharkar will illustrate. When reading this poem one student teacher commented on the importance of 'having a cultural understanding and a sensitive approach to attitudes and beliefs and understanding the religious backgrounds of my pupils' and another noted that it was 'so useful, especially for me realizing certain gaps in my own knowledge that I want to fill'. Augmenting subject knowledge in areas of relative weakness is important for all teachers. In this case knowing more about Islam was important for teachers in a multicultural school with a large Muslim population and is a valid and humane way of approaching professional learning with cultural sensitivity. One student teacher realized that she needed to know far more about different interpretations of 'jihad' in Islam, as well as the cultural practices of her pupils such as showing respect by removing one's shoes upon entering a house.

Learning to 'read' religious practices is vital in a plural society (Pike, 2008a, 2009c, 2010c), as is learning from different cultures and religious traditions. Clearly, different members of a class will perceive the central protagonist in 'The Right Word' variously as a 'freedom fighter', a 'terrorist', a 'martyr' or a boy who is like a member of the family and it is helpful to know what influences their views:

> knowledge of the qualitatively different ways in which a class of students understands a given religious phenomenon provides teachers with critical information about their pre-understandings prior to the start of the learning sequence. (Hella and Wright, 2009, p. 58)

Religiously motivated practices are often 'read' and interpreted differently, often to the extent of opinions being polarized. Indeed Hella and Wright note that 'in contexts in which the ultimate nature of reality and meaning of life is fundamentally disputed religious education must necessarily be a critical process' and they suggest that 'phenomenography and the Variation Theory of Learning offer potentially useful tools for the construction of an appropriate pedagogy for critical religious education' (Hella and Wright, 2009, p. 62).

It has been suggested that 'phenomenographic analysis of students' experiences may identify a tension between their own perceptions of dress codes as central to Islam and the curriculum's identification of submission to the will of Allah as a more critical issue' (Hella and Wright, 2009, p. 62). Seeing how other readers 'read' such 'signs' can also be helpful in understanding the world in which they live. The wearing of the burqa by some Muslim women in Western countries is a good example. Two high profile male readers recently publicly expressed very different interpretations of women wearing the burqa. Sarkozy seemed to believe that the burqa should not be worn in a 'secular' country such as France, whereas Obama stated that it is not for a state to tell its ethnic minority citizens what to wear. What one believes, one's assumptions and presuppositions, influences the reading of phenomena. The burqa may be seen as a symbol of the oppression of women or as a demonstration of the freedom to express one's religion. It is important to note, however, that:

> Variation Theory addresses key principles of learning that are more fundamental than understanding contested interpretations of an object of learning. According to the theory, variation is necessary for any learning to take place: for example, to discern the air temperature on a particular day as cold, you must have previous experience of variation in air temperature. (Hella and Wright, 2009, p. 65)

Such variation, or aesthetic distance, can valuably be provided by literary experiences and by pedagogy that facilitates and legitimates such experiences. Pedagogy for response to literature, informed by Variation Theory may inform ethical English where students do not just *learn about* but *learn from* religion so that they 'read' their world well. To do so requires the use of one's rational, affective, aesthetic and spiritual faculties.

Avoiding imaginative failure and learning from religion

A consideration of the spiritual, moral and religious dimensions of English is essential not least because teacher development cannot be based upon the positivism and empiricism of the technical model. To develop holistically as a teacher is to develop as a person who is inherently spiritual, moral and 'religious'. Beliefs and values matter in humane and ethical English that has a holistic approach to the development of teachers as human beings. It should not surprise us that, as Parker Palmer has noted, many teachers are increasingly prepared to draw upon spiritual and religious traditions to inform their professional practice. Ethical English will be 'religiously literate' and will enable teachers and students to 'learn from religion', preventing what we might term a 'imaginative failure'. An example of C. S. Lewis's 'imaginative failure' as his friend J. R. R. Tolkien called it, prior to his conversion to Christianity, will illustrate how necessary it is to 'learn from religion':

> Lewis complained that he could not see any personal relevance for himself in the story of Christ. . . . Tolkien pointed out that this was, as much as anything, an imaginative failure on Lewis' part. When Lewis came across myths . . . he was moved . . . he was prepared to 'feel the myth as profound and suggestive of meanings beyond my grasp even tho' I could not say in cold prose "what it meant" '. He stopped short of understanding Christianity because when he thought about that, he laid aside the receptive imagination with which he allowed himself to appreciate myth and became rigidly narrow and empiricist. He should understand that the story of Christ is simply a true myth . . . one must be content to accept it in the same way. . . . Tolkien argued, 'doctrines' which are extracted from the 'myth' are less true than the 'myth' itself. The ideas are too large and too all-embracing for the finite mind to absorb them'. That is why the divine providence revealed himself in story. (Wilson, 1991, pp. 125–6)

Once Lewis had overcome his 'imaginative failure', he came to see Christian truth claims or doctrines in a similar way to Tolkien but stressed that spiritual *experience* underpinned doctrine and not just myth.

This emphasis upon the 'spirit' of religious teaching is important educationally. In Part One we looked at the relevance of spirituality (apart from religion) to English teaching and it is important here in Part Three not to leave spirituality out of any reflection upon the importance of religion. Lewis describes meeting an old RAF officer who had felt 'the tremendous mystery' when he was 'out alone in the desert at night' but did not believe all the 'neat little dogmas and formulas' about God that Lewis outlined, on the grounds that compared to the experience in the desert 'they all seem so petty and pedantic and unreal' (Lewis, 1981/1952, p. 131). Lewis, perhaps as a result of his own experience of 'myth' and aesthetic or spiritual response to myth, was not unsympathetic and admitted:

> when he turned from that experience to the Christian creeds, I think he really was turning from something real to something less real. In the same way, if a man has once looked at the Atlantic from the beach, and then goes and looks at a map of the Atlantic, he also will be turning from something real to something less real: turning from real waves to a bit of coloured paper. (Lewis, 1981/1952, p. 131)

For Lewis, 'religion' and 'spirituality', 'myth' and 'doctrine' or 'experience' and 'truth claim' could not be divorced. Rather than being binary oppositions they were each parts of a hidden wholeness:

> The map is admittedly only coloured paper, but there are two things you have to remember about it. In the first place, it is based on what hundreds and thousands of people have found out by sailing the real Atlantic. In that way it has behind it masses of experience just as real as the one you could have from the beach; only, while yours would be a single glimpse, the map fits all those different experiences together. In the second place, if you want to go anywhere, the map is absolutely necessary. As long as you are content with walks on the beach, your own glimpses are far more fun than looking at a map. But the map is going to be more use than walks on the beach if you want to get to America. (Lewis, 1981/1952, p. 131)

If one's experience of 'being' in English means that one cannot accept the materialist hypothesis (but believes in human freedom, dignity and creativity), nor the humanist position (that declares ultimate truth and value is 'man-made') then one might conceivably look outside of oneself to the 'map'. C. S. Lewis says of faith: 'So it is a sort of Rubicon. One goes across; or not. But if one does, there is no manner of security against miracles' (Lewis, 1960, p. 98). As we have seen here, English is not short on 'miracles'.

Study questions

1   How do your beliefs and values inform your professional learning?

2   How would you describe your worldview?

3   How does your worldview inform your beliefs about English and how it should be taught?

4   How can your professional learning be more authentic and true to your fundamental commitments?

5   What is your 'walking on the beach'?

6   How do you turn to the 'map'?

Appendix 1: A self-audit of subject knowledge for teachers of English

1. Literacy and linguistic terms (drawn from National Literacy Strategy documents and National Curriculum English Programmes of Study for Key Stages 3 and 4 [DfE, 2013a, 2013b, 2013c, 2014]).

Using the list below, create a chart of terms you are unfamiliar with or do not have a ready definition for then add a definition and example. A sample chart has also been included below.

Term	Definition	Example
Digraph	Two letters which represent one sound	*ch* in tea*ch*er *sh* in *sh*out

abstract noun	assonance	cohesion
accent	asterisk	cohesive device
acronym	auxiliary verb	colloquial
acrostic	bilingual	colon
active voice	blank verse	comma
adjective	blend	common noun
adverb	blurb	comparative
adverbial	calligram	complement
alliteration	character	compound word
ambiguity	cinquain	conjunction
antonym	clause	connectives
apostrophe	cliché	consonant
article	cloze	contraction
ascender	coherence	cue

dash

decode

derivation

descender

determiner

dialect

dialogue

dictionary

digraph

diminutive

diphthong

direct object

direct speech

double negative

elegy

ellipsis

empathy

epic

epitaph

etymology

eulogy

exclamation

exclamation mark

fable

finite verb

free verse

full stop

genre

glossary

grammar

grapheme

phoneme

haiku

homograph

homonym

homophone

hyphen

idiom

imagery

imperative

indirect object

indirect speech

infinitive

inflection

intonation

intransitive verb

jingle

layout

legend

limerick

logograph

main clause

metalanguage

metaphor

mnemonic

modal verb

modifier

morpheme

morphology

myth

non-chronological writing

noun phrase

object

onomatopoeia

onset

palindrome

paragraph

participle

parenthesis

passive voice

personification

phoneme

phonics

phonology

phrase

plural

possessive

predicate

prefix

preposition

prepositional phrase

progressive

pronoun

proper noun

prose

pun

punctuation

question

question mark

rap

received pronounciation

register

relative clause

rhyme

riddle

rime

root word

scan

schwa

segment

semantic field

semi-colon

sentence

-complex

-compound

-simple

shape poem

simile

singular

skim

slang

sonnet

speech marks

split diagraph

standard English

stanza

statement

stress

story board

subject

subjunctive

subordinate

subordinate clause

suffix

superlative

syllable	text type	verb
synonym	theme	vowel
synopsis	thesaurus	word
syntax	transitive verb	word class
tautology	trigraph	word family
tense	unstressed	writing frame

2. Literary authors (taken from different incarnations of the National Curriculum for English). Audit your knowledge by indicating next to each author listed below the texts you have read. Try to add when you read different texts (school, University, personal reading, etc.). Identify the authors you should read. When prioritizing read what is on your school's scheme of work, GCSE and A-level specification first so that your reading is most relevant to what you may need to teach in the classroom.

Leila Aboulela, Chinua Achebe, Chimamanda Ngozi Adichie, Maya Angelou, Simon Armitage, Matthew Arnold, W. H. Auden, Jane Austen, Alan Ayckbourn, J. G. Ballard, Samuel Beckett, Alan Bennett, James Berry, William Blake, Robert Bolt, E. K. Brathwaite, Charlotte Brontë, Emily Brontë, Kevin Brooks, Elizabeth Barrett Browning, Robert Browning, John Bunyan, Robert Burns, Lord Byron, Willa Cather, Geoffrey Chaucer, William Congreve, John Clare, Gillian Clarke, Samuel Taylor Coleridge, Wilkie Collins, William Congreve, Joseph Conrad, Wendy Cope, Daniel Defoe, Anita Desai, Charles Dickens, Emily Dickinson, Berlie Doherty, John Donne, Keith Douglas, Arthur Conan Doyle, John Dryden, Douglas Dunn, George Eliot, T. S. Eliot, U. A. Fanthorpe, Henry Fielding, E. M. Forster, Brian Friel, Robert Frost, Athol Fugard, Elizabeth Gaskell, Graham Greene, William Golding, Oliver Goldsmith, Nadine Gordimer ,Thomas Gray, Willis Hall, Sophie Hannah, Thomas Hardy, David Hare, Tony Harrison, Seamus Heaney, Ernest Hemingway, George Herbert, Robert Herrick, Susan Hill, Gerard Manley Hopkins, Ted Hughes, Aldous Huxley, Elizabeth Jennings, Lloyd Jones, James Joyce, Henry James, Dennis Kelly, John Keats, Philip Larkin, D. H. Lawrence, Harper Lee, Laurie Lee, Doris Lessing, Joan Lingard, Liz Lochhead, Robert Lowell, Katherine Mansfield, Christopher Marlowe, Andrew Marvell, Arthur Miller, John Milton, Arthur Miller, Adrian Mitchell, Edwin Muir, Les Murray, R. K. Narayan, Bill Naughton, Grace Nichols, Ridjal Noor, Sean O'Casey, George Orwell, Wilfred Owen, Dorothy Parker, Brian Patten, Doris Pilkington, Harold Pinter, Sylvia Plath, Alexander Pope, J. B. Priestley, H. H. Richardson, Christina Rossetti, Willie Russell, Diane Samuels, Peter Shaffer, William Shakespeare, Jo Shapcott, G. B. Shaw, Owen Sheers, Mary Shelley, Percy Bysshe Shelley, R. B. Sheridan, R. C. Sherriff, Stevie Smith, Alan Sillitoe, Joe Simpson, Wole Soyinka, Muriel Spark, Edmund Spenser, John Steinbeck, Robert Louis Stevenson, Jonathan Swift, Rabindranath Tagore, Mildred Taylor, Alfred Lord Tennyson, Ngugi wa

Thiong'o, Dylan Thomas, Edward Thomas, R. S. Thomas, William Trevor, Anthony Trollope, Henry Vaughan, Derek Walcott, Evelyn Waugh, H. G. Wells, Arnold Wesker, Robert Westall, Oscar Wilde, Tennessee Williams, William Wordsworth, Sir Thomas Wyatt and W. B. Yeats.

3. Literary terms

Audit your knowledge of the following list of literary terms. If you do not understand some of these terms and would not be confident explaining them to a class of students then you need to write out their definitions with examples.

An excellent text to use is *A Glossary of Literary Terms* by M. H. Abrams and Geoffrey Harpham (2011).

alienation effect	dramatic monologue	malapropism
allegory	dystopia	marxist
alliteration	elegy	melodrama
allusion	emotive	memoir
ambience	empathy	metaphor
ambiguity	enjambement	metaphysical
anachronism	epic	meter
anecdote	epigram	mock
antithesis	epithet	monologue
aphorism	euphemism	morpheme
archetype	fable	myth
assonance	farce	narrative
autobiography	feminist	narrator
ballad	figurative	new criticism
bathos	first-person	novella
biography	form	octave
blank verse	genre	ode
burlesque	haiku	omniscient
caesura	hamartia	oxymoron
canon	hermeneutics	parable
catharsis	hubris	paradox
comic relief	humanism	parody
conceit (metaphysical)	hyperbole	pastoral
connotation	iambic pentameter	pathos
courtly love	imagery	pentameter
diachronic	irony	persona
diction	journal	personification
didactic	lampoon	phoneme
dramatic irony	lyric	picaresque

prose

protagonist

pun

refrain

rhetoric

rhyme

rhythm

romantic

sarcasm

satire

scenario

semantics

semiotics

sestet

sign

simile

soliloquy

sonnet

stanza

stress (syllable)

style

subplot

surrealism

suspense

symbol

synchronic

syntax

tale

theme

thesis

third-person

tone

touchstone

tragedy

tragic flaw

tragic hero

tragic irony

tragicomedy

travesty

utopia

verse

wit

Appendix 2: UK Standards for teachers (2012)

Teachers make the education of their pupils their first concern, and are accountable for achieving the highest possible standards in work and conduct. Teachers act with honesty and integrity; have strong subject knowledge, keep their knowledge and skills as teachers up-to-date and are self-critical; forge positive professional relationships; and work with parents in the best interests of their pupils.

PART ONE: TEACHING

TS1 A teacher must set high expectations which inspire, motivate and challenge pupils

- Establish a safe and stimulating environment for pupils, rooted in mutual respect
- Set goals that stretch and challenge pupils of all backgrounds, abilities and dispositions
- Demonstrate consistently the positive attitudes, values and behaviour which are expected of pupils.

TS2 Promote good progress and outcomes by pupils

- Be accountable for pupils' attainment, progress and outcomes
- Plan teaching to build on pupils' capabilities and prior knowledge
- Guide pupils to reflect on the progress they have made and their emerging needs
- Demonstrate knowledge and understanding of how pupils learn and how this impacts on teaching
- Encourage pupils to take a responsible and conscientious attitude to their own work and study.

TS3 Demonstrate good subject and curriculum knowledge

- Have a secure knowledge of the relevant subject(s) and curriculum areas, foster and maintain pupils' interest in the subject, and address misunderstandings

- Demonstrate a critical understanding of developments in the subject and curriculum areas, and promote the value of scholarship
- Demonstrate an understanding of and take responsibility for promoting high standards of literacy, articulacy and the correct use of standard English, whatever the teacher's specialist subject
- If teaching early reading, demonstrate a clear understanding of systematic synthetic phonics
- If teaching early mathematics, demonstrate a clear understanding of appropriate teaching strategies.

TS4 Plan and teach well-structured lessons

- Impart knowledge and develop understanding through effective use of lesson time
- Promote a love of learning and children's intellectual curiosity
- Set homework and plan other out-of-class activities to consolidate and extend the knowledge and understanding pupils have acquired
- Reflect systematically on the effectiveness of lessons and approaches to teaching
- Contribute to the design and provision of an engaging curriculum within the relevant subject area(s).

TS5 Adapt teaching to respond to the strengths and needs of all pupils

- Know when and how to differentiate appropriately, using approaches which enable pupils to be taught effectively
- Have a secure understanding of how a range of factors can inhibit pupils' ability to learn, and how best to overcome these
- Demonstrate an awareness of the physical, social and intellectual development of children, and know how to adapt teaching to support pupils' education at different stages of development
- Have a clear understanding of the needs of all pupils, including those with special educational needs; those of high ability; those with English as an additional language; those with disabilities; and be able to use and evaluate distinctive teaching approaches to engage and support them.

TS6 Make accurate and productive use of assessment

- Know and understand how to assess the relevant subject and curriculum areas, including statutory assessment requirements
- Make use of formative and summative assessment to secure pupils' progress
- Use relevant data to monitor progress, set targets and plan subsequent lessons
- Give pupils regular feedback, both orally and through accurate marking, and encourage pupils to respond to the feedback.

TS7 Manage behaviour effectively to ensure a good and safe learning environment

Have clear rules and routines for behaviour in classrooms, and take responsibility for promoting good and courteous behaviour both in classrooms and around the school, in accordance with the school's behaviour policy

- Have high expectations of behaviour, and establish a framework for discipline with a range of strategies, using praise, sanctions and rewards consistently and fairly
- Manage classes effectively, using approaches which are appropriate to pupils' needs in order to involve and motivate them
- Maintain good relationships with pupils, exercise appropriate authority, and act decisively when necessary.

TS8 Fulfil wider professional responsibilities

- Make a positive contribution to the wider life and ethos of the school
- Develop effective professional relationships with colleagues, knowing how and when to draw on advice and specialist support
- Deploy support staff effectively
- Take responsibility for improving teaching through appropriate professional development, responding to advice and feedback from colleagues
- Communicate effectively with parents with regard to pupils' achievements and well-being.

PART TWO: PERSONAL AND PROFESSIONAL CONDUCT

A teacher is expected to demonstrate consistently high standards of personal and professional conduct. The following statements define the behaviour and attitudes which set the required standard for conduct throughout a teacher's career.

A. Teachers uphold public trust in the profession and maintain high standards of ethics and behaviour, within and outside school, by:

- Treating pupils with dignity, building relationships rooted in mutual respect and at all times observing proper boundaries appropriate to a teacher's professional position
- Having regard for the need to safeguard pupils' well-being, in accordance with statutory provisions
- Showing tolerance of and respect for the rights of others
- Not undermining fundamental British values, including democracy, the rule of law, individual liberty and mutual respect, and tolerance of those with different faiths and beliefs
- Ensuring that personal beliefs are not expressed in ways which exploit pupils' vulnerability or might lead them to break the law.

B. Teachers must have proper and professional regard for the ethos, policies and practices of the school in which they teach, and maintain high standards in their own attendance and punctuality.

C. Teachers must have an understanding of, and always act within, the statutory frameworks which set out their professional duties and responsibilities.

		Strands within Teachers' Standards				
		1	2	3	4	5
Teachers' Standards — Part 1: Teaching	TS1	Chapters 1, 2, 5, 6, 9, 10, 11, 12	Chapters 1, 5, 6, 10, 11, 12	Chapters 1, 2, 5, 6, 7, 8		
	TS2	Chapter 1	Chapter 1	Chapter 6	Chapters 9, 10, 11, 12	Chapters 2, 6
	TS3	Chapter 2	Chapters 1, 9, 10, 11	Chapters 6, 7, 8	Chapters 6, 7, 8	
	TS4	Chapters 2, 7	Chapter 2	Chapters 7, 8	Chapters 3, 4	Chapters 1, 2, 5, 9, 10, 11
	TS5	Chapter 3	Chapter 2	Chapters 7, 9	Chapters 3, 10,	
	TS6	Chapter 3	Chapter 3	Chapter 3	Chapters 2, 3	
	TS7	Chapters 2, 5, 6, 7, 8	Chapters 2, 6, 7, 8	Chapters 2, 6	Chapters 1, 2, 6	
	TS8	Chapters 2, 4	Chapters 3, 4	Chapters 3, 4	Chapters 4, 8, 12	Chapters 2, 3, 9, 10, 11, 12
Part 2: Personal and professional conduct	A	Chapters 2, 3, 4, 5, 6, 10, 11	Chapters 5, 6, 10, 11	Chapters 5, 9, 10, 11	Chapters 5, 7, 8, 9, 11, 12	Chapters 3, 5, 7, 8, 9, 11, 12
	B	Chapters 1, 7, 8, 12				
	C	Chapters 7, 8, 12				

UK Teachers' Standards addressed in each chapter

Chapter 1: TS1 (1,2,3), TS2 (1,2), TS3 (2), TS4 (5), TS5 (4), TS7 (4); Pt2 B

Chapter 2: TS1 (1,3), TS2 (5), TS3 (1), TS4 (1,2,5), TS5 (2), TS6 (4), TS7 (1,2,3,4), TS8 (1,5); Pt2 A(1)

Chapter 3: TS3 (2,3), TS4 (4), TS5 (1,4), TS6 (1,2,3,4), TS8 (5); Pt2 A (1,5)

Chapter 4: TS3 (2,3), TS4 (4), TS8 (1,4); Pt2 A (1)

Chapter 5: TS1 (1,2,3), TS4 (5), TS7 (1); Pt2 A (1,2,3,4,5)

Chapter 6: TS1 (1,2,3), TS2 (3,5), TS3 (3,4), TS7 (1,2,3,4); Pt2 A (1,2)

Chapter 7: TS1 (3), TS3 (3,4), TS4 (1,3), TS5 (3), TS7 (1,2); Pt2 A (4,5), B, C

Chapter 8: TS1 (3), TS3 (3,4), TS4 (3), TS7 (1,2), TS8 (4); Pt2 A (4,5), B, C

Chapter 9: TS1 (1), TS2 (4), TS3 (2), TS4 (5), TS5 (3), TS8 (5); Pt2 A (3,4,5)

Chapter 10: TS1 (1,2), TS2 (4), TS3 (2), TS4 (5), TS5 (4), TS8 (5); Pt2 A (1,2,3)

Chapter 11: TS1 (1,2), TS2 (4), TS3 (2), TS4 (5), TS8 (5); Pt2 A (1,2,3,4,5)

Chapter 12: TS1 (1,2), TS2 (4), TS8 (4,5); Pt2 A (4,5), B, C

Bibliography

Abrams, M. H. (1958/1953), *The Mirror and the Lamp: Romantic Theory and the Critical Tradition*. New York: Norton.

Abrams, M. H. and Harpham, G. G. (2011), A *Glossary of Literary Terms*. 10th edn. Boston: Wadsworth.

Adamson, A. (2005), *The Lion, The Witch and The Wardrobe*. Walt Disney/ Walden Media.

Albright, J. (2002), 'Being in Authority, Being an Authority: Disrupting Students'/ Teachers' Practices in Literacy Education', *Teaching Education*, 13(3), 289–303.

Almond, B. (2010), 'Education for Tolerance: Cultural Difference and Family Values', *Journal of Moral Education*, 39(2), 131–43.

Alter, E. and Kermode, F. (eds) (1987), *The Literary Guide to the Bible*. Cambridge, MA: Harvard University Press.

Altrichter, H., Posch, P. and Somekh, B. (1993), *Teachers Investigate their Work. An Introduction to the Methods of Action Research*. London: Routledge.

AQA (2010), *Digital Anthology*. Available online at: www.anthology.aqa.org.uk.

Aristotle (1987), *The Nicomachean Ethics*. J. E. C. Weldon (trans.). New York: Prometheus Books.

— (2013), *Metaphysics*. W. D. Ross (trans.). Adelaide: University of Adelaide, eBooks@Adelaide.

Arnold, M. (1908), 'General Report for the Year 1880', in F. S. Marvin (ed.). *Reports on Elementary Schools, 1852–1882*. London: HMSO, pp. 200–17.

— (1988/1879), 'Preface to Wordsworth's Poems', in R. Selden (ed.), *The Theory of Criticism – From Plato to the Present*. London: Longman, 498–500.

Arthur, J. (2003), *Education with Character*. London: Routledge.

— (2005), 'The Re-emergence of Character Education in British Education Policy', *British Journal of Educational Studies*, 53(3), 239–54.

— (2010), *Of Good Character: Exploring Virtues and Values in 3–25 Year-olds*. Exeter/Charlottesville, VA: Imprint Academic.

Atkinson, J. (1995), 'How Do We Teach Pre-twentieth Century Literature?' in R. Protherough and P. R. King (eds), *The Challenge of English in the National Curriculum*. London: Routledge, pp. 48–64.

Auden, W. H. (1962), *The Dyer's Hand and Other Essays*. London: Faber and Faber.

— (1968), *Secondary Worlds*. New York: Random House.

Banks, C. A., Cortés, C. E., Hahn, C. L., Merryfield, M. M., Moodley, K. A., Murphy-Shigematsu, S., Osler, A., Park, C. and Parker, W. C. (2005), *Democracy and Diversity: Principles and Concepts for Educating Citizens in a Global Age*. Seattle, WA: Center for Multicultural Education, College of Education, University of Washington. Available online at: http://depts. washington.edu/centerme/DemDiv.pdf, accessed 28 December 2007.

Barnes, D. and Todd, F. (1977), *Communication & Learning in Small Groups*. London: Routledge & Kegan Paul.

Barnes, L. P. (2010), 'Enlightenment's Wake: Religion and Education at the Close of the Modern Age', in K. Engebretson, M. de Souza, G. Durka and L. Gearon (eds), *International Handbook of Inter-religious Education, Part 1: The Philosophical and Theoretical Aspects of Inter-religious Education*. Dordrecht: Springer, pp. 25–40.

— (2014), *Education, Religion and Diversity. Developing a New Model of Religious Education*. Oxon/New York: Routledge.

Barnes, L. P. and Wright, A. (2007), 'Romanticism, Representations of Religion and Critical Religious Education', *British Journal of Religious Education*, 28(1), 65–77.

BBC 'State Multiculturalism Has Failed, Says David Cameron', http://www.bbc.co.uk/news/uk-politics-12371994, accessed 5 December 2011.

Beadle, P. (2010), *How to Teach*. Carmarthen, Wales: Crown House Publishing.

Benton, M. (1995), 'From "A Rake's Progress" to "Rosie's Walk": Lessons in Aesthetic Reading', *Journal of Aesthetic Education*, 29(1), 33–46.

Benton, M. and Benton, P. (1998), *New Touchstones 14–16*. London: Hodder and Stoughton.

Benton, M., Teasey, J., Bell, R. and Hurst, K. (1988), *Young Readers Responding to Poems*. London: Routledge.

Berkowitz, M. and Bier, M. (2004), 'Research-based Character Education', *The Annals of the American Academy of Political and Social Science*, 591(1), 72–85.

Bible, The (1611), *Authorised Version*. Cambridge, MA: Cambridge University Press.

Biesta, G. and Lawy, R. (2006), 'From Teaching Citizenship to Learning Democracy: Overcoming Individualism in Research, Policy and Practice', *Cambridge Journal of Education*, 36(1), 63–79.

Black, P. and Wiliam, D. (1998), *Inside the Black Box: Raising Standards through Classroom Assessment*. London: KCL.

Black, P., Harrison, C., Lee, C., Marshall, B. and Wiliam, D. (2003), *Assessment for Learning: Putting It Into Practice*. Maidenhead: Open University Press.

Blake, N. (1996), 'Against Spiritual Education', *Oxford Review of Education*, 22(4), 443–56.

Bloom, A. (1987), *The Closing of the American Mind*. London: Penguin.

Bohlin, K. (2005), *Teaching Character Education through Literature*. London and New York: RoutledgeFalmer.

— (2014), 'Virtue – An Argument Worth Rehearsing', *Journal of Character Education*, 10(1), 53–9.

Booth, W. C. (2005), 'American Foreword', in K. E. Bohlin, *Teaching Character Education through Literature. Awakening the Moral Imagination in Secondary Classrooms*. London/New York: RoutledgeFalmer, pp. ix–x.

Bottery, M. (2003), 'The End of Citizenship? The Nation State, Threats to Its Legitimacy and Citizenship Education in the Twenty-first Century', *Cambridge Journal of Education*, 33(1), 101–22.

Bousted, M. (2000), 'Rhetoric and Practice in English Teaching', *English in Education*, 34(1), 12–23.

Brass, J. (2011), 'Sunday Schools and English Teaching: Re-reading Ian Hunter and the Emergence of "English" in the United States', *Changing English*, 18(4), 337–49.

Brown, G. (2007), 'We Need a United Kingdom', *Daily Telegraph*, 13 January.

Bryant, I. (1996), 'Action Research and Reflective Practice', in D. Scott and R. Usher (eds), *Understanding Educational Research*. London: Routledge, pp. 106–19.

Burke, K. J. and Segall, A. (2011), 'Christianity and its Legacy in Education', *Journal of Curriculum Studies*, 43(5), 631–58.

Burtonwood, N. (2000), 'Must Liberal Support for Separate Schools be Subject to a Condition of Individual Autonomy?' *British Journal of Educational Studies*, 48(3), 269–84.

Callan E. (1997), *Creating Citizens*. Oxford: Oxford University Press.

Cameron, D. (2011), 'PM's Speech at Munich Security Conference 5th February 2011', http://www.number10.gov.uk/news/pms-speech-at-munich-security-conference/, accessed 5 December.

Cameron, L. (2003), *Writing in English as an Additional Language at Key Stage 4 and Post 16*. OFSTED (HMI 1094).

Canter, L. (2010), *Assertive Discipline: Positive Behavior Management for Today's Classroom*. 4th edn. Bloomington, IN: Solution Tree.

Canter, L. and Canter, M. (2001), *Assertive Discipline: Positive Behavior Management for Today's Classroom*. 3rd edn. Bloomington, IN: Solution Tree.

Carr, D. (2004), 'On the Grammar of Religious Discourse and Education', *Zeitschrift fur Erziehungswissenschaft*, 7(3), 380–93.

— (2007), 'Character in Teaching', *British Journal of Educational Studies*, 55(4), 369–89.

Carr, W. (1993), What is an Educational Practice? in M. Hammersley (ed.), *Educational Research: Current Issues*. London: Open University/Paul Chapman Publishing, 160–76.

Chiang, H. M. and Maslow, A. (eds) (1977), *The Healthy Personality: Readings*. London: Van Nostrand.

Chubb, P. (1902), *The Teaching of English in the Elementary School and the Secondary School*. New York: Macmillan.

Cicero, M. T. (1942), *De Oratore*, E. W. Sutton (trans.). Cambridge, MA: Harvard University Press.

Clarke, S., Dickinson, P. and Westbrook, J. (eds) (2010), *The Complete Guide to Becoming a English Teacher*. London: Sage Publishing.

Clouser, R. (1999), *Knowing with the Heart – Religious Experience and Belief in God*. Downers Grove, Illinois: IVP Downers Grove.

— (2005), *The Myth of Religious Neutrality. An Essay on the Hidden Role of Religious Belief in Theories* (rev. edn). Notre Dame, IN: University of Notre Dame Press.

Cohen, L., Mannion, L. and Morrison, K. (2000), *Research Methods in Education*. 5th edn. London: RoutledgeFalmer.

Copley (2005), *Indoctrination, Education and God*. London: SPCK.

Cremin, H. (2011), 'Reading Teachers/Teaching Reading – Why Teachers Who Read Make Good Teachers of Reading', *English Drama and Media*, 19, 11–18.

Crick, B. (2007), 'Citizenship: The Political and the Democratic', *British Journal of Educational Studies*, 55(3), 235–48.

— (2000), *Essays on Citizenship*. London: Continuum.

Cross Reference Project, Crossref-it.info.

Crystal, D. (2010), *Begat The King James Bible & the English Language*. Oxford: Oxford University Press.

Darwin, C. (1859/1968), *On the Origin of Species by Means of Natural Selection. The Preservation of Favoured Races in the Struggle for Life.* Harmondsworth: Penguin.

— (1887), 'Letter to W. Graham, July 3, 1881' https://darwinproject.ac.uk/letter/entry-13230, accessed 14 July 2014.

Davies, C. (1996), *What is English Teaching?* Buckingham: Open University Press.

Davies, I. (2012), 'Perspectives on Citizenship Education', in J. Arthur and H. Cremin (eds), *Debates in Citizenship Education.* Oxon: Routledge, pp. 32–40.

Davies, I., Gorard, S. and McGuinn, N. (2005), 'Citizenship Education and Character Education: Similarities and Contrasts', *British Journal of Educational Studies*, 53(3), 341–58.

Davis, M. (1992), 'Censorship Update', *The Council Chronicle* [National Council of Teachers of English], 2(1), 13.

Davison, J. (2005), 'British Foreword', in K. E. Bohlin, *Teaching Character Education through Literature. Awakening the Moral Imagination in Secondary Classrooms.* London/New York: RoutledgeFalmer, pp. xi–xii.

Day, C. (1998), 'Working with the Different Selves of Teachers: Beyond Comfortable Collaboration', *Educational Action Research*, 6(2), 255–74.

Dewey, J. (1934), *Art as Experience.* New York: Perigee Books.

— (2002/1966), *Democracy and Education.* New York: Macmillan.

DES (1986), *English from 5 to 16: Second Edition (Incorporating Responses).* London: HMSO.

DfE (2011), 'The National Strategies APP in English', *Teaching and Learning Resources* (http://webarchive.nationalarchives.gov.uk/20110809091832/http://teachingandlearningresources.org.uk/secondary/english/app-english).

— (2012), *Teachers' Standards – Guidance for School Leaders, School Staff and Governing Bodies.* London: HMSO.

— (2013a), *National Curriculum in England: English Programme of Study – Key Stage 3.* London: HMSO, https://www.gov.uk/government/uploads/system/uploads/attachment_data/file/244215/SECONDARY_national_curriculum_-_English2.pdf.

— (2013b), *National Curriculum in England: English Programme of Study – Key Stage 4.* London: HMSO, https://www.gov.uk/government/uploads/system/uploads/attachment_data/file/331877/KS4_English_PoS_FINAL_170714.pdf.

— (2013c), 'Glossary for the Programmes of Study for English', https://www.gov.uk/government/uploads/system/uploads/attachment_data/file/244216/English_Glossary.pdf.

— (2014), *Statutory Guidance National Curriculum in England: English Programmes of Study.* https://www.gov.uk/government/publications/national-curriculum-in-england-english-programmes-of-study/national-curriculum-in-england-english-programmes-of-study, updated 16 July 2014.

DfEE (2001), *Key Stage 3 National Strategy: Framework for Teaching English: Years 7, 8 and 9.* London: HMSO.

DfES (2002), *Access and Engagement in English.* London: DfES Publications.

— (2004), *Literacy in Citizenship* (ref: 0258–2004). London: HMSO.

Dickens, A. G. (1982/1959), *Lollards and Protestants in the Diocese of York.* London: The Hambledon Press.

Donne, J. (1987/1627), 'Meditation XVII', in A. Raspa (ed.), *John Donne Devotions upon Emergent Occasions.* Oxford/New York: Oxford University Press, pp. 86–7.

Dooyeweerd, H. (1955), *A Critique of Theoretical Thought*. Philadelphia, PA: Presbyterian and Reformed.

Doug, R. (2011), 'The British Schools' National Curriculum: English and the Politics of Teaching Poetry from "different cultures and traditions"', *Journal of Curriculum Studies*, 43(4), 439–56.

Dymoke, S. (2003), *Drafting and Assessing Poetry*. London: Paul Chapman Publishing.

Dymoke, S. and Hughes, J. (2009), 'Using a Poetry Wiki: How Can the Medium F Support Pre-service Teachers of English in their Professional Learning about Writing Poetry and Teaching Poetry Writing in a Digital Age', *English Teaching: Practice and Critique*, 8(3), 91–106.

Easthope, A. (1991), *Literary into Cultural Studies*. London: Routledge.

Education Reform Act 1988 (London: HMSO).

Education Schools Act 1992 (London: HMSO).

Edwards, D. and Mercer, N. (1987), Common Knowledge. London: Routledge.

Edwards, J. R. (1988), 'A Review of the Language Trap', in N. Mercer (ed.), *Language and Literacy from an Educational Perspective, Vol.1: Language Studies*. Milton Keynes: Open University Press, pp. 190–8.

Eisner, E. (2002), *The Educational Imagination*. New Jersey: Merrill Prentice Hall.

Eliot, G. (1967/1876), 'Letter to Frederic Harrison', in F. R. Leavis, *Introduction to Silas Marner*. Harmondsworth: Penguin, pp. 9–10.

Eliot, T. S. (1932), *Selected Essays, 1917–1932*. London: Faber and Faber.

— (1935), 'Religion and Literature', *Selected Essays*. London: Faber and Faber.

Elliott, J. (1991), *Action Research for Educational Change*. Buckingham: Open University Press.

Ellis, V. (2011), 'Editorial: The Rhetorics of English in Education', *Changing English*, 18(3), 245–9.

Elshtain, J. B. (2008), 'The Abolition of Man: C. S. Lewis's Prescience Concerning Things to Come', in D. Baggett, Gary R. Habermas, and Jerry L. Walls (eds), *C. S. Lewis as Philosopher – Truth, Goodness and Beauty*. Downers Grove, IL: IVP Academic, pp. 85–94.

Evans, Dr R. I. (1968), *B. F. Skinner – the Man and His Ideas*. New York: E. P. Dutton & Co.

Fish, S. (1980), *Is There a Text in This Class? The Authority of Interpretive Communities*. Cambridge, MA: Harvard University Press.

Fox, G. (1993/1664), *Christ the Light of the World*. Gloucester, UK: George Fox Fund, New Foundation Fellowship.

Francis, L. J. (2000), 'Who Reads the Bible? A Study among 13–15 Year Olds', *British Journal of Religious Education*, 22(3), 165–72.

Friere, P. and Macedo, D. (1987), *Literacy: Reading the Word and World*. South Hadley, MA: Bergin and Garvey.

Gabler, M. and Gabler, N. (1982), 'Mind Control through Textbooks', *Phi Delta Kappan*, 64(2), 96–7.

Gallagher, S. V. and Lundin, R. (1989), *Literature through the Eyes of Faith*. San Francisco, CA: HarperCollins.

Gaulthier, C. (1992), 'Between Crystal and Smoke or, How to Miss the Point in the Debate about Action Research', in W. F. Pinar and W. M. Reynolds (eds), *Understanding Curriculum as Phenomenological and Deconstructed Text*. New York: Teachers College Press, pp. 184–94.

Gearon, L. and Brown, M. (2003), 'Active Participation in Citizenship', in L. Gearon (ed.), *Learning to Teach Citizenship in the Secondary School*. London and New York: RoutledgeFalmer, pp. 203–24.

Ghandhi, M. (1958), *The Last Phase Vol II*. Ahmedabad, India: Navajivan Publishing House.

Goodwyn, A. (2011), *The Expert Teacher of English*. Abingdon, UK: Routledge.

Goodwyn, A. and Findlay, K. (1999), 'The Cox Models Revisited: English Teachers' Views of their Subject and the National Curriculum', *English in Education*, 33(2), 19–31.

Graham, G. (1994), 'Liberal vs Radical Feminism Revisited', *Journal of Applied Philosophy*, 11(2), 155–70.

Gray, J. (1983), *Mill on Liberty: A Defence*. London: Routledge & Kegan Paul.

Green, K. (1999), 'Defining the Field of Literature in Action Research: A Personal Approach', *Educational Action Research*, 7, 105–23.

Green, R. L. and Hooper, W. (1979/1974), *C. S. Lewis: A Biography*. Glasgow: Fount Paperback.

Grimes, M. L. and Belote, S. B. (1994), 'Reclaiming the Canon: The Case for Adolescent Literature', in M. Hayhoe and S. Parker (eds), *Who owns English?* Buckingham and Philadelphia, PA: Open University Press, pp. 85–9.

Grove, N. (1998), *Literature for All – Developing Literature in the Curriculum for Pupils with Special Educational Needs*. London: David Fulton.

Guardian,The: Doward, J. (2011), 'David Cameron's Attack on Multiculturalism Divides the Coalition', *The Guardian*, originally in The Observer, Sunday 6 February http://www.guardian.co.uk/politics/2011/feb/05/david-cameron-attack-multiculturalism-coalition.

Hábl, J. (2011), 'Character Formation: A Forgotten Theme in Comenius's Didactics', *Journal of Education and Christian Belief*, 15(2), 141–52.

Hall, K. (2003), *Listening to Stephen Read – Multiple Perspectives on Literacy*. Buckingham: Open University Press.

Halliday, M. (1978), *Language as Social Semiotic*. London: Edward Arnold.

Halstead, J. M. (1995), 'Voluntary Apartheid? Problems of Schooling for Religious and Other Minorities in Democratic Societies', *Journal of the Philosophy of Education*, 29(2), 257–72.

— (1999), 'Teaching about Homosexuality: A Response to John Beck', *Cambridge Journal of Education*, 29(1), 131–6.

— (2004), 'An Islamic Concept of Education', *Comparative Education*, 40(4), 517–29.

— (2007), 'Editorial – Islamic Values: A Distinctive Framework for Moral Education?', *Journal of Moral Education*, 36(3), 283–96.

— (2011), 'Is Moral Education Working? Extracts from the Diary of a Twenty-first Century Moral Educator', *Journal of Moral Education*, 40(3), 339–47.

Halstead, J. M. and Pike, M. A. (2006), *Citizenship and Moral Education: Values in Action*, London and New York: Routledge.

Hand, M. (2006), 'Against Autonomy as an Educational Aim', *Oxford Review of Education*, 32(4), 535–50.

Harrison, C. (2004), *Understanding Reading Development*. London: Sage.

Hattersley, R. (1998), 'Reading to Make us Glad', in B. Cox (ed.), *Literacy is Not Enough – Essays on the Importance of Reading*. Manchester: Manchester University Press, pp. 50–2.

Hawkins, M. (2006), *Making the Grade*. media-education.gov.uk.

Hay, D. and Nye, R. (2006), *The Spirit of the Child.* London: Jessica Kingsley.

Haydon, G. (1997), *Teaching about Values: A New Approach.* London: Cassell.

Heater, D. (1999), *What is Citizenship?* Cambridge, MA: Polity Press.

Hegel, G. W. F. (1997), 'Introduction to Aesthetics', in D. E. Cooper (ed.), *Aesthetics: The Classic Readings.* Oxford: Blackwell, pp. 137–49.

Hella, E. and Wright, A. (2009), 'Learning "about" and "from" Religion: Phenomenography, the Variation Theory of Learning and Religious Education in Finland and the UK', *British Journal of Religious Education,* 31(1), 53–64.

Higgins, C. (2010), 'Work and Flourishing: Williams' Critique of Morality and Its Implications for Professional Ethics', *Journal of Philosophy of Education,* 44(2–3), 211–36.

Hirsch, Jr, E. D. (1987), *Cultural Literacy: What Every American Needs to Know.* Boston, MA: Houghton Mittlin.

Holbrook, D. (1964), *English for the Rejected.* Cambridge, MA: Cambridge University Press.

— (1979), *English for Meaning.* Windsor, UK: NFER.

Honey, J. (1988), 'The Language Trap: Race, Class and Standard English in British Schools', in N. Mercer (ed.), *Language and Literacy from an Educational Perspective, Vol.1: Language Studies.* Milton Keynes: Open University Press, pp. 163–89.

Hook, P. and Vass, A. (2011), *Behaviour Management Pocketbook.* Hampshire: Teachers' Pocketbooks.

Hooper, W. (1996), *C. S. Lewis: A Complete Guide to his Life and Works.* New York: Harper San Francisco.

Hourd, M. (1949), *The Education of the Poetic Spirit.* London: Heinemann.

Huebner, D. E. (1999/1962), 'The Art of Teaching', in V. Hills (ed.), *The Lure of the Transcendent.* New Jersey: Laurence Erlbaum, pp. 23–35.

Hunter, J. D. (2000), *The Death of Character.* New York: Basic Books.

Iser, W. (1971), 'Indeterminacy and the Reader's Response in Prose Fiction', in J. Hillis Miller (ed.), *Aspects of Narrative.* Columbia: Columbia University Press, pp. 3–30.

— (1978), *The Act of Reading: A Theory of Aesthetic Response.* Baltimore, MD: Johns Hopkins University Press.

Jackson, R. (2003), 'Should the State Fund Faith-based Schools? A Review of the Arguments', *British Journal of Religious Education,* 25(2), 89–102.

Jacobs, A. (2001), *A Theology of Reading: The Hermeneutics of Love.* Boulder, CO: Westview Press.

Jaeger, W. (1960), *The Theology of the Early Greek Philosophers.* New York: Oxford University Press.

James, W. (1929), *The Varieties of Religious Experience.* New York: Longmans.

Jarvis, F. W. (1993), 'Beyond Ethics', *Journal of Education,* 175(2), 59–74.

Jasper, D. (1999), 'How Can We Read the Bible?', in L. Gearon (ed.), *English Literature, Theology and the Curriculum.* London: Cassell, pp. 9–26.

Jauss, H. R. (1982), *Toward an Aesthetic of Reception.* Minneapolis, MN: University of Minnesota Press.

Johnstone, P. (2011), 'English and the Survival of Multiculturalism: Teaching "Writing from Different Cultures and Traditions"', *Changing English,* 18(2), 125–33.

Jones, C. (ed.) (2009), *A Short History of Parliament: England, Great Britain, the United Kingdom, Ireland and Scotland*. Woodbridge: The Boydell Press.

Kant, I. (2003), *Groundwork for the Metaphysics of Morals*. A. W. Wood (ed. and trans.). New Haven, CT: Yale University Press.

King, A. and Ketley, M. (1939), *The Control of Language: A Critical Approach to Reading and Writing*. London: Longmans, Green & Co.

Koch, R. and Smith, C. (2006), *Suicide of the West*. London and New York: Continuum.

Kristjánsson, K. (2013), 'Ten Myths about Character, Virtue and Virtue Education – Plus Three Well-Founded Misgivings', *British Journal of Educational Studies*, 61(3), 269–87.

Küng, H. (1986), *Christianity and the World Religions*. Gorden City, NY: Doubleday.

Kymlicka, W. (2003), 'Two Dilemmas of Citizenship Education in Pluralist Societies', in A. Lockyer, B. Crick, and J. Annette (eds), *Education for Democratic Citizenship: Issues of Theory and Practice*. Aldershot: Ashgate, pp. 47–63.

Langer, S. (1957), *Problems of Art – Ten Philosophical Lectures*. London: Routledge and Kegan Paul.

Leavis, F. R. (1948), *The Great Tradition*. London: Chatto and Windus.

Letter to William Graham, Down, 3 July 1881, in F. Darwin (ed.), *The Life and Letters of Charles Darwin, Including an Autobiographical Chapter,*. London: John Murray, 1887, 1, 315–16.

Letter of 100 academics to Michael Gove (20 March 2013), 'The Danger of the New National Curriculum Proposals – Michael Gove Has Prioritised Facts over Creativity', *The Telegraph*, telegraph.co.uk, accessed online 14 February 2014.

Lewis, C. S. (1950), *The Literary Impact of The Authorised Version*. The Ethel M. Wood Lecture delivered before the University of London on 20 March 1950. (London: The Athlone Press).

— (1960/1947), *Miracles*. London: Collins/Fontana.

— (1960), *Studies in Words*. Cambridge, MA: Cambridge University Press.

— (1967a), 'On Ethics', in W. Hooper (ed.), *Christian Reflections*. London: Geoffrey Bles, pp. 44–56.

— (1967b), 'The Poison of Subjectivism', in W. Hooper (ed.), *Christian Reflections*. London: Geoffrey Bles, pp. 72–81.

— (1971/1964), *The Discarded Image. An Introduction to Medieval and Renaissance Literature*. Cambridge, MA: Cambridge University Press.

— (1978/1943), *The Abolition of Man: Reflections on Education with Special Reference to the Teaching of English in the Upper Forms of Schools*. Glasgow: Fount.

— (1980/1969), 'The Anthropological Approach', in W. Hooper (ed.), *Selected Literary Essays*. Cambridge: Cambridge University Press, pp. 301–11.

— (1981/1952), *Mere Christianity*. London: Fount.

— (1989/1950), *The Lion, the Witch and the Wardrobe*, in *Tales of Narnia*. London: Collins/ WH Smith.

— (1989/1955), *The Magician's Nephew*, in *Tales of Narnia*. London: Collins/ WH Smith.

— (1989/1952), *The Voyage of the Dawn Treader*. London: Collins/Lion.

— (1996/1943), 'Equality', in W. Hooper (ed.), *Compelling Reason – Essays on Ethics and Theology*. London: Fount, pp. 28–31.

— (1996/1944), 'Democratic Education', in W. Hooper (ed.), *Compelling Reason – Essays on Ethics and Theology*. London: Fount, pp. 39–43.

— (1996/1958), 'Willing Slaves of the Welfare State', in W. Hooper (ed.), *Compelling Reason – Essays on Ethics and Theology*. London: Fount, pp. 176–82.

— (2002/1965), 'Screwtape Proposes a Toast', in C. S. Lewis (ed.), *The Screwtape Letters*. New York: Harper Collins, pp. 177–80.

— (2005/1943), *Perelandra* [*Voyage to Venus*]. London: Harper Collins.

— (2005/1945), *That Hideous Strength*. London: Harper Collins.

Lickona, T. (1991), *Educating for Character – How Our Schools Can Teach Respect and Responsibility*. New York: Bantam Books.

— (2004), *Character Matters*. London: Touchstone.

Long, J. (2000), 'Spirituality and the Idea of Transcendence', *International Journal of Children's Spirituality*, 5(2), 147–61.

Loomis, S. and Rodriguez, J. (2009), *C. S. Lewis: A Philosophy of Education*. New York: PalgraveMacmillan.

Luke, A., Carrington, V. and Kapitzke, C. (2003), 'Textbooks and Early Childhood Literacy', in J. Marsh (ed.), *Handbook of Early Childhood Literacy*. London: Falmer, pp. 249–57.

Maag, J. W. (2004), *Behavior Management: From Theoretical Implications to Practical Applications*. 2nd edn. London: Wadsworth/Thompson Learning.

MacIntyre, A. (1990), *Three Rival Versions of Moral Enquiry*. Notre Dame, IN: Notre Dame University Press.

Manguel, A. (1997), *A History of Reading*. New York: Viking.

Marshall, B. (1998), 'English Teachers and the Third Way', in B. Cox (ed.), *Literacy Is Not Enough – Essays on the Importance of Reading*. Manchester: Manchester University Press, pp. 109–15.

— (2000), 'A Rough Guide to English Teachers', *English in Education*, 34(1), 24–41.

Marshall, B. and Wiliam, D. (2006), *English in the Black Box*. London: KCL.

Maslow, A. (1943), 'A Theory of Human Motivation', *Psychological Review*, 50, 370–93.

— (1987/1954), *Motivation and Personality*. New York: Harper Row.

Mathieson, M. (1975), *The Preachers of Culture: A Study of English and Its Teachers*. London: Allen and Unwin.

McCrum, R., Cran,W. and MacNeil, R. (1986), *The Story of English*. New York: Viking Penguin.

McCulloch, R. and Mathieson, M. (1995), *Moral Education through English*. London: David Fulton.

McGrath (2001), *In the Beginning: The Story of the King James Bible and How It Changed a Nation, a Language and a Culture*. London: Hodder and Stoughton.

McGuinn, N. (2004), 'Romantic Words and Worlds', in D. Stevens and N. McGuinn, *The Art of Teaching Secondary English: Innovative and Creative Approaches*. London: Routledge Falmer, pp. 51–72.

McLaughlin, T. H. (1995), 'Liberalism, Education and the Common School', *Journal of Philosophy of Education*, 29(2), 239–55.

— (1999), 'Beyond the Reflective Practitioner', *Educational Philosophy and Theory*, 31(1), 9–25.

— (2000), 'Citizenship Education in England: The Crick Report and beyond', *Journal of Philosophy of Education*, 34(4), 541–70.

McNiff, J., Lomax, P. and Whitehead, J. (1996), *You and Your Action Research Project*. London: Routledge.

McNiff, J. and Whitehead, J. (2006), *All You Need to Know About Action Research*. London: Sage.

Medway, P. (2010), 'English and Enlightenment', *Changing English*, 17(1), 3–12.

Mill, J. S. (1914/1859), 'On Liberty', in J. S. Mill (ed.), *Utilitarianism, Liberty & Representative Government*. London: J. M. Dent & Sons, pp. 65–170.

Milton, J. (1895), in E. E. Morris (ed.), *Tractate of Education*. London: Macmillan, pp. 1–27.

Modood, T. (2007), *Multiculturalism: A Civic Idea*. Cambridge, MA: Polity.

Moorhead, A. (1969), *Darwin and the Beagle*. London: Hamish Hamilton.

Muijs, D. and Reynolds, D. (2001), *Effective Teaching*. London: Paul Chapman Press/Sage.

Mulhall, S. and Swift, A. (1996), *Liberals and Communitarians*. Oxford: Blackwell.

Myhill, D. and Warren, P. (2005), 'Scaffolds or Straightjackets? Critical Moments in Classroom Discourse', *Educational Review*, 57(1), 55–69.

Newbolt, H. (1921), *The Newbolt Report: The Teaching of English in England*. London: HMSO.

Newby, M. (1997), 'Literary Development as Spiritual Development in the Common School', *Journal of Philosophy of Education*, 31(2), 283–94.

Nicolson, A. (2011), 'The Bible of King James', *National Geographic*, 220(6), 36–61.

Nye, R. (1998), 'Relational Consciousness: A Key to Unlocking Psychological Facets of Children's Spirituality', Paper presented at the *International Seminar on Religious Education and Values 13–16 July 1998*.

OFSTED (1994), *Framework for the Inspection of Schools. Revised Edition, May*. London: OFSTED.

— (2004), *Promoting and Evaluating Pupils' Spiritual, Moral, Social and Cultural Development*. London: OFSTED.

— (2012), *Moving English Forward – Action to Raise Standards in English*. London: OFSTED.

O'Malley, R. (1950), 'Measuring the Inner Light', *The Use of English*, 2(1), 20–5.

Osler, A. and Starkey, H. (2005), *Citizenship and Language Learning: International Perspectives*. Stoke on Trent: Trentham.

Palmer, P. (1993), *To Know as We Are Known: A Spirituality of Education*. New York: Harper Collins.

— (1998), *The Courage to Teach – Exploring the Inner Landscape of a Teacher's Life*. San Francisco, CA: Jossey-Bass.

Pascal, B. (1966), *Pensées*, A. J. Krailsheimer (trans.). London: Penguin.

Peng, Y. (2011), *The New Teaching Requirements and the Influence of Assessment: A Case Study of College English Reform in China*. PhD thesis, Huddersfield: Huddersfield University.

Phillips, M. (2002/1996), *All Must Have Prizes*. London: Time Warner Paperback.

Pike, M. A. (1999), 'Reading the Writer Reading the Reader', *Use of English*, 51(1), 41–52.

— (2000a), 'Boys, Poetry and the Individual Talent', *English in Education*, 43(4), 41–55.

— (2000b), 'Keen Readers: Adolescents and Pre-twentieth Century Literature', *Educational Review*, 52(1), 13–28.
— (2000c), 'Pupils' Poetics', *Changing English – Studies in Reading and Culture*, 7(1), 45–54.
— (2000d), 'Spirituality, Morality and Poetry', *International Journal of Children's Spirituality*, 5(2), 177–92.
— (2001), 'Adolescents as Active Readers', in *TOPIC Practical Applications of Research in Education (NFER)*, 26, 1–4.
— (2002a), 'Aesthetic Distance and the Spiritual Journey: Educating for Morally and Spiritually Significant Events across the Art and Literature Curriculum', *International Journal of Children's Spirituality*, 7(1), 9–21.
— (2002b), 'Action Research and English Teaching: Ideology, Pedagogy and Personal Growth', *Educational Action Research*, 10(1), 27–44.
— (2002c), 'The Most Wanted Text in the West: Rewards Offered for Reading the Bible as Literature', *The Use of English*, 54(1), 29–42.
— (2003a), 'The Canon in the Classroom: Students' Experiences of Texts from Other Times', *Journal of Curriculum Studies*, 35(3), 355–70.
— (2003b), 'From Personal to Social Transaction: A Model of Aesthetic Reading', *Journal of Aesthetic Education*, 37(2), 61–72.
— (2003c), 'On Being in English Teaching: A Time for Heidegger?', *Changing English – Studies in Reading and Culture*, 10(1), 91–9.
— (2003d), 'From the Picture to the Diagram? Literacy and the Art of English Teaching', *The Use of English*, 54(3), 211–16.
— (2003e), 'The Bible and the Reader's Response', *Journal of Education and Christian Belief*, 7(1), 37–51.
— (2003f), 'Belief as An Obstacle to Reading: The Case of the Bible?', *Journal of Beliefs and Values – Studies in Religion and Education*, 24(2), 155–63.
— (2004a), *Teaching Secondary English*. London: Sage/Paul Chapman Publishing.
— (2004b), Editorial 'The Spiritual Gift of Reading', *International Journal of Children's Spirituality*, 9(2), 123–6.
— (2004c), 'Well-being through Reading: Drawing upon Literacy and Literature in Children's Spiritual Education', *International Journal of Children's Spirituality*, 9(2), 155–62.
— (2004d), 'Aesthetic Teaching', *Journal of Aesthetic Education*, 38(1), 20–37.
— (2005a), *Teaching Texts from Other Times*. Teacher development Agency report.
— (2005b), 'Reading and Responding to Biblical Texts in a Christian School', in C. Ota and C. Erricker (eds), *Spiritual Education – Literary, Empirical and Pedagogical Approaches*. Brighton: Sussex Academic Press, pp. 189–201.
— (2005c), 'The Challenge of Christian Schooling in a Secular Society', *Journal of Research on Christian Education*, 13(2), 149–66.
— (2005d), 'Citizenship Education and Faith Schools: What Should Children in Christian Schools Understand and Appreciate about a Liberal and Secular Society?', *Journal of Education and Christian Belief*, 9(1), 35–46.
— (2006a), 'Measuring the Inner Light: Assessing Creativity and Spirituality in English', *The Use of English*, 57(3), 214–22.
— (2006b), 'From Beliefs to Skills: The Secularization of Literacy and the Moral Education of Citizens', *Journal of Beliefs and Values – Studies in Religion and Education*, 27(3), 281–9.

— (2007a), 'The State and Citizenship Education in England: A Curriculum for Subjects or Citizens?', *Journal of Curriculum Studies*, 37(4), 471–89.

— (2007b), 'Values and Visibility: The Implementation and Assessment of Citizenship Education in Schools', *Educational Review*, 59(2), 215–29.

— (2007c), 'Transactional Reading as Spiritual Investment', *Journal of Education and Christian Belief* (Special issue on Teaching Spiritually Engaged Reading), 11(2), 83–9.

— (2007d), *Faith in Students*. ESRC Report. Leeds: University of Leeds.

— (2007e), *English in the New Vocational Diplomas: An Analysis of Principal Learning* QCA. London: Qualifications and Curriculum Authority.

— (2007f), *An Analysis of Principal Learning in Three Accredited Specifications for the Creative and Media Specialised Diploma* QCA. London: Qualifications and Curriculum Authority.

— (2008a), 'Reading the Signs of the Times: Semiotic Engagement for Ethical Learning', *Journal of Curriculum Studies*, 40(4), 541–50.

— (2008b), 'Faith in Citizenship? On Teaching Children to Believe in Liberal Democracy', *British Journal of Religious Education*, 30(2), 113–22.

— (2009a), 'Judeo-Christian Sources of Character Education: Learning from England's Most Academically Improved Academy', *Journal of Research in Character Education*, 7(1), 25–40.

— (2009b), 'The Emmanuel Schools Foundation: Sponsoring Transformation in England's Most Improved Academy', *Management in Education*, 23(3), 139–43.

— (2009c), 'Religious Freedom and Rendering to Caesar: Reading Democratic and Faith-based Values in Society, Schools and Citizenship Education', *Oxford Review of Education*, 35(2), 133–46.

— (2010a), 'A Tale of Two Schools: Comparing and Contrasting Jacobus Fruytier Scholengemeenschap in the Netherlands and Bradford Christian School in England', *Journal of Beliefs & Values: Studies in Religion & Education*, 31(2), 181–90.

— (2010b), 'Christianity and Character Education: Faith in Core Values?', *Journal of Beliefs & Values: Studies in Religion & Education*, 31(3), 311–21.

— (2010c), 'Faith Schools in the Twenty-first Century', *Educational Review*, 62(2), 243–5.

— (2010d), 'Transaction and Transformation at Trinity: Private Sponsorship, Core Values and Christian Ethos at England's Most Improved Academy', *Oxford Review of Education*, 36(6), 749–65.

— (2011a), 'Reading Research on Core Values, Christian Ethos and School Transformation at England's Most Improved Academy: A Reply to Bragg et al.', *Oxford Review of Education*, 37(4), 567–70.

— (2011b), 'Ethical English Teaching: Learning Democratic Values or Living by the Tao?', *Changing English: Studies in Culture and Education*, 18(4), 351–9.

— (2011c), 'Human Rights, Citizenship and Religious Education', in Barnes, L. P. (ed.), *Debates in Religious Education*. London: Routledge, pp. 109–19.

— (2011d), 'Ethics and Citizenship Education', in J. Arthur and H. Cremin (eds), *Debates in Citzenship Education*. London, Routledge, pp. 181–93.

— (2011e), 'The Value of Christian-Ethos Schooling for Secular Students', *Journal of Research in Christian Education*, 20(2), 1–17.

— (2011f), 'Developing as an Ethical English Teacher: Valuing the Personal and Poetic in Professional Learning', *English in Education*, 45(3), 224–35.

— (2012a), 'The Trees of Knowledge and Life Growing Together in the Educational Vision of C. S. Lewis', *Changing English: Studies in Culture and Education*, 19(2), 249–59.

— (2012b), *Core Values, Student Learning and School Transformation* AHRC Research Project gtr.rcuk.ac.uk

— (2013), *C. S. Lewis: Teacher for our Time*. Cambridge: The Lutterworth Press.

— (2014), 'C. S. Lewis: Christian Educator for a Post-Christian Era', *Sehnsucht*, 7/8, 63–88.

Popper, K. (1959), *The Logic of Scientific Discovery*. London: Routledge & Kegan Paul.

Porter, R. (2001), *The Enlightenment*. New York: Palgrave.

Postman, N. (1968), 'Linguistics and Relevance', *The Use of English*, 20(1), 3–9.

— (1992), *Technopoly: The Surrender of Culture to Technology*. New York: Alfred Knopf.

Powell, R., Chambers Cantrell, S. and Adams, S. (2005), 'Saving Black Mountain: The Promise of Critical Literacy in a Multicultural Society', in G. Moss (ed.), *Critical Reading in the Content Areas 2004/2005*. Dubuque, IA: McGraw Hill, pp. 12–19.

QCA (1998), *The Promotion of Pupils' Spiritual, Moral, Social and Cultural Development: The Contribution of Subject Teaching in Secondary Schools and Colleges*. London: HMSO.

— (1999), *The National Curriculum for England: Citizenship*. London: QCA.

Rawls, J. (1971), *A Theory of Justice*. Cambridge, MA: Belknap Press.

— (1999), *The Idea of Public Reason Revisited in The Law of Peoples*. Cambridge, MA: Harvard University Press.

Raz, J. (1988), *The Morality of Freedom*. Oxford: Oxford University Press.

Reimer, K. S. and Furrow, J. L. (2001), 'A Qualitative Exploration of Relational Consciousness in Christian Children', *International Journal of Children's Spirituality*, 6(1), 7–23.

Richards, I. A. (1929), *Practical Criticism: A Study of Literary Judgement*. London: Routledge & Kegan.

Rogers, B. (2000), *Behaviour Management: A Whole-school Approach*. London: Paul Chapman Publishing.

Rosenblatt, L. (1968), *Literature as Exploration*. London: Heinemann.

— (1978), *The Reader, the Text, the Poem: The Transactional Theory of the Literary Work*. Carbondale, IL: Southern Illinois University Press.

— (1985), 'The Transactional Theory of the Literary Work: Implications for Research', in C. Cooper (ed.), *Researching Response to Literature and the Teaching of Literature*. Norwood, NY: Ablex, pp. 33–53.

Sachs, J. (2005), 'How to Build a Culture of Respect', *Demos Lecture, 18 May*. http://www.chiefrabbi.org/speeches/demos2005.htm, accessed 5 October 2005.

Sadler, R. (1998), 'Formative Assessment: Revisiting the Territory', *Assessment in Education*, 5(1), 77–84.

SCAA (1995), *Spiritual and Moral Development*. London: HMSO.

Schleiermacher, F. (1959), *Hermeneutik nach den Handaschriften*. Heidelberg: C.Winter.

Schofield, J. W. (1993), 'Increasing the Generalizability of Qualitative Research', in M. Hammersley (ed.), *Educational Research: Current Issues*. London: OpenUniversity Press/Paul Chapman Publishing, pp. 91–113.

Schön, D. (1983), *The Reflective Practitioner: How Professionals Think in Action*. New York: Basic Books.

Schrag, F. (1999), 'Why Foucault Now?', *Journal of Curriculum Studies*, 31(4), 375–83.

Scruton, R. (2002), *The West and the Rest: Globalization and the Terrorist Threat*. London: Continuum.

Selden, R. and Widdowsen, P. (1993), *A Reader's Guide to Contemporary Literary Theory*. New York: Harvester Wheatsheaf.

Shafiq, M. (2011), 'David Cameron and Multiculturalism' (http://www.ramadhanfoundation.com/CAMERONMULTICULTURALISM050211.htm), accessed 6 February 2014.

Simons, H. and Humble, S. (1978), *From Council to Classroom: An Evaluation of the Diffusion of the Humanities Curriculum Project*. Basingstoke, MA: Macmillan Educational.

Skinner, B. F. (1965/1953), *Science and Human Behaviour*. New York: The Free Press.

— (1971), *Beyond Freedom and Dignity*. Harmondsworth: Penguin.

— (1974), *About Behaviourism*. New York: Random House Publishing.

Slote, M. (1997), 'Agent-based Virtue Ethics', in R. Crisp and M. Slote (eds), *Virtue Ethics*. Oxford: Oxford University Press, pp. 239–62.

Smith, D. (2001), 'Spirituality and Teaching Methods: Uneasy Bedfellows?', in R. Best (ed.), *Education for Spiritual, Moral, Social and Cultural Development*. London & New York: Continuum, pp. 52–67.

Smith, D. and Shortt, J. (2001), 'Editorial: Hallowing the Curriculum?', *Journal of Education and Christian Belief*, 5(1), 3–7.

Somekh, B. (1989), 'Action Research and Collaborative School Development', in R. McBride (ed.), *The In-Service Training of Teachers*. London: Falmer Press, pp. 160–7.

Stables, A. (2005), *Living and Learning as Semiotic Engagement: A New Theory of Education*. Lewiston, NY/Lampeter: Edwin Mellen Press.

Stables, A., Morgan, C. and Jones, S. (1999), 'Educating for Significant Events: The Application of Harre's Social Reality Matrix across the Lower Secondary Curriculum', *Journal of Curriculum Studies*, 4(31), 449–61.

Standish, P. (2010), 'What Is the Philosophy of Education?', in R. Bailey (ed.), *The Philosophy of Education: An Introduction*. London/New York: Continuum, pp. 4–20.

Stenhouse, L. (1975), *An Introduction to Curriculum Research and Development*. London: Heinemann.

Stern, J. (2009), *The Spirit of the School*. London: Continuum.

Stevens, D. (2010a), 'A Freirean Critique of the Competence Model of Teacher Education, Focusing on the Standards for Qualified Teacher Status in England', *Journal of Education for Teaching*, 36(2), 187–96.

— (2010b), *Radical Romantic Pedagogy: An Exploration of the Tradition and Viability of a Synthesis of Romantic and Radical Visions of Education, Focusing on the Teaching of English at Secondary Level in England*. Doctoral thesis, Durham University. Available at Durham E-Theses Online: http://etheses.dur.ac.uk/489/.

— (2011), 'Critically Enlightened Romantic Values and English Pedagogy: A Response to Peter Medway', *Changing English*, 18(1), 45–56.

Stevens, D. and McGuinn, N. (2004), *The Art of Teaching Secondary English: Innovative and Creative Approaches.* London: RoutledgeFalmer.

Stibbs, A. (1998), 'Language in Art and Art in Language', *Journal of Art and Design Education,* 17(2), 201–9.

— (2001), 'For How Long, Where, and with Whom: Narrative Time, Place and Company as Generic Distinguishers and Ideological Indicators', *Changing English,* 8(1), 35–42.

Sutcliffe, J. (2012), 'Elocution Lessons: Who Wants to Speak the Queen's English?', *The Independent.* Thursday 19 January 2012.

Tankard, P. (2007), 'Didactic Pleasures: Learning in C.S. Lewis' Narnia', *VII: An Anglo-American Literary Review,* 24, 65–86.

Tanner, H. and Jones, S. (2006), *Assessment: A Practical Guide for Secondary Teachers.* London: Continuum.

Taylor, C. (1989), *Sources of the Self: The Making of the Modern Identity.* Harvard: Harvard University Press.

Taylor, G. P. (2006), *Sin, Salvation & Shadowmancer,* as told to B. Smietana. Grand Rapids, MI: Zondervan.

TDA (2009), *Including Students with SEN and/or Disabilities in Secondary English.* London: HMSO.

Tillich, P. (1951), *Systematic Theology.* Chicago, IL: University of Chicago Press.

Time magazine (1971), September 20. *Skinner's Utopia: Panacea, or Path to Hell?*

Vygotsky, L. (1971), *The Psychology of Art.* Cambridge, MA: MIT.

— (1978), *Mind in Society.* Cambridge, MA: MIT.

Wachlin, M. G. (1997), 'The Place of Bible Literature in Public High School English Classes', *Research in the Teaching of English,* 31(1), 7–50.

Wang, S. R. (2006), 'Promoting College English Reform to Improve the Teaching Quality of China's Higher Education', *Foreign Language World,* (5), 2–6.

Ward, M. (2008), *Planet Narnia. The Seven Heavens in the Imagination of C. S. Lewis.* Oxford: Oxford University Press.

Watson, J. B. (1924), *Behaviourism.* New York: Norton.

Wheen, F. (2004), *How Mumbo-jumbo Conquered the World.* London: Fourth Estate.

White, J. (1991), 'The Justification of Autonomy as an Educational Aim', in B. Spiecker and R. Straughan (eds), *Freedom and Indoctrination in Education – International Perspectives.* London: Cassell, pp. 84–93.

Wilshaw, M. (2012), 'Raising Standards in Literacy', *speech given at Thomas Jones Primary School 15 March 2012.*

Wilson, A. N. (1991), *C. S. Lewis: A Biography.* London: Flamingo.

— (2009), 'Religion of Hatred: Why we should no Longer be Cowed by the Chattering Classes Ruling Britain who Sneer at Christianity', *The Daily Mail,* 11 April 2009.

Wilson, E. (2009), *School Based Research: A Guide for Education Students.* London: Sage.

Wilson, J. (1991), 'Religious (Moral, Political, etc.) Commitment, Education and Indoctrination', in B. Spiecker and R. Straughan (eds), *Freedom and Indoctrination in Education-International Perspectives.* London: Cassell, pp. 42–50.

Wolterstorff, N. (2004), *Educating for Shalom. Essays on Christian Higher Education*, C. W. Joldersma and G. G. Stronks (eds), Grand Rapids, MI: Eerdmans.

Wood, R. C. (2003), *The Gospel According to Tolkien Visions of the Kingdom in Middle-earth*. Louisville, KY: Westminster John Knox Press.

Wordsworth, D. (1897), *Journals of Dorothy Wordsworth*, 1, W. Knight (ed.), http://www.archive.org/stream/journalsofdoroth027709mbp/ journalsofdoroth027709mbp_djvu.txt.

Wordsworth, W. (1988/1802), 'Preface to Lyrical Ballads', in S. Gill (ed.), *William Wordsworth*. Oxford: Oxford University Press, pp. 595–615.

— (1988/1799), 'The Prelude', in S. Gill (ed.), *William Wordsworth*. Oxford: Oxford University Press, pp. 375–590.

Wright, A. (2000), *Spirituality and Education*. London: Falmer, Routledge.

— (2003), 'Freedom, Equality, Fraternity? Towards a Liberal Defence of Faith Community Schools', *British Journal of Religious Education*, 25(2), 142–52.

Yandell, J. (2008), 'Exploring Multicultural Literature: The Text, the Classroom and the World Outside', *Changing English*, 15(1), 25–40.

Yin, R. K. (1994), *Case Study Research: Design & Methods*. Thousand Oaks, CA: Sage.

Index